Hugh M.
2-15

73-0!

Bears Over Redskins:

The NFL's Greatest Massacre

Lew Freedman

Blue River Press
Indianapolis, Indiana

73-0! Bears Over Redskins: The NFL's Greatest Massacre

ISBN 10: 1935628402
ISBN 13: 9781935628408

Cover Design by Phil Velikan

Cover photo: The faces of owner-coach George Halas and
quarterback Sid Luckman reflect the happy occasion as the
Chicago Bears were beating the Washington Redskins, 73-0.
Luckman was personally selected by Halas to introduce the
modern T-formation to the football world. 1940-Washington,
DC (Copyright Bettmann/Corbis / AP Images)

Interior Design by Dave Reed

Printed in the United States of America

10 9 8 7 6 5 4 3 2 1

Published by Blue River Press
2402 N. Shadeland Ave., Suite A
Indianapolis, IN 46219

www.brpressbooks.com

Distributed by Cardinal Publishers Group

Tom Doherty Company, Inc.

www.cardinalpub.com

CONTENTS

ACKNOWLEDGMENTS

I would like to offer a very special thanks to the Pro Football Hall of Fame library, particularly researcher Jon Kendle, for so much assistance.

The use of research materials, including newspaper clippings from the 1940 NFL season, championship game reports on the 73-0 NFL title game, and magazine stories about the players and their era, as well as books covering the history of the Chicago Bears and Washington Redskins, was invaluable.

– Lew Freedman

PREFACE

The world is both a larger and smaller place in the 2000s than it was in 1940. Larger because the earth's population is now about 7.1 billion; in 1940 it was around 2.3 billion.

It is smaller because almost every acre of land on the planet has been explored whereas in the 1940s neither Mount Everest nor any of the other Asian mountains standing higher than 26,300 feet had been climbed. It is smaller, too, because the world is much more tightly connected through computer capability, international telephone calling, and air travel.

Pro football maintains a bigger footprint on the American sports landscape by far in the 2000s than it did on December 8, 1940 when the Chicago Bears met the Washington Redskins for league honors. In 1940, the undisputed most popular team sport nationwide was Major League Baseball – even if there were no teams located in the Deep South or West of St. Louis.

Also rated much higher in popularity and importance in the years immediately after the Great Depression, as they had been ranked for years, were boxing (especially the heavyweights), and horse racing (especially the Triple Crown races of the Kentucky Derby, the Preakness Stakes and the Belmont Stakes). While pro football was gaining larger audiences, college football was still seen as the form of the sport that more people cared about – Boola, boola and the old college try.

The more knowledgeable fan had come to realize that pro football featured a higher caliber player than undergraduates suiting up for the alma mater. Chicago Bears owner George Halas had spent two decades making that case for the public and sometimes taking on exhibition games between his club and a college team, mainly with the goal of crushing the foe.

Organized professional football was two decades old in 1940. The National Football League had undergone tremendous growing pains, weeding out teams from small Midwestern cities that had dreamed of being part of it. Canton, Ohio, Akron, Ohio, Hammond, Indiana had all owned franchises, but those teams and communities couldn't keep up.

With the exception of Green Bay, Wisconsin, which continues to be an anomaly in the present NFL, the biggest cities in the United States, notably the population centers of the East and Midwest were represented in the league. The New York Giants, the Philadelphia Eagles, the Pittsburgh Steelers, the Chicago Bears, the Washington Redskins, the Detroit Lions, the Chicago Cardinals, and the Cleveland Rams made up most of the league. The Cardinals moved to St. Louis and then on to Arizona. The Rams moved to Los Angeles and then on to St. Louis. But by 1940 the NFL was basically a big-city league.

Although there was some small-scale professional basketball in 1940, there was no National Basketball Association, which was not formed until after World War II. The National Hockey consisted of six teams, two, the Montreal Canadiens and the Toronto Maple Leafs, in Canada, plus the Boston Bruins, Chicago Blackhawks, Detroit Red Wings, and New York Rangers. It has only been since the late 1960s that hockey began to take root in other cities around the United States.

All daily activity halted when the World Series was underway. The nation held its breath, sitting in living rooms beside the radio when the heavyweight crown was at stake. Otherwise sport did not play as significant a part in daily lives as it does now. There was no game of the week on TV. Fans did not hang on the name announced of every NFL draft pick. Communities did not throw championship parades that attracted a million fans along the route.

Nor were individuals (outside of Olympic champions such as Jesse Owens, fighters like Joe Louis, or the crème de la crème of baseball stars) lionized beyond the boundaries of their playing fields. The 1940 NFL rushing champion was Byron "Whizzer" White, who gained all of 514 yards on the ground and while an excellent player became much better known later in life for serving 31 years as a U.S. Supreme Court Justice.

The World Series concluded a few months before the NFL title game. The Cincinnati Reds captured a thrilling seven-game series from the Detroit Tigers. Reds manager Bill McKechnie was later enshrined in the Baseball Hall of Fame, as was slugging catcher Ernie Lombardi. During that era it was unusual that the American League was not represented by the New York Yankees.

Between 1936 and 1943, the 1940 season was the only year in which the Yanks did not reach the Series. They won the crown six times and lost in the Series once during the eight-year span. Joltin' Joe DiMaggio had quite a bit to do with that success under Hall of Fame manager Joe McCarthy.

Remarkably, Louis was the heavyweight champ from 1937 to 1949, making a record 25 title defenses. His reign made him one of the best-known men in the country and the world and his personality, grace, and integrity helped improve race relations around the United States.

In hockey, the Boston Bruins won the Stanley Cup in 1939 and 1941, with the Rangers capturing the National Hockey League championship in 1940. It was an era of tight checking and low scores and the 1939-40 season NHL scoring champ was Boston's Milt Schmidt with just 22 goals and 52 points.

Of more import to most Americans was the recently completed presidential election. On November 5, approximately a month prior to the December 8 NFL championship game, President Franklin Delano Roosevelt won re-election to the nation's highest political office over Republican challenger Wendell Wilkie. Originally elected in 1932, the former governor of New York was elected to his third four-year term. This was the first time Americans had voted for the same man for president in three victorious elections. Roosevelt, of course, would win election for a fourth time in 1944. After Roosevelt died in office federal law was changed to prohibit one president from serving more than two terms.

Roosevelt had guided the country through the Great Depression and had introduced a variety of plans to put the nation back to work. In 1940, there were still ripple effects vibrating through the economy holding back many workers.

Looming more gloomily in 1940, however, was the prospect of war. When the Armistice declaring the end to "The Great War" was imposed in 1918, many felt that the terrible casualty list and horror created by more sophisticated weaponry would lead to the end of wars between countries as a way to settle their disputes. Two decades later that ferocious war would be renamed World War I because there was a World War II.

Germany had been disarmed following World War I, but the extremely dogmatic, nationalistic Adolf Hitler rose to power throughout the 1930s, masking his intentions of world domination and extermination of the world's population of Jews and other minorities in the interests of establishing a "pure Aryan" race. For the most part the world looked the other way as Hitler amassed power and realists were shouted down.

On September 1, 1939 Germany invaded Poland, triggering what became worldwide hostilities carrying well into 1945. The United States officially stayed out of the war because of the clamor of isolationists. Great Britain did not. Numerous American flyers volunteered to fight the Germans under the English flag by 1940 and flew in the Battle of Britain.

A tug-of-war of diplomacy raged and it seemed inevitable that the United States would at some point form an alliance with England and other Western European nations. Keenly aware of the world situation Roosevelt used the time to build American military might. It was difficult to ignore the signs and not to believe war was coming. On September 16, right at the beginning of the pro football season, Congress enacted the Selective Training and Service Act of 1940. The legislation required that all young men between the ages of 21 and 35 register with their local draft boards. This was the first time in American history that Congress had called for draft registration in peacetime.

While the likelihood of the United States being embroiled in another war was on the minds of young men around the country, when the Bears and Redskins took the field for their athletic war on December 8, the country was still almost exactly one year shy of committing to participation in a shooting war.

INTRODUCTION

Chicago History Museum
NFL title game ball signed by Bears, 1940.
That day, our Chicago Bears crushed the Washington Redskins
73-0 in a packed Griffith Stadium.

Photo provided by Chicago History Museum ICHi-65142

They ran out of footballs.

During the 1940 National Football League championship game, the Chicago Bears scored so many touchdowns – 11 – that by the fourth quarter the officials were running short on footballs because so many extra-point kicks were being boomed into the stands and kept by fans at Griffith Stadium in Washington, D.C.

On December 8, 1940 the Bears obtained the most resounding sort of revenge in the history of pro football, a beat-down so thorough that nearly 75 years later the result still astounds. That day the Bears stampeded over the Washington Redskins by the unbelievable, never-again-matched plurality of 73-0.

Never has another NFL game been such a one-sided massacre. Never has another NFL championship game been such a thorough wipeout. The enduring theme of competition in the National Football League is the phrase, "any given Sunday." By that it is meant that on any day, in any game, either team can win because the level of parity in the sport is that equal.

One of the remarkable things about that humongous 73-0 score is that the "any given Sunday" rule of thumb is accurate. On the face of it any football fan would conclude just by glancing at the score that the game was a mismatch. Going by the numbers – that day – the conclusion is accurate. However, there was no hint leading up to the contest that the result would be so lopsided. Indeed, the game figured to be a close one and only a few weeks earlier the Redskins had defeated the Bears, and the final score of the preceding game was 7-3. Who would have imagined that barely three weeks later a rematch between the same teams would produce a point total of 73 for one team?

There was every reason to believe that the NFL title game of 1940 would be a close one, hard-fought, and perhaps decided at the end, as the clock was ticking down. There was nothing in either team's makeup that would enable anyone to predict a final result that made history for its extreme nature.

Same men, same coaches, same players, same uniforms, going after the biggest prize in the game, so there never was any evidence to suggest why this one game, on this given day, provided the most stunning final score in league history. It was inexplicable then and it is inexplicable now. The closest thing to any explanation is that the Chicago Bears played the perfect game and the Washington Redskins had the worst on-field day of their lives.

The game is notable for its uniqueness – that score is tattooed on the minds of any football history buffs. The fact that there never has there been a larger margin of victory, despite the many, many seasons played since, involving more and more teams as the league expanded, makes it more remarkable.

Just about every season in college football there is a game, or maybe even a few, that turn out in a similar manner, with one team riding roughshod over the other and scoring touchdowns as if they were fast-break lay-ups. But that is attributable more to scheduling than anything else. A powerhouse team does some lower-level college a favor by scheduling it and offering a nice share of the gate. Bears versus Redskins was a different animal because each was a champion. The Bears won the Western Division and the Redskins won the Eastern Division. These teams were the best of the best.

Many of those involved in the game were also the best of the best in the NFL at the time. Between owners, coaches and players, 12 individuals with connections to the Bears and Redskins were later elected to the Pro Football Hall of Fame in Canton, Ohio.

On the Washington side, owner George Preston Marshall was a colorful, say-what-was-on-his-mind promoter who employed an agile mind to help develop rules that would make the sport more popular. Yet he was also close-minded enough to avoid signing any African-American players for his roster for decades and until he was pressured to do so in the 1960s.

Besides Marshall, Washington coach Ray Flaherty, quarterback Sammy Baugh, two-way end Wayne Millner, and lineman Turk Edwards, were all selected for the Hall of Fame.

Across the field, Bears owner and coach George Halas, who helped invent the NFL, was a member of the Hall's first class in 1963. From that 1940 championship team he was joined by quarterback Sid Luckman, halfback George McAfee, and Clyde "Bulldog" Turner, an offensive lineman-center who many consider one of the best to ever play the game. Also, linemen Joe Stydahar, Danny Fortmann, and George Musso were elected to the Hall.

A key factor in the game was the Bears' mastery of the T formation offense, where three backs line up behind the quarterback. During that time period the T formation, which later became the most prominent offensive formation in the sport, was used only by selected teams. In college play, Stanford and Notre Dame had used it to great effect. Stanford's coach Clark Shaughnessy has been called "the father of the T formation," which is not quite accurate since a form of the formation was used in the 1880s. More accurately, he can be credited with advancing the T. In particular, during the lead-up to the Bears-Redskins fight for the crown, Shaughnessy worked with the Bears to help Halas smooth rough edges.

The National Football League was founded in 1920, but from the first year of play through 1932, the league's annual champion was chosen based on having the best record, not in a head-to-head game with another opponent. That changed in 1933 when the league split into two divisions and conducted an annual post-season title game between the division winners.

Much later, after the American Football League was created, a merger was effected, and a multi-tiered playoff system was instituted, it took victory in several post-season games to claim a championship. Most of the early games were close. Only periodically did one team completely dominate another in the championship.

Some of the other worst beatings in championship games were: Cleveland Browns 56, Detroit Lions 10 in 1954; Detroit Lions 59, Cleveland Browns 14 in 1957, San Francisco 49ers 55, Denver Broncos 10 in 1990; Dallas Cowboys 52, Buffalo Bills 17 in 1993; and Seattle Seahawks 43, Denver Broncos 8 in 2014. But in terms of scorched earth, no result compares to Bears 73, Redskins 0.

No one who played in that 1940 game ever forgot it, nor did anyone who witnessed it, though it would have been more fun for spectators if the game had been played in Chicago rather than D.C. On anniversaries, 10 years, 30 years, and beyond, sportswriters revisited in print the vicious storm that visited itself upon the Redskins that day. In those retrospective articles the participants were asked to comment until there came a time when all those who suited up had passed away.

Red Smith, the wordsmith who won a Pulitzer Prize for commentary as a sports columnist for The New York Times, rode a time machine back to 1940 to discuss the game in 1979, and made a joke about it, relying on readers' and fans' knowledge of the sports betting spreads that bookies concocted.

Smith penned that a sportswriter from Philadelphia lamented the 73-0 result while on the train home. "I blew a tough bet today," he said. "I had the Redskins and 72 points."(1)

No odds-maker gives infinity as the point spread, but that's what it would have taken to win such a bet on Bears-Redskins in the most peculiar and surprising NFL championship contest.

73-0!

Bears Over Redskins:

The NFL's Greatest Massacre

THE SETTING

While it is not certain if the term "bulletin board material" made its debut as a result of Washington Redskins owner George Preston Marshall opening his big mouth, it is certainly true that it played a role in provoking an angry mood from the Chicago Bears and inspiring them into a phenomenal performance.

On November 17, 1940 the Redskins defeated the Bears, 7-3, at Griffith Stadium in Washington. In the aftermath of the game some Bears players said that they never should have lost. They felt they were the superior team and didn't feel the result was just.

Marshall, who could be as loud as a ship's foghorn in the night, bristled at the comments. Rather than merely being content with the victory and proof of superiority based on the scoreboard, he retaliated verbally, though not right away. At the end of the regular season, the Redskins owned a 9-2 record. That was good enough to capture the National Football League's Eastern Division title. The Bears finished 8-3 and that was good enough to take the Western Division crown. The regular-season results set up the match between the Bears and the Redskins for the league title.

One day during the week of practice leading up to the final game of the year, it came to the attention of Bears coach George Halas that Marshall was popping off. Marshall called the Bears whiners and complainers and summed them up as a bunch of crybabies and did so more than once.

"Halas plastered all the stories on the locker room bulletin board," said Bears end Ken Kavanagh. (1)

It is doubtful that Halas had a subscription to the Washington Post, or any other D.C. newspaper, but friends made sure he got hold of the newspaper clippings and just as it said in the future cliché, the Bears did have a bulletin board handy hanging on the wall. Halas made no comment, but the players read Marshall's remarks and seethed.

Although surely other examples of ill-timed verbosity abound down through the years, Marshall's foolish comments definitely contributed to the modern-day glut of bland pre-game observations by players who don't want to be blamed for inciting the enemy.

Truth be told that the Bears did believe they were the better team and so did odds-makers who installed Chicago as a 21-point favorite for the title game. However, the Redskins, as they had proven on the field just three weeks earlier, were a worthy adversary, and were working their way up to becoming the Bears' biggest rival of the era.

The NFL origins story places a group of enthusiastic, not-necessarily wealthy men crowded into a Hupmobile showroom in Canton, Ohio in 1920. There were not enough available seats for the bunch that turned out with the goal of starting an organized professional football league and some sat on the running boards of the cars. Halas was in the room and being present at the creation was just one of his claims to fame when he emerged as the player-coach of the Decatur Staleys. Long after tossing his cleats into a storage box, and long after the Staleys morphed into the Bears, Halas was a power in owners' meetings.

Actually, the name of the fledgling league in 1920 was the American Professional Football Association (it didn't become the NFL until 1922 at the time the Staleys moved to Chicago). Any fans that can name the teams that played out the inaugural season should appear on "Jeopardy" because they are trivia geniuses. Among the clubs were the Akron Pros, the first champs, the Rock Island Independents, the Canton Bulldogs (who provided Jim Thorpe, the world's greatest athlete of the first half of the 20th century as league president), the Dayton Triangles, the Buffalo All-Americans, the Columbus Panhandles and the Moline Universal Tractors.

Within a decade all of the mid-sized cities (except Green Bay, Wisconsin) would be on the outside of the candy store looking in through the glass window, replaced by teams representing the nation's biggest popular centers. Throughout the 1920s and into the first years of the 1930s, franchises came and went like migratory birds.

In 1932, the Newark Tornadoes went out of business and the franchise rights reverted to the NFL. George Marshall was hovering and scooped up the club and installed it in Boston. Boston's National League baseball team was the Boston Braves, the same team that is currently the Atlanta Braves and made stopover in Milwaukee. Marshall chose the nickname Redskins because as far as he was concerned one Indian was like another and he thought the local fans would identify with his team because of the Braves.

Between 1932 and 1934, the Redskins played mediocre ball, finishing 4-4-2, 5-5-2, and 6-6 in consecutive years. Originally, Marshall shared ownership with three partners, but after just one year and a $50,000 loss, he bought them all out. Marshall was not one to share the stage with any other egos. In 1935, Boston slumped, falling to 2-8-1. Marshall, who was one of those shoot-first-and-ask-questions later desperadoes, fired his coach and hired Ray Flaherty as the new field boss. It was the right move.

It took a while for the Redskins to jell under Flaherty, but they made a late-season surge and won the Eastern Division with a 7-5 record, setting up a championship game against the Packers. The Redskins held the rights to host the championship game, but Marshall had soured on Boston fans. When only 4,813 fans turned out for the Redskins' last home game, he yanked the championship game from the city and the contest was played at the Polo Grounds in New York.

Marshall never returned to Boston, maybe not even to switch trains. Once he pulled the title game he decided Boston was not worthy of his presence and shifted the team to Washington for the start of the 1937 season. The Redskins were even better, a team on the rise, finishing 8-3 and moving into a second straight NFL championship game.

There they found the Chicago Bears. The Bears won championships in 1932 and 1933 and four times had been runner-up in the 1920s. Chicago finished the '37 regular season with a 9-1-1 record and figured to sweep past the Redskins. Instead, the Redskins prevailed, 28-21.

Flaherty was proving to be an excellent coach, but even more importantly, the Redskins had themselves the most glittering of the league's new stars at quarterback. The NFL draft was instituted in 1936 and Jay Berwanger, a halfback out of the University of Chicago who won the 1935 Heisman Trophy was the first player ever selected. He was the No. 1 choice of the Philadelphia Eagles and the No. 1 choice of all-time.

Berwanger emerged from college demanding $1,000 a game in salary. The Eagles recoiled at the price and traded him to the Bears. Halas offered a seasonal salary of $13,500 to Berwanger, but he turned it down to preserve his amateur status and try out for the U.S. Olympic team in the decathlon. He didn't make it, but when Halas wouldn't budge from his salary offer, Berwanger went into private business and never played a down of pro football.

The Redskins were more fortunate. In 1937, their No. 1 pick was Sammy Baugh, the exceptional quarterback from Texas Christian University. Although Baugh injured his knee in the title game versus the Bears he came off the bench to lead a rally that gave Washington its first championship.

This was the start of one of the greatest careers in NFL history. At a time when teams were just adapting to the forward pass as a weapon that would equal the running game in importance, Baugh was a ready-made quarterback. Beyond that he became an All-Pro as a defensive back and punter, as well. No other player in league history has ever been as brilliantly versatile.

Unlike Marshall in 1940, who belittled the Bears leading up to that championship encounter, Halas played a different sort of hand as the days dwindled down to the 1937 title game. "That's the greatest football team ever put together," Halas said of his opponents. He also noted that all 11 Redskin starters could be all-stars. (2)

It is not likely that Halas really believed that. Certainly, he felt his team would win the game. But even though he was also known as someone who was prone to issuing loud, ill-conceived statements, this was one time he played the aw-shucks football coach role. As it turned out, the Redskins may not have been the best team the imagination could field, but it was good enough to beat his Bears on December 12, 1937 at Wrigley Field in Chicago.

That game increased the Redskins' stature. It was the team's first title and gave the players some swagger. It also put them on the Bears' enemies list, to some degree. They were in opposite divisions, but they did meet during the regular season once in a while. In 1938, Chicago clobbered Washington, 31-7. In 1939 the teams did not play. During the 1940 regular season there was that low-scoring 7-3 Redskins victory. That was the prelude to the 1940 championship game.

The game was set for Griffith Stadium, home of the baseball Washington Senators, a ballpark that had served that team since 1911 when it replaced a wooden park on that same site constructed in 1891. When it opened the park was named National Park, but in 1920 the name was changed to honor Senators owner Clark Griffith.

The Setting

Although there was always the chance that the Bears-Redskins showdown might be played in wintry conditions, fans were anxious to see a rematch. Once the pairings were clear, the announcement that the game was a sell-out was made three-and-a-half hours after the ticket windows opened. There were 35,752 tickets available and they evaporated as quickly as if a sunrise melted ice on the ground with its rays. Washington saved 2,000 tickets for the Bears to distribute.

In the days leading up to the game, the worry was not so much about snow and ice, but whether anyone would drown on the grassy field. It was as if a monsoon had hit D.C. A 12-hour rain poured heavily and interrupted Redskins' planned practices. Three days shy of the championship, Washington coach Ray Flaherty chose to refrain from a hard workout for his men, partially fearful that someone might pull a muscle on the slippery ground.

A planned hard go was reduced to a lecture and calisthenics upon the muddy turf. Throughout the season Flaherty had been very open with the newspaper reporters from his hometown Washington outlets. They were permitted to watch practice every day all season long – until this day. What was different was the arrival of Chicago newspapermen from the Windy City. Flaherty barred the visiting scribes from the workout and to be consistent he also shut out the hometown writers.

It was Flaherty's outlook that the Chicago sportswriters came to D.C. early in order to spy on the Redskins and pass on their knowledge to the Bears' organization.

"They were sent on ahead to scout for the Bears," Flaherty said. (3)

Whether he truly believed that, was just being careful, or didn't want anything he was including in the game plan to slip out in any newspaper story, no one was quite sure. Everyone got a little bit of a chuckle when Flaherty met with the newsmen and explained the success of Washington's season by saying, "Luck. That's all. We get a lot of breaks." (4)

He must have rated the Chicago sportswriters' gullibility quite high to issue such a simple-minded statement. It was his way of dodging saying anything of substance to them. Flaherty did add one other observation, though there was nothing secret about it. He praised quarterback Baugh for his role in the successful regular season.

"Sammy Baugh is having his greatest year," Flaherty said. "He reported much heavier than ever before and he retained the extra heft throughout the season. It made him a stronger player and we were able to use him more than before." (5)

Meanwhile, whether the Redskins knew it or not, the Bears were getting some last-minute tutoring from Stanford coach Clark Shaughnessy on how best to employ the T formation offense. There was one casual comment in the Chicago Tribune that Shaughnessy had been traveling from Palo Alto, California, Stanford's location, to visit relatives in Minnesota and dropped in on Bears workouts. That observation understated the aid he offered to George Halas and his Bears.

Shaughnessy got to know Halas when he had coached at the University of Chicago. Stanford was coming off of a miserable 1-7 season in 1939 and although others were deemed more popular choices, the Cardinal officials hired Shaughnessy. Stanford had been wedded to the single-wing offense and Shaughnessy judged correctly that it wasn't a lack of talent holding the Cardinal back on the gridiron, but the wrong choice of offense. He installed the T formation, with three backs lined up behind the quarterback forming the T, and led Stanford to an unbeaten season.

Shaughnessy drilled the Cardinal overtime to absorb his new style and with Frankie Albert at quarterback and such offensive threats as Hugh Gallarneau, Stanford shocked the Pacific Coast Conference and the nation in the autumn of 1940. When Halas summoned Shaughnessy for a little fine-tuning with the T formation, he was fresh off of a 9-0 Stanford season.

During a dead period between the end of the regular season and the Rose Bowl, Shaughnessy provided a little bit of instruction for Chicago quarterback Sid Luckman. It was a crash course, not as thorough as his teaching of Albert, but Luckman was a quick study and picked up some knowledge that helped him against the Redskins. Of course the way the game turned out it might not have mattered if Luckman called elementary school touch football plays rather than indulging at all in a sophisticated offense.

Years later, between 1951 and 1962, Shaughnessy actually joined the Bears' coaching staff full-time as an assistant coach.

The doors to Redskins practice were also closed the next day, two days until kickoff, but Flaherty met with reporters and did reveal that rookie running back Bob Hoffman, who was suffering from a knee injury, would not play except as a last resort. Sports reporters pretty much had to guess what Flaherty was up to and since they had to satisfy their editors 1,000 miles away in Chicago, they had to write something in their stories. Speculation leaned towards the likelihood of the Redskins relying on Baugh's passing arm more than anything else. Naturally, any of the animals in the Washington Zoo might have been smart enough to reach the same conclusion since Baugh was the main man in the offense.

By the time December 8 rolled around the reporters had little to report. The sell-out crowd figure was announced ahead of time at 36,034 and the gate receipts were figured at $112,508. To that point in NFL history the dollar total was a record for a championship game. The winner's share of the pot was estimated to be about $900 per player.

During that era even the biggest stars and most valuable players on offense such as Baugh, would double as defensive players. Throughout the entire season, 34 players appeared on the Redskins' roster. Likewise the Bears. The 2013 roster maximum for an NFL team was 53 players. In 1940, there was less money for the champs to divide and fewer players earned a share.

Although fans of the Chicago Bears may believe that their favorite team has always been attached to the sobriquet "Monsters of the Midway," that is not true. They also may not even comprehend what the Midway is. In 1893, when the World's Columbian Exposition, aka The World's Fair, was held in Chicago the ground zero of the amusements was on the south side of the University of Chicago campus known as the Midway Plaisance. Although Chicago's World's Fair had a limited run, the word "midway" has been used to describe the center of games and rides at carnivals and fairs ever since. The area itself where the Midway Plaisance existed, is currently a Chicago park.

The description "Monsters of the Midway" was first applied to the University of Chicago Maroons football team coached by the legendary Amos Alonzo Stagg because of its geography. However, in 1939 the school dropped college football and soon after, with the Bears emerging as a powerful club in 1940, the name was transferred to the pro franchise. It has stuck with the Bears ever since and the Bears definitely proved themselves worthy of the nickname.

George Halas was a gritty guy. He had played college football at the University of Illinois and borrowed his alma mater's orange and blue team colors for the Bears. He played Major League baseball very briefly for the New York Yankees, inhabiting right field for a short time before the Yankees acquired Babe Ruth from the Boston Red Sox. It was his allegiance to the Chicago Cubs that led him to strike a deal with that club to use Wrigley Field as the Bears' home park. By nature he was a no-frills man who believed that the high quality of pro football would sell itself. This was basically the same outlook as Major League owners took. Neither Halas nor baseball magnates were much for promotion.

George Preston Marshall was cut from different cloth. He was a showman at heart, a blood brother of P.T. Barnum. Not long after he moved the Redskins from Boston to Washington he dreamed up the concept of a team fight song. Marshall liked the rah-rah feel of college football. And yes, was seen on the sidelines wearing a fur coat.

Marshall talked up the notion of a team song and between the end of the 1937 season and the start of the 1938 season he had himself one. The lyrics were written by his wife Corinne, and the music was written by his Redskins band leader, Barnee Breeskin, the conductor of a 110-piece band. They did not create a symphony worthy of the pen of Mozart, but "Hail To The Redkins" became a favorite in D.C. A version of the song is still played at Redskins games, but the lyrics have been adjusted to be less controversial due to what was perceived to be offensive to Native Americans and allegiance to the Southern states that formed the Confederacy.

In part, lyrics employed in 1940 and still in use now, include, "Hail Victory! Braves On The Warpath!" (6)

A few days before the Bears-Redskins hoedown, Marshall tweaked Halas a little while bragging some on himself.

"The Redskins present professional football just like Northwestern or Notre Dame presents college football," Marshall said. "The Bears, for instance, present it like the Cubs present baseball. Here we get all the trimmings of college football. Every seat is reserved. Season tickets are sold. For your money you get the best in the sport, the best in music and some laughs," (7)

As far as Marshall was concerned his massive Redskins band could play "Hail To The Redskins" repeatedly, until the brass sounds left Halas no recourse but to cover his ears in despair.

George Halas, left, owner and coach of the Chicago Bears, shakes hands with **Ray Flaherty**, Washington Redskins coach, after the Bears beat the Redskins, 73-0, in a National Football League championship game in Washington, D.C., on Dec. 8, 1940. At right is **George Marshall**, owner of the Redskins. (AP Photo)

OWNERS AND COACHES

The photograph of George Preston Marshall says it all. The man, his team and show business were all rolled into one in the picture of Marshall wearing a full-fledged, colorful Indian head dress. You wouldn't catch George Halas in a Bear suit and Wellington Mara was too distinguished a giant of a man to pretend to be a New York Giant like Gulliver.

No doubt it never even crossed Marshall's mind to blush. Marshall was born in 1896 in Grafton, West Virginia, and although he liked to imagine himself a very sophisticated gentleman the rural South was never quite shaken out of him. This was particularly true in race relations. He could be a prickly boss, actions led him to being labeled a racist, yet he could be a fan-friendly showman. His wife Corinne, for 22 years between 1936 and 1958, was an actress before they wed. And Marshall admitted that his first love was acting, but he wasn't good enough at it to make a living.

One way or another Marshall always seemed to be on stage. He held court at D.C.'s famous Duke Zeibert restaurant, and often in his classy hotel room. He could, however, joke about his biggest moment on the stage. He said it came in 1914 when he was performing in a play in Winnipeg and the manager asked him to make an announcement to the audience.

"Once I brought a house down," Marshall said. "I doubt any actor ever got the wild, spontaneous ovation I got from delivering just one line. I walked out in front of the curtain and said, 'The United States has just declared war on Germany.' Boy, those Canadians went wild." (1)

Never the retiring sort, sometimes Marshall's injection of opinion into an argument produced good results. He served with Halas on a National Football League committee in the early 1930s that modified rules opening up the game to more offense and more reliance on passing. This was before Marshall owned the rights to Sammy Baugh, so the move was not designed with self-interest in mind. Marshall believed that a freer passing game would lead to more touchdowns and more entertainment for the fans.

Marshall, like many owners, was first a businessman, then a sports impresario. He made his money from a chain of laundries founded by his father and based in the Washington, D.C. area. That made it easier for Marshall to shift the Redskins from Boston to D.C. Marshall also owned a basketball team in the 1920s called the Palace Five Laundrymen – his first foray into sports. The team was hung out to dry in 1928 when it folded.

Whether Marshall anticipated the future because of his love of show business, or helped shape the future, it didn't take long after he purchased the Redskins for him to establish a lively halftime show. The Redskins band was a key element in those displays, but Marshall took a hand in choreographing more elaborate shows, as well. When the Redskins played a home game around Christmas, fans were guaranteed a live show splashy enough to compete with the other live show – the football game. The halftime show featured Santa Claus arriving on a dog sled, or perhaps a Mississippi steamboat, or even Santa floating out of a helicopter wearing a parachute.

Marshall took an almost childish pleasure out of the trappings of show business, but when it came to business he could be intransigent, and stern. In his later years he was better known for his frown than his smile and his white hair was neatly parted and gave him the authoritative look of a CEO. That was appropriate because when Marshall wanted something he got it. If not, he raised his voice rather loudly in protest, whether that was in a restaurant or at an NFL board meeting. Marshall had no patience with anything that bored him. He abhorred dullness and sought to remedy any such situation as swiftly as possible.

One thing about Marshall – he was consistent. That meant for better or for worse. He was always willing to try new things that fine-tuned the product and enhanced the game of professional football and he remained Redskins owner long enough that he was still going strong years into 1960s era of commissioner Pete Rozelle.

"Mr. Marshall was an outspoken foe of status quo when most were content with it," Rozelle said. "All of us who participate in some form of the game, and those millions who enjoy viewing it, are beneficiaries of what his dynamic personality helped shape over more than three decades." (2)

That was diplomatic commentary and looking on the bright side because Marshall was in other ways an NFL embarrassment. In the 1930s and the early 1940s, there were no African-American players in the league. After World War II, when Jackie Robinson broke the color barrier in Major League baseball and the Los Angeles Rams re-broke the color barrier in the NFL by hiring Woody Strode and Kenny Washington, Marshall stood out as a staunch opponent of pro football integration.

His stance remained firm throughout the 1940s and 1950s and into the 1960s. During that era the Redskins were the southernmost located NFL team and their fan base extended throughout the Deep South. Marshall did not want to alienate those supporters, even the ones who never made it to a game in Washington, D.C. Marshall was one of the first owners to recognize the value of television, formed his own television network, and splashed Redskins games on the tube across the South.

Although the lyrics of the Redskins fight song officially read, "Fight For Old D.C." When the mood struck him, Marshall ordered it to be sung as "Fight For 'Ol Dixie." While the NFL was steadily integrating and terrific African-American ballplayers joined every other team in the league, the Redskins' roster remained all-white into the early 1960s. It literally took an act of government for Marshall to make changes.

For years Marshall actively fought integration, sometimes with words, always with actions. One of his most severe critics with the Washington Post was sports columnist Shirley Povich who actually out-lasted Marshall in their jobs. Povich once wrote that the Cleveland Browns' fantastic fullback Jim Brown "integrated the end zone." He tweaked Marshall in print for not signing black ballplayers and Marshall verbally retaliated with comments such as, "We'll start signing Negroes when the Harlem Globetrotters start signing whites." Marshall was wrong. In fact, the Redskins did beat the Globetrotters on that integration front – but under duress. (3)

It took until the presidential administration of John F. Kennedy for the Redskins to integrate and it took a serious threat to force Marshall to act. In the NFL draft following the 1960 season, the Redskins selected 20 players. All of them were white. At that time Washington was building a new stadium that eventually would be known as Robert F. Kennedy Stadium following his assassination, but initially was called

District of Columbia Stadium when it opened in October of 1961. Marshall signed a 30-year lease to play in the new stadium, but one day he received an unwelcome piece of mail from Secretary of the Interior Stuart Udall. Since the stadium was being built with public funds and it would be under the jurisdiction of the Capital Parks system and Udall, Marshall was informed his team would not be allowed to play in it unless he integrated the franchise.

Marshall's public response very much was typical of his personality. He said, "I didn't know the government had the right to tell a showman how to cast the play." In this case, it did. To illustrate how dramatically Marshall was on the wrong side of history, he was supported by members of the American Nazi Party (less than two decades after the end of World War II), who demonstrated while waving signs that read, "Keep Redskins White." (4)

Marshall capitulated. He traded for Cleveland Browns all-star running back Bobby Mitchell, who was later chosen for the Pro Football Hall of Fame and after retirement worked for the Redskins' front office for 35 years.

Those ugly battles came long after the showdown against the Bears in 1940, but were all part of Marshall's complex character. Still, some of Marshall's memorable contests of will involved the Bears and dated back more than a quarter of a century. In 1943, while in attendance at a Bears-Redskins game at Wrigley Field, Marshall became so incensed the on-field doings that he raced down an aisle towards the field and standing behind the Bears' team bench waiting for the end of the first half and a likely confrontation with George Halas.

Marshall's greatest contribution to the 1940 game itself was his mouthing off in the week leading up to the contest when he labeled the Bears crybabies and whiners. For once, Halas, known to be quite bombastic, did not say anything to his team to rile it up any more than it had been already by those newspaper clips on the bulletin board. Halas let Marshall's own words hang him.

If there was a Mount Rushmore of famous Chicago sports figures, Halas' jaw would be foremost in the chiseling. He was pugnacious and his mug told the story. Born in 1895, Halas was Chicago all of the way. Halas' family was Czech-Bohemian and he grew up in one of Chicago's cloistered, ethnic neighborhoods. A wonderful athlete,

Halas played football, basketball and baseball at the University of Illinois in Champaign and he earned a degree in civil engineering, an academic honor he did not put to use as the owner-coach-player for the Staleys and the Bears.

Halas served in the U.S. Navy during World War I (and re-entered the Navy during World War II). A two-way end, in 1919 he was the Most Valuable Player in the Rose Bowl for the Illini. A successful minor-league baseball player, Halas earned a call-up from the New York Yankees in 1919.

Listed as a switch-hitter, standing six feet tall and weighing just 165 pounds, Halas appeared in 12 games for New York, but did not hit his weight. His lifetime batting average was .091. That amounted to two singles in 22 at-bats. Before that year was out, Halas was back on the gridiron, representing the Hammond Pros for $75 a game prior to joining up with the fledgling NFL.

Halas played pro ball through 1928, mainly as an end, and his listed weight for that sport was 182 pounds. Halas put the growl into the Bears with his ferocious demeanor, on the field and in leading other men. The most memorable play involving Halas as an active player would have been a career highlight for anyone.

During a 1923 game against the Oorang Indians, Halas forced a fumble by the great Jim Thorpe as his team threatened from the two-yard-line en route to a 26-0 victory. Halas scooped up the ball, spun around and began sprinting the other way. Thorpe regained his equilibrium and started the chase. Thorpe, the gold medalist in the 1912 Olympic decathlon, was a faster runner than Halas, but the ground was slippery and Halas cut back and forth.

Halas ran as if being pursued by a fire-breathing dragon, which in a sense he was. He said later that he could hear Thorpe's pounding steps closing in on him and always marveled that he had escaped a flying tackle. Somehow Halas made it safely to the other end zone and set a National Football League record for longest punt return of 98 yards, a mark that lasted for decades.

By 1940, Halas was turning 45, long removed from pulling on the pads. He was more identifiable by his fedora than his jersey. He was down to filling two roles – owner and coach, instead of three. During some of the darkest days of the Great Depression Halas came very close to losing financial control of the Bears (that remains in his family to this day) and was bailed out by friends and a bank at the last possible minute. It has been theorized that by coming up through the ranks when the NFL was shaky and every dollar was dear caused Halas to retain his thriftiness even when the NFL was a smooth-running, big-money institution and owners had to pay big bucks for players.

There is little doubt that Halas was old school, but that was pretty much because he opened the old school and became the last man standing from his era.

It took two Redskins, Marshall, and coach Ray Flaherty, to equal Halas's one-man output for the Bears. Flaherty was born near Spokane on a farm in Lamont, Washington in 1903 and played his college football for Gonzaga. He was an accomplished end who turned pro in 1926 for the short-lived Los Angeles Wildcats, who played all of their games on the road.

The 6-foot, 190-pound, red-headed Flaherty also played for the New York football Yankees, and the New York Giants, through 1935, with the exception of 1930. Flaherty experienced a rather odd sports shift in the middle of his pro football career, taking time out that year to play minor-league baseball and coach the Gonzaga Bulldogs for just that one season. Flaherty's major claim to fame as an offensive end was leading the NFL in receptions with 21 in 1932.

When Marshall became dissatisfied with his losing coach as time grew short in Boston, Flaherty was tapped to lead the Redskins. During his seven seasons coaching the Redskins, Flaherty won four division titles and two NFL titles. He is also credited with inventing the screen pass in 1937, Sammy Baugh's rookie year. While Halas only had to answer to himself for his coaching moves, Flaherty had to answer to the picky Marshall. However, he laid down the law early in his tenure. Marshall may have been the owner and the boss, but he hired Flaherty to coach and he, Flaherty, was going to do the coaching, not Marshall. Somewhat surprisingly, Marshall acquiesced to his coach standing up to him.

"I never had any trouble with Mr. Marshall," Flaherty once said. "He came down to the bench one day and I sent him back into the stands. He never came down again." (5)

Certainly, Flaherty was confident enough assuming his new role as field leader. When he accepted Marshall's offer to coach he declared that he would take the Redskins to a title or resign. That was a bold statement, but he did come through with the club's first crown in 1937. Flaherty made a quick transition from player to coach at a young age – he was only 33 his first season at the helm – but earned the respect of the Redskins because he knew the game and like a military officer commanding a platoon understood how to lead men.

"He knew football, but his biggest asset was in knowing how to handle players," said one of the 1940 linemen, Jim Barber. "He knew when to chew a fanny or to pat somebody on the back. The players liked him, but he was no patsy." (6)

One thing that may have made Flaherty an attractive hire for Marshall was the smarts he displayed with the Giants in 1934. New York met the Bears for the NFL title that year. It was a frigid day in December and the field was icy. It was Flaherty, who knew exactly how slick the field was from running pass patterns, who prompted Giants coach Steve Owen to hurriedly obtain rubber sole shoes. The Giants rounded up sneakers, wore them for the second half and ran away from Chicago for the title.

"We got up that morning," Flaherty said. "It was early December and it was down near zero. The general manager of the team called me from the field to say it was frozen, so when I got back from church I told our equipment manager to find us some tennis shoes. Since it was a Sunday and no football team had ever used tennis shoes before, we had a difficult time finding any. But it so happened that our clubhouse boy was also the clubhouse boy at Manhattan College, so he ran over and rounded up all of the tennis shoes he could find. I had him busy dyeing them black so the Bears wouldn't steal the idea." (7).

Given that football teams never wore tennis shoes, Flaherty got the idea from a brief personal experience.

"The reason I knew about the shoes," he said, "is that I used them once at Gonzaga University when I had a bruised heel. The field was frozen that day, too, and while the other guys were slipping and sliding, I was able to run all over the place." (8)

New York topped Chicago 31-13 that day. It was one time that Halas was out-smarted. And it was one game that always stuck in his craw. It was not clear if Halas knew that Flaherty, the opposing Redskins coach, played a significant role in the Bears' sneaker humiliation, but he would have relished revenge in the 1940 championship game.

When he wasn't playing or coaching football, Flaherty was an active outdoorsman. Although he won two titles with the Redskins, he described his greatest thrill in sports being when he shot an elk in Idaho that was bearing down on him full blast just as hard as one of those nasty Bears linemen like George Musso. There are many other big-toothed, long-clawed beasts of the wild considered more deadly than a bull elk, but Flaherty nearly lost a key argument with one anyway.

Flaherty was a few days into a group hunt in the Bitterroot Mountains and he was deep in the hills with two others when he spied a likely target grazing 200 yards distant. Flaherty was armed with a .35-caliber rifle when he crawled 50 yards closer to the animal and snapped off a shot. The bullet seemed to slap against the elk's body, but rather than slowing it down, the impact caused the elk to lose its temper and charge at Flaherty, who shot again. And again and again. The elk did pause, but only briefly, and kept on roaring at him.

"He looked bigger than a mastodon," Flaherty said. (9)

On his fifth shot, Flaherty downed the elk inside of 100 yards from him. He added a kill shot up close and then figured out that every one of his bullets had struck home. The elk, weighing more than 1,000 pounds, was just that tough.

It wasn't quite the same as out-foxing Halas with the sneakers, but Flaherty feared for his own safety while he maintained a cool head in his battle with the elk. Out-thinking the opponent is a key element in any kind of competition.

"Coaching is like playing a checker game," Flaherty said. "You are in competition with the other coach to outguess him." (10)

Applying Flaherty's definition, he was definitely outguessed by Halas on December 8, 1940. More sports experts make the comparison between coaching and chess rather than checkers, and there is no doubt that Flaherty's squad was checkmated by the Bears that day.

LIVE FROM WASHINGTON, D.C.

When kickoff rolled around at 2 p.m. on December 8, 1940, the audience for the eighth National Football League championship game was built around 36,034 fans in Washington's Griffith Stadium. But for the first time there was an additional audience, ghostlike in its attendance.

Some 20 years into its existence, the NFL was encroaching on the big time, though it is not clear if league president Carl Storck was aware of it through the action of granting radio air rights to the Mutual Broadcasting System.

It is ironic that one of the milestone moments in league history – the national broadcast of the title game for the first time – occurred when the highest office in the NFL was in turmoil.

Jim Thorpe was the first commissioner of organized pro football, chosen for his name recognition. Thorpe held the post in 1920 and 1921, yielding to Joe Carr, whose much more significant reign as the league established its footing lasted until 1939. Carr passed away that year and was succeeded by Storck.

Storck was one of the league founders in 1920 and in the 1920s was owner and coach of the Dayton Triangles. He ascended to the league presidency in 1939 when Carr died, but due to his own fragile health stayed on the job only through 1941.

Storck was in office when the Bears met the Redskins for the title in 1940 and when the game was broadcast. The Mutual Broadcasting System was founded in 1934 and went out of business in 1999. Mutual was a major player in broadcasting for decades, and particularly in the sports realm. Baseball's All-Star game, the World Series, and Notre Dame football were staples of the network's broadcasting lineup.

Beyond that, during the golden age of radio, such shows that lured entire families into crowding around their living room radio the way TV shows in the future would, could be heard on the Mutual system. They included "The Lone Ranger," "The Adventures of Superman," and "The Shadow."

Broadcasts of live sporting events, beginning with radio, continuing with the advent of regular television, and following with Cable-TV and eventually streaming over the Internet, were about to change how Americans related to their favorite sports and teams.

Only a year after the NFL was founded, the first college football game was broadcast on the radio, a contest between Texas and Mechanical College of Texas (now known as Texas A&M). The event took place on November 25, 1920.

Less than a year later, the first Major League Baseball game was broadcast on August 5, 1921 when KDKA in Pittsburgh aired a Pittsburgh Pirates-Philadelphia Phillies game with Harold Arlin at the microphone. Only two months later the first World Series was aired.

The year 1939 was a huge one in television broadcasting history. NBC introduced regular programming of variety shows, circus acts and dramas and before very long threw sports into the mix, too. The very first televised sporting event, of all things, was a May 17, 1939 baseball game between Princeton and Columbia. The famous radio announcer Bill Stern handled the game.

During this experimental and pioneering age the shows and events were telecast on W2XBS in New York, which had a broadcast signal of roughly 50 miles.

On August 26, 1939, the first Major League Baseball game was televised, showing the Cincinnati Reds versus the Brooklyn Dodgers. The announcer was Walter "Red" Barber. His nickname was "The Ol' Redhead," and Barber's was a familiar voice on New York City area radio.

Nearly two months later, the first telecast of a pro football game occurred, with the opponents being the Brooklyn Dodgers and the Philadelphia Eagles. Televised football is ubiquitous in the 2000s during the autumn months and well into winter, but it had to start somewhere.

One of pro football's biggest problems in the early days of the NFL was proving to fans that the caliber of play was better than the quality of the college game. College football had been part of the sporting landscape longer and some fans found it difficult to believe that the pros that were not highly paid, were really better than the best college teams. This was one aspect about trying to establish the league that drove George Halas. He was so irritated by the argument that he took advantage of every opportunity he could manufacture to match the Bears against collegians. When the squads played he showed no mercy to the college boys.

College football, which ranked higher in the sports hierarchy in newspaper coverage during the 1920s and 1930s than the pros, saw its games televised before NFL games were. It was hoped by NFL supporters that when both were aired it would become obvious to football fans that the caliber of play was much better in the pros.

Of course, in 1939, there were hardly more television sets owned by the public in New York City than there might be for sale in the average Wal-Mart these days. When the Eagles and Dodgers kicked off there were just 1,000 TV sets in New York's six boroughs. The act of televising the game was so underpublicized that even players who played in it never knew they were part of the historic league first TV game.

"I certainly wasn't aware of it," said Brooklyn tackler Bruiser Kinard. (1)

Unlike the modern day broadcast booth, often crammed with three people clamoring for attention, and a team of four or five handling a halftime report, the first game was broadcast by a solo artist named Alan Walz. An athlete in his younger days, Walz had played football for New York University and been a New York City Golden Gloves boxing champ who made his career as a broadcaster.

"I remember the game," Walz said of the Eagles-Dodgers match 42 years after it was played. "Pro football was a great game to do by television and the excitement of doing the game was fun." (2)

The broadcast was not without its technical challenges. TV was in its infancy and equipment was far from being as sophisticated as it became in future decades.

"It was late October on a cloudy day," Walz said, "and when the sun crept behind the stadium there wasn't enough light for the cameras. The picture would get darker and darker and eventually it would be completely blank and we'd revert to a radio broadcast. I would sit with my chin on the rail in the mezzanine boxes and the camera would be over my shoulder." (3)

The initial broadcast was considered enough of a success that the other Dodgers games were shown that year, too. Walz said the audience built and was interactive in the sense that suggestions on how to improve this newfangled operation would be mailed in to Walz.

"We were selling television at the time and people had to believe in television," he said. (4)

There was no halftime analysis. When the clock ticked down at the end of the second quarter and the teams ran into the locker room, the TV station also took an intermission. Rather than Walz, or a team of commentators filling the time, music or other programming from the radio would fill the gap until it was time for the second-half kickoff.

Walz did post-game interviews with players, but often the sky was so dark by then, the cameras could not produce a useful picture.

"Players probably thought I was just another of the radio men there," Walz said. (5)

The field was wide open as far as programming went. There were no nationally syndicated deals around, partially because lacking foresight most of the owners of professional sports teams did not recognize that they could build an audience for their product by showing games to fans for free. They were certain that radio first, and then TV, would cut into home attendance. Reality demonstrated that the broadcasting of games merely whet the appetite of the sports fans to watch his heroes in person.

It was never trouble to sell out a baseball All-Star game or the World Series and both were such big news that fans wanted to listen or watch them even if they couldn't obtain tickets because of sellouts. It stood to reason to Mutual Broadcasting System officials that the same type of support might be forthcoming from fans that could not make it to Griffith Stadium for the NFL title game in 1940, a game that in any case was sold out.

Choosing to broadcast the NFL championship game was a worthwhile gamble for Mutual, too, because of its standing against the other national broadcast groups. Mutual may have had more affiliate stations, but they tended to be in smaller markets, so that held down advertising compared to NBC, CBS, ABC and DuMont.

If Mutual could secure a long-term agreement to work with the NFL, it might better compete with the other radio networks. However, Mutual was just a little bit ahead of its time. NFL popularity did not mushroom until the late 1950s.

Still, for the serious 1940 NFL fan who wanted to hear what was happening in the championship game as it unfolded, Mutual was the way to go and that fan was rewarded by hearing one of the finest broadcasters of all time. Just as he had pioneered baseball on television, Red Barber pioneered football on national radio.

Barber was born in Columbus, Mississippi in 1908. During his broadcasting heyday of the 1930s, 1940s, and 1950s, he developed a reputation as a brilliant baseball announcer. However, much like the professional athletes of the times who made a pittance in salary compared to modern-day players, broadcasters could not afford to specialize only in one sport and were also in the market for off-season jobs.

He did not come from a wealthy family and Barber hitch-hiked to college at the University of Florida in Gainesville and held a part-time job as a janitor while an undergraduate. He made his debut in radio with one of the most unlikely and least sexy of readings that ever jump-started a major broadcaster's career.

One day in 1930 the student radio station came up short when the scheduled agricultural professor failed to show up to read a paper on the air. Barber was enlisted and made his sparkling debut by reading a piece entitled, "Certain Aspects Of Bovine Obstetrics." It might be surmised than even a 73-0 football game held more drama. However, Barber was not exactly baffled by football. After solving the station's problem as a fill-in, he gained the chance to do some sports. His very first assignment was the University of Florida's season-opening football game that season.

Barber played high school football and became the station's Florida football broadcaster because his predecessor left school to join his father's law firm. Barber said he was paid 35 cents an hour for the work and the only time during his long professional broadcasting career when he was a fan and rooted for the team he was covering was this very beginning.

"I was a fan for six-and-a-half football games," he said. "I was a red-hot Florida Gator fan. I hadn't learned the necessity for pre-game preparation. I was having a great time." When powerhouse Alabama appeared to face Florida, Barber asked Coach Wade Wallace if he could lend him a spotter to identify the Crimson Tide players during the action. Wallace said he could count on a third-string guard who had been hit in the head and was too injured to play. Florida was holding 'Bama and seemed prime for an upset, a fact that Barber noted on air. The only problem was that Wallace pulled a fast one and did not start his usual first team, the one that had so thoughtfully been provided to Barber by the injured player. "I looked at the Alabama spotter's face and it was a pale green. I leaned off the mike and asked, "Are you sick?" He said, 'Yes, and you're going to be sicker. That's the first team coming in.'" The toughest moment Barber faced in broadcasting followed when he said to his audience, "Forget everything I've said about Alabama's first team." (6)

After that, Barber said, he devoted his time to learning his craft, going to practices, talking with coaches and players, and he no longer cared who won or lost, only about doing a good job, so he wouldn't lose his job.

Barber's smooth tones were much better known in the world of baseball than in the world of football and he is more closely identified with broadcasting baseball. Still, Barber gained football broadcast experience by announcing the football Dodgers games, the New York Giants football team's games, and Princeton games.

Agreeing to broadcast the 1940 title game between Chicago and Washington really amounted to just another off-season gig for Red Barber. Handling a big football game was as much evidence of his versatility as it was contributing to his bank account so he could put food on the table leading up to Christmas.

SID LUCKMAN

Sid Luckman was the favorite son. During his 63 years associated with the Chicago Bears, George Halas never pursued another player harder, was willing to pay his price more readily at the time, or bonded more closely than he did with the Bears star quarterback of the 1940s.

Besides those who were really related to Halas who worked in the Bears' offices over the decades, the troika of players that came closest to becoming family – as adopted sons, so to speak – were Luckman, Mike Ditka, and Gale Sayers. The relationships were not identical – Ditka was the wayward son. But Halas-Luckman ties never wavered, from the moment Halas showed up at Luckman's apartment to convince the young man to become a Bear who was planning to skip pro football, and throughout the rest of their lives.

Luckman was born on November 21, 1916 in Brooklyn, New York. During Luckman's youth baseball was the biggest sport in the United States and especially in New York. The New York Giants thrived under manager John McGraw. The Brooklyn Dodgers had their own following. And the New York Yankees, who obtained Babe Ruth, became the team of the Roaring Twenties. Yet those were also the early days of the New York Giants football team in the young National Football League.

The thing of it was, Luckman loved football and while many of his friends favored playing baseball in the streets he preferred the pigskin game.

"When I was a young boy growing up in Brooklyn, we used to play football for hours on the cobblestone streets," he said. "It was something I felt I had to do, be part of football. My favorite team was Notre Dame where Knute Rockne was the head coach. One day (in 1931), it was announced over the loudspeaker that Rockne was killed in a plane crash. I sat by the radio and cried. It taught me a lesson. You never know in life what the good Lord has in store for you." (1)

Luckman's high school was Erasmus Hall, the producer of numerous famed sports alumni for the borough of Brooklyn, including boxing promoter Bob Arum, basketball star Billy Cunningham, chess champion Bobby Fischer, Hall of Fame pitcher Waite Hoyt, and world-class swimmer Eleanor Holm. Barbra Streisand is also an alum, but was too busy memorizing the songbook to cope with the playbook. Decades later, the Erasmus football field was named after Luckman.

Handsome, with wavy hair, the 6-foot, 197-pound Luckman, who played in the era of leather helmets with no face masks, was heavily influenced by his high school football coach Paul Sullivan.

"He believed in discipline, dedication and desire, motivation to be successful, not only in football, but in life," Luckman said. (2)

Sullivan also believed in Luckman and he wrote to Columbia University football coach Lou Little endorsing him.

"Here is a boy who is a grand competitor and, as you know, a fine forward passer," Sullivan penned about Luckman. "But he's more than that. He loves the game to the extent that he'll work at it hour after hour in an attempt to excel. You can't possibly pile too much on him. He'll take it, and he'll be the first man on the practice field the next afternoon, asking for more." (3)

Luckman had the smarts for an Ivy League education, but as the years passed Little feared he was going to lose his star. Luckman threatened to drop out of college to go to work and help support his mother during the mid-1930s. Luckman was a product of a single-family home since his father had died when he was young. But as a result of Little's intervention Luckman worked as a chauffeur for Little's wife and university professors, did some baby-sitting, and helped counsel students in financial need.

Halas recognized that the T formation was the wave of the future in pro ball, but that style of play needed a savvy quarterback to be run smoothly. After scouting Luckman during his senior year Halas knew the kid was the player he had to have. Only Luckman planned for a business career and rebuffed Halas's suggestions that he play pro ball. It was a little bit odd given his childhood and high school zest for the game, as described by Sullivan, but he seemed to think his football days were behind him.

A great believer in his own persuasive powers, Halas traded two players and a draft choice to the lowly Pittsburgh Steelers to ensure that the Bears had no worse than the second pick in the player draft and despite Luckman's discouraging words Halas plucked him in the 1939 draft as the quarterback wrapped up his senior year.

As soon as he graduated, Luckman got married – his wife's name was Estelle – and now that he had invested a draft choice in Luckman Halas journeyed to New York and took another run at signing Luckman. The answer was still no.

Even Little was impressed with how passionately Halas chased his man and any time the Bears leader made contact he passed on the information to Luckman.

"A persistent man, that Halas," Little said. "He's set on nabbing you, one way or another. And he's certainly got enough money to dish out." (4)

Halas made a third pass at Luckman, again visiting him in New York in his new apartment. Estelle was sold before Sid and helped convince him that he should give the NFL a try. It also did not hurt that Halas waved a salary of $5,000 at him. In 1939 that was big money for a recent college graduate.

"You and Jesus Christ are the only two people I'd pay this to," Halas informed Luckman. And Halas was not at all sure that Jesus Christ had the kind of arm the Bears needed. And although he was Jewish, Luckman replied, "Thank you, Coach. You put me in great company." (5)

Although he didn't say it out loud at the time, Halas was hoping Luckman might stand out in the great company of the Redskins' Sammy Baugh.

As a New Yorker all of the way in the pre-World War II years, Luckman's traveling had been pretty much limited to Columbia away games in the Northeast and forking over small change for subway rides. To him Chicago was the largest dot on the map in the Midwest and he knew little else about it.

"I had never been further than Buffalo," Luckman said. "I really thought Chicago was where cowboys were still around." (6)

Since the T formation had long before fallen out of favor and needed modernizing and tweaking, Luckman had to learn how to master it from the playbook drawn up by Halas. He wasn't even used as the quarterback for the first few games of the 1939 season and he often stayed up late doing his homework.

Six games into the season, on October 22, with the Bears on their way to an 8-3 record, Luckman got the call to start at QB in New York, against the Giants, the team he rooted for as a kid. He later said that the experience was very stressful and he was nervous playing in front of his relatives, fellow students and coaches from Columbia and other New Yorkers. It was not the best game of his life, though Luckman did throw an important touchdown pass, and Chicago lost 16-14. But he did earn the regular quarterback job and held it for a decade.

"I didn't know left from right or right from left," he said. "I was so high-strung." (7)

Luckman gained seasoning in 1939 and by December of 1940 and the championship game against the Redskins he had proven to be the real deal. After his edgy beginnings, he was unflappable on the field and during his career, which culminated with election to the Pro Football Hall of Fame, Luckman led the Bears to four titles. Decades after his retirement he is still considered the greatest Bears quarterback of all time. Halas' instincts were correct – Luckman was the perfect fit for Chicago.

Halas was crusty and often profane, regarded as a cheapskate when it came to paying his men generous salaries, but he was a complex character who was loyal to his players and displayed his generosity quietly when one of them, or a family member, suffered a serious setback. Luckman respected Halas and admired what he accomplished with the Bears and the league as a whole and always praised him.

"Halas was a tough disciplinarian, a human being beyond anyone's imagination, a best friend," Luckman said. "He was and always will be the NFL. He made it. His dreams and visions came true." (8)

Luckman did extraordinary things on the field under Halas' guidance. He was a five-time All-Pro. He threw 137 career touchdown passes during an era when passing was more like 35 percent of the offense compared to running, and he established the one-game record of throwing seven TD passes in a game, a mark that has never been broken, though it has been tied by a handful of other players.

As a rookie, Luckman was definitely still feeling his way. He appeared in all 11 Bears games, but he certainly didn't strain his arm, making only 51 attempts all season. Luckman was a more active passer in 1940 during the regular season leading up to the title game, that year tossing 105 passes. Still, he only heaved four touchdown passes while flinging nine interceptions. When he showed up at his first Bears training camp, Luckman was taken aback by the size and speed of the pros who had it all over the college boys he had been playing against. It took him time to adjust to the better athletes and the more sophisticated offense. But those watching him closely recognized that he had the goods to be a true leader.

Although Luckman seemed somewhat perturbed that the Bears had not gone undefeated in 1940, he did ache for a chance to play the Redskins in the championship game. He was well aware that Washington supporters, notably owner George Preston Marshall, had been agitating the waters after the 7-3 loss on November 17.

"We had taken enough badgering to keep us plenty riled up," Luckman said. He felt a little bit guilty because the Bears had nearly stolen that regular season game from the Redskins when Luckman hurled a potential touchdown pass to halfback George McAfee that fell incomplete. The Bears felt McAfee didn't make the catch because he was held in the end zone – the source of Marshall's complaints about the Bears being crybabies. "Then Washington jockeys started to label us "rulebook weepers," among other things. Was there a better time to make them swallow those words?" (9)

The newspaper reports out of Washington had been hanging on the bulletin board for a few days and mostly Halas just let his players gaze at them. At one point, as kickoff approached, he showed how irritated those Marshall comments fanned by sportswriters left him. "The guy ought to be sued for libel!" Halas roared. (10)

It is likely that Halas got more satisfaction out of what was to come on the field at Griffith Stadium than he would have from a day in court. For the rest of his life, more than 40 years worth, Halas cackled, grinned, or pursed his lips in satisfaction any time he spoke about the 1940 championship game.

As for Luckman, who was going to start a career in the trucking business in Manhattan before Halas steered him in a new direction, he gained fame and fortune from playing pro football. He became one of

Chicago's most legendary athletes, a reputation that still stands strong six decades after his retirement and many years after his death. He met high-powered businessmen because of his glorious days on the gridiron and after he stopped playing he continued in the game as an assistant coach, always in demand, with the Bears and other teams, as an expert on the T formation. In 1948, around the time he authored his autobiography, Luckman also wrote a book called "Passing For Touchdowns" which offered instructions about quarterbacking for young players and for those who either did not play for the teams he tutored or attend clinics he ran.

Right off the bat in the book Luckman lets readers who may not have observed the obvious know that he is a passing man, a firm believer in the fact that the passing game livened up the sport.

"Football in its early days was at best a dull game," Luckman wrote. "The offense at the time consisted mostly of a series of line bucks, with occasional cracks around end...passing was a distinct rarity. Then came the forward pass." (11)

Luckman was one of a handful of key figures arriving on the scene in a timely manner who pushed the forward pass forward as a weapon. Not even Luckman or any of those other pioneers would ever have dreamed how the passing game has evolved and by the 2010s became predominant. While Luckman may have appreciated a Peyton Manning becoming one of the few quarterbacks to equal his seven-touchdowns-in-a-game record, he would have been flabbergasted to hear that the Denver Broncos QB threw 55 of them during the 2013 season and gained 5,477 yards through the air in a single season. Luckman may have been in love with passing, but those statistics would have been as alien to him as learning that a Martian was throwing out the first pitch at a Cubs game.

Reflecting on his seven-touchdown game versus the New York Giants and other big-game TD passes he threw, Luckman said, "There's no more thrilling play in football. But by the same token there's no type of offensive maneuver which requires more in the way of teamwork on the part of every man." (12)

The business opportunities he gained access to through his success on the field made Luckman a millionaire.

"I can never repay the Bears for making my life a more enchanting life," Luckman said. (13)

One of those enchanting days as an athlete occurred on the big stage, in the championship game versus the Redskins in 1940. Athletes dream of playing for all of the marbles, of playing for the title, of getting the chance to win a ring. By 1940, Halas had been coaching the Bears for 20 years. He had earned his share of success. The Bears were a traditional power, a terror of the league. For Luckman, this was something new. He was a second-year professional in his first championship game and he could not know what was to come once he stepped out onto the field in front of a hostile crowd.

Just before the locker room door was opened and the Bears poured out of their sanctuary to run onto the gridiron, Halas provided some last words, a pep-talk paragraph to inspire his players. He reminded them of the recent 7-3 loss to Washington and played it up, wanted them to think about it as the game began.

"You have one great advantage over the Redskins today," Halas said. "An important score to even up. Those guys have been strutting about the past two weeks like half-lit roosters, raving about a flimsy four-point edge. I'm thinking in bigger terms than that – much bigger. I want to show them how a real big-league outfit operates. If I had taken the kind of razzing that you boys did, why, I'd want to whale the daylights out of anyone attached in any way to Washington." (14)

Halas did not often prepare or deliver pep talks, so it was clear this was a meaningful occasion to him. When Halas spoke to his team just before a game that team listened.

"I can almost see him in front of me now," Luckman said 55 years later, "delivering one of the few inspirational speeches he ever gave us. He said that we were the greatest football team in the nation and that he wanted us to prove it to George Marshall and the Redskins, to the nation, and most important, to prove it to ourselves. 'Now go out there and play the football you are capable of playing,' said Halas. After that we all ran to that damn door to break it down and get out there on that field." (15)

The Bears thundered out of the locker room and onto the field, but Halas grabbed Luckman and pulled him back for a private word. It was last-minute advice offered to his leader and verbally and by written word. Halas had studied Washington's defense from the previous game and jotted down some fresh plays that he shared with Luckman, hoping there would be a chance to employ them and surprise the Redskins.

"Coming down here I scribbled a pet play on each of these cards," Halas said. "I'd like you to try these, Sid, if Washington keeps the same formation (it) did in the game two weeks back. The first play should test the defense and the second should carry you to the goal." (16)

At this late hour Halas slipping Luckman some fresh plays was pretty much redundant. When Halas talked of whipping the Redskins he was really preaching to the choir. The Bears may have lost that regular-season showdown, but to a man they believed they were the better team and were intensely focused on proving it. Chicago was most assuredly ready to go.

"We hoped they would use the same defense the next time," Luckman said, "and we vowed we would get to the championship game. We worked for weeks against their defense. Even though we had lost that pre-title game, we still marched up and down the field." (17)

In some ways the 1940 championship game was the making of Sid Luckman as a star. He was well-known in some quarters, especially New York, and soon enough would be featured on the cover of Life Magazine with the teaser headline of "Best Passer." But as kickoff approached for that important game there was no doubt that Luckman was overshadowed completely by Sammy Baugh.

Quarterbacks may be the face of the sport in the modern era, but it was possible that in 1940 – before the era of football on TV several times a weekend and with newspapers covering their own teams but no others – it was possible for a fan to be familiar with just one quarterback in Baugh. Luckman elevated his stature that cold day.

It was the true beginning for Luckman, who would achieve so much in the game, and who would become so beloved in Chicago. The tete-a-tete with Halas reinforced their relationship at an early stage. That closeness remained long after Luckman retired from the sport and after Halas gave up coaching and became a full-time front-office man.

Halas passed away in 1983 and he was ill for a lengthy period of time before his demise. For whatever particular motive he chose to pen a letter to Luckman during the final months of his life – perhaps as a reminder to the player he first met as a fresh-faced collegian.

"My boy," Halas wrote, "my pride in you has no bounds. You were the consummate player. You added a luster to my life that will never tarnish." (18)

Halas was not known for his sentiment, but his phrasing was certainly sentimental. He was clearly in a serious mood, or perhaps he might have added, "We'll always have Washington."

Slingin' Sam, passer par excellence, in a practice session with the Washington Redskins, shows the form that won him fame. Right now, Baugh is in his 18th season with the team, setting passing records right and left. (Copyright Bettmann/Corbis / AP Images)

SLINGIN' SAMMY BAUGH

Sammy Baugh, the cowboy from Texas, made the Washington Redskins. Baugh's arm was a singular weapon at a time when few National Football League teams thought much about passing and fewer still possessed a quarterback with a cannon arm. Such quarterbacks are rare enough species at any time, but in the Pleistocene era of passing, Baugh's skill was almost magical.

George Preston Marshall's Redskins showed signs of life as they exited Boston. With the arrival of both the Redskins and Baugh simultaneously in Washington, Marshall struck gold, and with the most unsophisticated of ranch-hewn men at the helm they stormed the nation's capital and spread the gospel of pro football into and throughout the South.

Baugh was a wiry 6-foot-2 and weighed about 185 pounds, no big-bodied truck in build. He had an innate toughness and started at quarterback as a rookie in 1937 after being drafted out of Texas Christian University. Until then the Redskins had been no particular rival of the Chicago Bears. Baugh's presence uplifted the Redskins into the elite category of the NFL.

Baugh was from tiny Sweetwater, Texas, progressed through TCU and on to Washington by the time he was 23. He had dreamed of becoming a Major League baseball player and his right arm served him well on the diamond, too. It was just that it was better suited to the gridiron.

There was no denying Baugh's all-around athleticism. Although it is difficult to compare eras and the all-around caliber of football play has dramatically changed, based on his contributions to Washington during his 16-season NFL career, it can be argued that Baugh is the greatest player in NFL history.

Clearly, he was one of the pioneers of the passing game and as quarterback led the Redskins to championship success. But beyond that, at different times during his NFL career, he was chosen All-Pro as a defensive back and as a punter. Three positions? Baugh was a legendary passer. Add in all-star play at two other positions and they have yet to define the word to cover that breadth of talent and achievement in the game. That's the kind of stuff a superior athlete achieves in high school. In the NFL? Not hardly.

Baugh arrived on the scene as the Redskins' No. 1 draft pick in 1937 and at a time when the league's football coaches were just beginning to open their minds and playbooks to the understanding that a passer could be a devastating offensive force. His opposite number with the Bears, Sid Luckman, was of the same vintage, a player coming along at just the right time to show what he had and to show what could be accomplished by a signal-caller armed with a bazooka.

For all of his own greatness, as a Hall of Famer, and certainly as one of the most appreciated Chicago Bears of all time, Luckman admired Baugh. Near the end of their careers, Luckman noted, "I just like to sit and watch him. Every time he throws, I learn something. Nobody is ever going to equal him, nobody." (1)

Baugh was born in 1914 in Temple, Texas and he was a two-time All-American for TCU. He was blue-eyed and raw-boned and played in the leather helmet days with no face mask. He was an infielder in baseball and mastered rodeo roping later. With Washington, Baugh led the NFL in passing six times, in punting five times and in interceptions once. One year he completed 70.2 percent of his passes – at a time when many other starting quarterbacks completed less than 50 percent. One season Baugh averaged 51.3 yards per punt. One year he intercepted 11 passes. He was so popular he was recruited to appear in a movie called "King of the Texas Rangers."

Texas was stamped all over Baugh. If the NFL had been playing in Dallas or Houston back then he no doubt would have angled to end up on one of their rosters. He wouldn't leave Texas unless he had to – especially in his latter years.

The word is often used now to describe a strong-armed quarterback with a gambler's gumption – gunslinger. But there was no prototype for a gunslinging quarterback when Baugh played. He pretty much invented it. He had a willingness to throw often and long and he could rally a team into a late-game comeback.

That style came naturally to him. Baugh followed football when he was younger, but all of the stars were either hulking tackles or running backs who tucked the ball under their arm and darted downfield by either finding holes or making them. There weren't many passers for a young player to model himself after and the offenses weren't yet geared to the thrower yet, either.

"When I was a boy, football was Jim Thorpe, Red Grange and the Four Horsemen of Notre Dame," Baugh said once. "But I was one of those boys who just liked to throw the damned thing." (2)

When Baugh was a boy growing up in the 1920s when those players ruled, he was called Sam by everyone and he preferred that, although in later years when sportswriters sung his praises he was more commonly referred to as Sammy. One reason he stuck with Sam was for autographs – it was faster to write than "Slingin' Sammy," what the public knew him as.

The boy who learned those big-time football names grew up in West Texas, 50 miles from Abilene. His father worked for the railroad, but Sam liked the country and from an early age he thought it would be nice to own his own spread. He made that come true with his football earnings. Baugh's earliest youth was spent in Temple, but his last two years of high school, when he moved from end to quarterback, were spent in Sweetwater.

Where others might find the natural weather of the 10,000-person town of Sweetwater to be somewhat bleak, something of the dryness and even the blowing sands set just right on Sam. He liked the gritty feel of the area, didn't even mind living in an area where rattlesnakes out-numbered humans. He was not one of those small-town guys just aching to get out and prove himself to the world, to move on and never look back. On the contrary, Baugh always came back to Texas.

Maybe Baugh latched onto the land to stay grounded because his father left the family and became a bootlegger, trained fighting cocks, and abandoned his wife for a girlfriend.

Baugh was a good, not great football player, a blocking back, and later denied stories written about his high school days of leading the Sweetwater team to state glory.

"But it just ain't true," Baugh said. "Hell, I was a long way from being the guy who led us to the playoffs." (3)

Baugh's sporting dream focused on baseball and he believed he was about to be offered a scholarship to Washington State University. But then he hurt his knee and that prospect vanished. After high school he played third base for an amateur team. He had no idea what he wanted to do in life. Then the baseball coach at the University of Texas stepped up and wooed him. Baugh was convinced Austin was the place for him, but when he showed up he was told he couldn't also play football. So responding to an earlier foray from TCU's Dutch Meyer he changed his mind and switched allegiances.

Meyer coached freshman football and was a huge influence on Baugh's life. Meyer believed in the passing game and he found his leader in Baugh. They were good for each other and by the time Baugh graduated he was a two-time All-American.

The Great Depression still held sway on the American economy when Baugh enrolled at Texas Christian in Fort Worth in 1934 and dusty West Texas suffered as much as any town in the land. Baugh did not come from money. He came from hard work, raised from his teens on by a single mother. College football was not nearly the big deal then as it is today, at least not in terms of national media coverage and with beloved university teams filling stadiums of 100,000 or more seats each Saturday.

Yet football was always big in Texas and TCU was a member of the Southwest Conference. Even then that counted for something. There was something in the game that connected it to the heart of the people in the Lone Star state. That remains true today. Those were glory years for TCU under Baugh and when he departed from the school he was nationally known.

If an All-American quarterback with Baugh's pedigree and resume comes available for the pro football draft in the 2000s he is likely to be a sought-after commodity. The quarterback is the franchise in the modern NFL. Not so in 1937. While the passing game was growing in importance, most pro teams were still built around the run. Most offensive formations were still geared to emphasize power football. The concept of the game-changer quarterback was not ingrained in the minds of pro team owners and coaches yet. One had to more or less be a visionary to see the future with a wide-open style taking over.

Benny Friedman had made some noise with the New York Giants. Green Bay coach Curly Lambeau recognized the changes coming and he paired quarterback Cecil Isbell and end Don Hutson. Luckman was still in college.

However, a few years earlier, Redskins owner George Marshall played a role in changing NFL rules to give more emphasis to the passing game so at least in theory he understood that passing could lead to more points and more entertainment for the fan dollar. As someone show business oriented he could relate to the idea of a marquee player, someone whose name alone would put fannies in the seats.

Marshall felt burned by his experience in Boston when he put a winning team on the field and a fan could still grow lonely sitting on the 50-yard-line. Marshall wanted a winner and he wanted a headliner who could light up the box office. Baugh was still contemplating a career in baseball when the Redskins gained negotiating rights to him through the NFL draft. Sweetwater High needed a new football coach and tempted Baugh. TCU offered to make him an assistant football coach and he planned to take that job.

Still, Baugh played out his college baseball senior year and went on the road with a summer team. The St. Louis Cardinals showed some interest. As the summer wound down and fall approached, Baugh was still not signed to play pro football. He had other options. Marshall really wanted Baugh on his team so he made an offer of $5,000. Baugh went to his old coach, Meyer, as a sounding board and Meyer said that was good pay and that many of his college assistants weren't collecting that much. Marshall then upped his offer to $8,000 and that tipped Baugh towards the Redskins.

"I figured I couldn't turn it down," Baugh said. (4)

The first time Marshall summoned Baugh to Washington, D.C. after he was selected with the team's No. 1 pick he requested Baugh dress as a cowboy. It was a nice show, but Baugh didn't actually sign his contract until months later and when he returned for the 1937 season he wore a suit, just as all of the politicians in D.C. did. Soon enough he would make his Redskins' No. 33 jersey more famous than the old cowboy boots and shirt that was supposed to advertise he was a Texas guy.

No matter. It wasn't long before anyone in the nation's capital gave a hoot what Sammy Baugh wore as long as he unleashed his rifle arm on their behalf. And that was something he did immediately upon taking control of the team's offense. The Redskins won their first championship that season, 28-21 over the Bears. It was a fine introduction for Chicago's George Halas and hardly the last time Baugh was a major blip on Papa Bear's radar screen.

In that first major showdown with the Bears Baugh threw for 352 yards and three touchdowns. You could say there was a new sheriff in town and the normally grumpy Halas tipped his fedora in Baugh's direction with a classy post-game observation.

"Baugh was a one-man team," Halas said. "He licked us by himself." (5)

Even in 1937 Baugh's exploits made him a nationwide phenomenon and he was asked to write a syndicated newspaper series about his young life to date. It should be noted that Baugh was recruited for the writing task barely more than a month into his Redskins' quarterbacking duties – he made that much of an impact that quickly. In the series Baugh took a little bit more credit for Sweetwater's on-field success in that lengthy dissection of his playing days to date. And he gave a lot of credit to Dutch Meyer for developing his skills as a quarterback and punter in college.

One thing Baugh did was clarify the origin of his nickname "Slingin' Sammy."

"Almost everybody in the country takes it for granted it is because I am a forward passer and that it was given to me because of football," he said. "But that is all wrong. The name, believe it or not, was given to me because of my baseball career." The moniker was pinned on him by a Fort Worth sportswriter for the way he threw the ball to first after fielding grounders at third. (6)

Baugh was still a rookie, but the teaser for the series distributed by the North American Newspaper Alliance already was calling him "the greatest forward passer football has ever known." (7) While not incorrect, it was premature.

Not terribly surprisingly, since stars in all sports over the decades from the 1930s into the 1960s, were routinely solicited to provide advice for youngsters wanting to follow in their footsteps, Baugh went over some of the fundamentals. He did have some interesting observations about the differences between college and professional football at a time when pro football was still attempting to eclipse the college game in popularity and was still trying to gain respect.

"…it's our bread and butter to win and play well," Baugh said. "And nobody is going to throw away his bread and butter without a struggle. Self-preservation is, after all, really the first law of nature. Fairer minded and clear thinking football fans know there is no let-up in professional football. As to the caliber of players, you can take it from me they are much better than in college. In the first place, professional players are the cream of the crop. They are the best players available at their positions. Thus, in every position a man is good. And his substitute is almost as good as the regular or first stringer. Blocking and tackling is better and harder. Defensively the teams are better. Pro ball, like anything else, is a swell career for a fellow who is good in his line." (8)

It is not clear whether or not this series was ghost-written, but the word "swell" was not the type of namby-pamby word that Baugh used in everyday conversation. His sentences were heavily sprinkled with "hell" and "damn" rather than swell. Even though he was a swell player.

By the end of the 1937 season, with that NFL title in the bank, the Sammy Baugh Fan Club membership list could not be easily tabulated. The adjectives flowed and the compliments gushed.

"Baugh is my all-time, all-around All-American as a player and a fellow," said Redskins teammate Wayne Millner. (9)

An opponent, Green Bay Packer tackle Lou Gordon, said of Baugh, "I've seen and played against (Ernie) Nevers, (Benny) Friedman, and (Harry) Newman, and Baugh is the greatest passer of them all." (10)

And he was really just getting started. To say that Baugh made a good first impression in 1937 was a bit of an understatement on the order of saying that talking pictures were revolutionizing the movies. Baugh established himself in a hurry and he, too, was in the vanguard of a revolution.

The passing game had arrived in pro football and was here to stay. While it doesn't seem much compared to the throwing habits of current-day quarterbacks Baugh heaved 171 passes as a rookie. That was shocking at the time. He gained 1,127 yards through the air. Baugh was no longer a newcomer in the NFL in 1940. He was a known quantity, just one that most defenses couldn't stop.

During the 1940 regular season Baugh tossed 177 passes and completed 111 of them for a completion rate of 62.5 percent, an average rate of success that did not become common until the 1970s and beyond. If the Bears and Halas were at all surprised by what Baugh pulled off in the 1937 championship game, they definitely understood that to win the 1940 crown they would have to contain Baugh.

The Bears had not played particularly well in the regular-season loss to the Redskins, the 7-3 defeat of three weeks earlier, but it gave Washington confidence and even if the Bears were angry, they were still smarting from a loss they wished to avenge.

There was no reason for the Redskins not to believe that they could duplicate the success. Baugh was no different than his teammates. Of course they thought they would win the championship in 1940. Although he did not say so until many years later, Baugh did say that he and his teammates were not happy about owner George Preston Marshall taunting the Bears about the loss.

"He put things in the paper running the Bears down," Baugh said. "You don't want to help the other team. You shouldn't say things like that." (11)

Marshall's rather infantile gloating gave Baugh pause, if not a headache. One irony of the Bears-Redskins confrontations of that era was the fact that starting in 1940 Chicago also had a star player from Sweetwater, Texas, as unlikely as that was. Lineman Clyde "Bulldog" Turner, whom some consider to be as a great a center as Baugh was a quarterback, passed his hometown boy on the way off the field on the day Washington bested Chicago, 7-3, in the regular season.

The teams were exiting the field, walking down the ramp that led to the locker rooms when Turner sidled up next to Baugh and said, "Just remember, we'll be seeing you bastards in three weeks. Don't forget that." (12)

At the moment that could easily have been construed as sour grapes, but Baugh did not respond in kind. He well knew that there was every chance the two squads would meet again in December. He kept his own counsel, unlike Marshall.

Baugh cringed when he read how Marshall popped off in the newspapers, belittling the Bears. Yes, Marshall did call them "crybabies." He added more, too. "Quitters," Marshall said. "They fold up when the going gets tough. Just look at what they did today. They don't know how to win a close game." (13)

Ouch.

Baugh may or may not have known that in addition to this ill-advised diatribe, Marshall also actually sent George Halas an inflammatory telegram. Apparently, that was just in case Halas didn't read the Washington newspapers. In part it read, "I hope I have the pleasure of beating your ears off next Sunday and every year to come. Justice is triumphant." (14)

In many ways this encounter was a dream come true for Marshall. Not only was he the owner of a top-notch football team – Baugh said he thought this was the best Redskins team he played on – but it was a hit at the box office, too. Washington was a power town and the Redskins represented the city that was at the seat of American power. Congressmen and Senators not only rooted for the Redskins, they wanted tickets to the big game at Griffith Stadium.

Marshall was in his element. He couldn't wait for kickoff. Marshall was like the father of the bride. All eyes in Washington were going to be on his Redskins. His star quarterback Sammy Baugh would shine and the 150-piece Redskins band would play the song of the day. At the end of the afternoon, in Marshall's mind, indeed justice would be triumphant.

Bill Osmanski (9), the Chicago Bears' full back, is under full steam racing for the Washington Redskins goal line on the second play of the NFL Championship game in Washington, D.C., Dec. 8, 1940. Osmanski went on a reverse around left end and ate up 68 yards for a touchdown. The Bears slaughtered the Skins, 73-0. Washington players trying to put a halt to Osmanski's gallop are **Ed Justice** (13), **Dick Farman** (21) and **Jimmy Johnston** (31). (AP Photo)

FIRST QUARTER

Looking back, it might be said with a certain amount of smirking that the Chicago Bears won the first play of the game and that was merely a harbinger of what was to come. Chicago won the coin toss and elected to receive the opening kickoff in the 1940 NFL championship game.

The temperature was a brisk 39 degrees for the 2 p.m. kickoff on December 8, but with the wind whispering at only 2 miles per hour the conditions were not extreme and could be handled by rugged football players felt to be impervious to weather.

The opening boot was the responsibility of Washington's Willie Wilkin, a bulky, 260-pound tackle out of St. Mary's College in California. A native of Utah, Wilkin was drafted in the 16th round by the Redskins in 1939. His kick was a deep one, fielded by Bears halfback Ray Nolting on his own three-yard-line.

Nolting was a trusted offensive weapon for Chicago. He came out of the University of Cincinnati and had been a fixture as a runner in the Bears' backfield since 1936. Although not as well-remembered as many other Chicago backs who came along, during his eight seasons with the Bears Nolting averaged 4.5 yards per carry and was a member of three world championship teams, as well as five Division champs.

The 5-foot-11, 185-pound back returned the kick 22 yards before being forced out of bounds. His return gave Chicago a first down on the 25-yard-line to start the offense.

Chicago's trademark had always been power, but coach George Halas and quarterback Sid Luckman opened with a slick play. The call was for a reverse by George McAfee that gained seven yards and immediately made the Redskins' defense uneasy because of its unpredictable nature.

That was not half the degree of surprise that greeted Washington on the next play from scrimmage. Luckman handed off to fullback Bill Osmanski who zipped around left end and saw nothing but open territory ahead. As the 5-11, 200-pound Osmanski steamed down the left sideline, two Washington defenders closed in. They converged on Osmanski at about the Redskin 30-yard-line and threatened to trap him. Nicknamed "Bullet Bill," Osmanski was a notable sprinter and ordinarily was unlikely to be caught from behind, though a tackler working an angle would have a shot. However, Chicago end George Wilson sprinted into the picture and the future coach of the Miami Dolphins and Detroit Lions managed to flatten both with one block. Wilson was a member of four Bears title teams, but surely he always wished he had the highlight film of that block available to show his men during his latter coaching days.

Osmanski finished off the run, a 68-yard gallop that was the most famous of his seven-year, World War II-interrupted career. Eventually, Osmanski became the answer to a trivia question: Who scored the first Bears touchdown in their 73-0 victory over the Washington Redskins? It was actually quite fitting that Osmanski scored that TD because he was a pivotal figure in that 7-3 loss to Washington three weeks earlier and as part of Marshall insulting the Bears as sore losers.

As the final seconds of that regular-season game ticked down Osmanski was roaming the Redskins' end zone as Luckman faded back and sought to pass. Osmanski represented the winning touchdown, but before the ball reached him, the Bears fullback said, Washington defender Frank Filchock pinned his arms down and another Redskin hit him. To Osmanski, and the other Bears, the officials should have whistled an infraction.

"The ball hit my chest and fell to the ground," Osmanski said. "We complained, but the officials refused to call a penalty, and the Redskins immediately called us crybabies." (1)

The title-game touchdown was very satisfying to Osmanski, who adjusted on the fly once he got around end.

"On the second play of the game I took the handoff and slanted off left tackle," Osmanski said. "The end had only been partially blocked, so I dipped to avoid him, something not in the playbook, and raced down the sidelines." (2)

He surely appreciated Wilson's hit, too. George Musso made the initial block that sprung Osmanski, but Wilson was downfield running a pass route and he delivered the smack to Washington's Jimmy Johnston and Ed Justice.

"George threw the greatest block I have ever seen," Osmanski said. "It not only disposed of Justice, but it flattened Johnston, too. All I had to do was run the rest of the way." (3)

Osmanski attended Holy Cross and was enshrined in the College Football Hall of Fame. He spent the rest of his life as a dentist and said the only reason he played pro football was that he was able to insure his hands against debilitating injury through Lloyd's of London. Halas wanted Osmanski, and he knew dentistry was his lifelong ambition, but he made Osmanski pay the premiums for the insurance policy himself.

Jack Manders kicked the extra point for a 7-0 lead 55 seconds into the game. In less than a minute the Bears had exceeded their total points from the previous game. While that explosive TD might have muffled Redskin fans' cheers they could not have imaged what was to follow and how their club would never be this close on the scoreboard again.

The Redskins were reeling from the quick strike, but they were also receiving the ball. It was Sammy Baugh's turn with the ball. Manders kicked off to Washington's Max Krause, who gathered in the pigskin on his own 10-yard-line. But a lapse in Bears coverage allowed Krause to wriggle free and rip off 51 yards. Krause, who won 14 letters in various sports in high school, came out of Gonzaga and had an eight-year NFL career. This proved to be his last contest, however, because he suffered a knee injury.

Krause's run was a gift for the Redskins, with field position on the Bears' 39. They could stifle Chicago's swiftly earned momentum. Baugh handed off to Johnston, who scampered for six yards to the Chicago 33. The play worked so well the Redskins did it all over again, Baugh to Johnston for a gain of five. For variety Baugh handed off to Justice, who gained two yards. That advanced the ball to the 26-yard-line. The next play was for no gain, Johnston shut down by the Bears' defense. On third-and-eight from the 26, Baugh ordered up a pass play.

This would be Washington's most memorable offensive play of the day. Right end Charley Malone, who made 20 grabs during the regular season, shimmied and shook and was open at the 5-yard-line. Baugh fired, the ball was on target, and the usually-reliable and definitely-wide open Malone dropped it. A follow-up 32-yard field-goal attempt missed, so the Redskins got nothing out of the drive and Chicago still led 7-0.

A couple of hours later a sportswriter who either had a sense of humor or only air between his ears, asked Baugh if things might have been different if Malone caught the pass and Washington had tied the score early in the first quarter. It was not reported whether or not Baugh eyed the questioner as if he had just emerged from a spaceship, but his reply was unequivocal and memorable.

"Yes," Baugh said, "it would have been 73-7 instead of 73-0." (4)

His answer had just the right amount of sardonic inflection. Of course, at the moment of Malone's miscue nobody could have pictured that the play was as close to scoring all day as the Redskins would get.

Chicago got the ball back on its own 20-yard-line after the kickoff. On the first play George McAfee was nearly caught behind the line of scrimmage, but shook off Bob Titchenal's tackle try and gained four yards. That was the beginning of a 17-play, bulldozer of an 80-yard Bears drive on which Luckman bothered just once to straighten his arm out to throw.

This was old-time, smash-mouth football as play after play the Bears' linemen opened up king-sized holes and the Bears' runners took turns darting through the gaps and moving the ball downfield a few yards at a time. Normally, it is thought that a long strike that swallows a big chunk of the field in one play is very demoralizing to a defense. But to trot out of the offensive huddle play after play and gouge holes in the line may make defenders seem even more futile.

During the first 16 plays of the drive, Nolting, McAfee and Osmanski took turns ripping gashes in the Redskins' defense. There was no defense really. Always the Chicago guards and tackles dug in, shot forward, and created space. The hard-running backs followed. It was as if a herd of elephants cleared the forest. Nolting rushed for 3, 3, 3, 2, 1, and 5 yards. McAfee rushed for 4, 6, 6, 3, and 2 yards. Osmanski ran for 22 yards early and it was Baugh, contributing in one of his other roles in the Redskins' defensive backfield, who possibly saved another touchdown by knocking him out of bounds. Osmanski also ran for six yards and was stopped at the line of scrimmage once.

The Bears were at the Washington 14-yard-line when things got a little funky. Luckman called a pass and hit Nolting on a flare that brought the ball to the 2. Luckman called Osmanski's number and the Bears had a brief fright when a hard hit from Washington's Ernie Pinckert popped the ball free. However, Chicago tackle Joe Stydahar scooped up the fumble and advanced it to within about a half yard of the goal-line, rescuing the drive.

On the next play Luckman did not give the ball to anyone. He held on and capitalized on a quarterback sneak for Chicago's second touchdown. This time Bob Snyder, who wore many hats, including backup quarterback, kicked the extra point for a 14-0 lead. This was a tell-tale drive. It was not a fluke, but a grind-it-out series of plays, hard work that produced a reward. The Bears pushed the Redskins around and once Luckman learned that they could do that he knew he could count on the running game being dominant and the passing game being a good supplement that could be utilized to keep the Redskins off-balance.

"We controlled them at the line of scrimmage," Luckman said. "We knew what they were going to do and we were able to attack them from every angle we could. They were unable to stop the power we generated. Whatever we did, we did right, and they did wrong. That was the start of the T formation in sports because after that game every team in the United States watched the Bears." (5)

Lee Artoe kicked off for the Bears and his boot sailed through the end zone for a touchback. That meant Washington started its possession on its own 20. Down by two touchdowns, it was still plenty early enough in the game, and the quarter, for the Redskins to mount a comeback. Washington had tested the Bears on the ground and had fairly good success on its first drive, although no points were scored. This possession Baugh, who generally passed more frequently than Luckman, and who in his prior experience learned that he could pick apart a defense and move the ball downfield in small chunks, just like running it, aired it out.

However, he discovered quite quickly that the Bears' defense was geared to him. Baugh faded back and the Bears sealed off routes. Baugh faded back and was hit by the pass rush. Chicago was suffocating him. On the first play Baugh completed a short pass to Johnston, but he was cornered behind the line of scrimmage and lost six yards. On the second play, back at the 14-yard-line, Baugh dropped back and facing a heavy rush threw incomplete.

On third down Baugh aimed for Bob McChesney and the pass again fell incomplete. Within moments the Redskins faced fourth down deep in their own territory. There was no choice for coach Ray Flaherty except to signal for a punt. This was an age of lack of specialization in pro football. In the 2000s the quarterback, regarded as the most important player on the field, is protected from harm through hard-fast rules. He is not used for anything but leading the offense, and counting on blockers to form a brick wall of defense for him.

In 1940 no quarterback was considered to be such hot stuff he couldn't also perform other duties. Baugh rarely came off the field. He was the QB on offense and a defensive back on the other side of the ball and when the Redskins faced the situation, he was the punter. Standing inside his 10-yard-line, Baugh tried to get distance on this kick. Only Chicago's George Musso busted through the line and got a piece of the ball. Partially blocked, the kick turned somewhat wobbly. Of all people, Luckman, doing double duty, too, was the receiver of the punt and he returned it three yards.

Washington had been hoping for a breather, the Bears taking over the ball far away, deep in their own territory. Instead, Chicago had a first down at the Redskins' 42. Most observers were likely ready for another series of inside handoffs with the Bears sticking to the ground and chewing up the turf a few yards at a time. Instead, back Joe Maniaci took the ball from Luckman and shot around left end. He accelerated as he turned the corner – nearly stepping out of bounds, but avoiding the miscue. When he straightened out he was in the clear.

Maniaci put distance between himself and all pursuers, going all of the way for the touchdown. Following an apparent share-the-wealth policy, Halas selected a third kicker to kick the extra point. Phil Martinovich got into the box score this way. So before the first period was over the Bears led 21-0.

Maniaci, who played collegiately at Fordham and later coached St. Louis University, was one of what seemed to be an endless supply of backs that Halas deployed when the mood hit him. Maniaci, who lived to be 100 years old, probably never had a sweeter memory than scoring this critical touchdown which gave the Bears all the confidence they needed to realize they would win the championship – even if the game had more than three quarters to play. The Redskins knew they were in trouble.

Washington was the beneficiary of a minor break on the kickoff. Lee Artoe's boot went awry and the Redskins took over on their 45-yard-line. It was good field position. But even worse for the Redskins than the 21-point deficit was the absence of Baugh when Washington's offense came onto the field again. He was shaken up on a hit and back-up Frank Filchock came in.

The Redskins' possession lasted three plays and out, although it might have been a bigger disaster since Filchock's first down pass to McChesney was caught, but then fumbled. Tackle Bo Russell recovered, but still the Redskins bogged down and had to punt.

The clock ran out on the first period before the Bears could score again. But those numbers – 21 – loomed large on the scoreboard after the initial 15 minutes of play. Washington still had a pulse, but barely. It was not clear if the Bears had made George Preston Marshall cry or whine yet, or not.

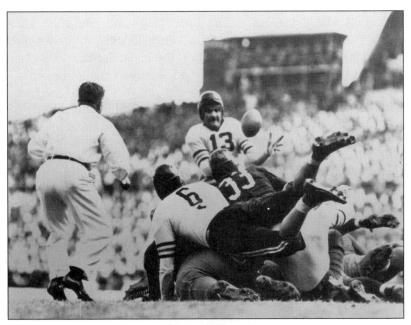

Chicago Bears Hall of Fame tackle **Joe Stydahar** recovers a loose ball in a 73-0 win over the Washington Redskins in a League Championship game on December 8, 1940 at Griffith Stadium in Washington, D.C. 1940 NFL Championship Game - Chicago Bears vs Washington Redskins - December 8, 1940 (AP Photo/NFL Photos)

A HALL OF FAME LINE

Yes, Sid Luckman was a great field general. Yes, the Chicago Bears were explosive. But the reason Luckman could recognize and say before the first quarter was even over that the Bears had control of the line of scrimmage was the Bears' coterie of fantastic linemen.

George Musso was a 6-foot-2, 262-pound guard and tackle who like his counterparts played both ways on offense and defense. He attended small Millikin University in Decatur, Illinois and was elected to the Pro Football Hall of Fame in 1982.

While Musso was one of the larger players of his era, Dan Fortmann was one of the smaller stellar linemen. He was 6 feet tall and weighed 210 pounds. Fortmann came out of Colgate University and was selected for the Hall of Fame in 1965.

The 6-4, 233-pound Joe Stydahar competed for both the University of Pittsburgh and West Virginia and was a Hall of Fame choice in 1967.

Clyde "Bulldog" Turner is considered one of the greatest linemen in pro football history and for decades was called the best center of all time. Turner, 6-1, 237 pounds, came out of the same hometown as Sammy Baugh, Sweetwater, Texas, played small-college ball for Hardin-Simmons, and his induction into the Hall of Fame occurred in 1966.

Four linemen playing together all advancing into the Hall of Fame made it difficult to run on the Bears, run past the Bears, or get past the line into the backfield to tackle the Bears who might be carrying the ball.

If you were the Redskins and you surveyed those sides of beef you might have been afraid, very afraid.

During Musso's 12-year stay with the Bears, Chicago won four NFL titles, seven Western Division titles, and the team's overall record was 104-26-6. That's how the Bears eased into the nickname of "The Monsters Of The Midway." Musso was definitely one of the monsters.

Musso's weight closed in on 270 pounds at a time when even

teammates on his own line weighed 60 pounds less. The 300-plus NFL lineman was a fact of the distant future. It was no wonder after seeing him up close in several big-time situations that Washington coach Ray Flaherty conjured up sincere flattery for Musso.

"George was one of the outstanding linemen of his time," Flaherty said. "His size and speed made him a difficult target, particularly on defense." (1)

Musso's nickname was "Big Bear," quite appropriate given his affiliation, and his trademark was making big plays during the career that spanned 1933 to 1944. That very much included a proficiency in blocking kicks, much as he did in the first quarter of the 1940 title game when he got a paw on Baugh's punt.

Offensively, when Bronko Nagurski was the Bears' powerhouse fullback, Musso was assigned to open holes. Nagurski was known for putting his head down and plowing ahead and once ripped through the end zone and crashed his head into the wall near a dugout at Wrigley Field.

"I am blocking for Nagurski and he waits for no one," Musso said. "If you don't open a hole he'll hit you in the back and the next time you will either open it or get out of the way quick." (2)

Musso was captain of the Bears for years, but his life easily could have turned in another direction. His father was a coal miner who had to be persuaded that Musso should bother to stay in school for high school, never mind college. One of Musso's line opponents at Millikin was Eureka College's Ronald Reagan. Musso out-weighed Reagan by close to 100 pounds, but in the end Reagan wielded more power than Musso during his later-in-life job as president of the United States. Interestingly, also as a collegian, Musso went head-to-head with another future president in Gerald Ford, then playing for Michigan.

Yet Reagan had more speed than Musso and could beat him sometimes employing that trait. When it was muscle against muscle, Musso won the match-ups. One of Musso's teammates, Red Grange, called him, "The Moose." (3)

"If I got him (Reagan) halfway standing up, I'd bowl him over," Musso said. "But he was smart enough most of the time to stay around the ankles. He was a damned nuisance, I'll tell you that." Musso asked him, "Why are you around my ankles all the time?" Reagan replied, "You take care of your position and I'll take care of mine." (4)

Politically, both Reagan and Ford outranked Musso, who after retiring from football became a crime stopper. He served as a parole officer and a deputy sheriff, and lost one election to become a sheriff. Then he was elected sheriff of Madison County in Southern Illinois. Musso certainly had the build of an enforcer. Don't mess with me, could have been his motto, same as it was on the gridiron.

One of the more humorous incidents during his tenure was leading a raid and finding more guilty parties involved than he had prepared for – so Musso called taxi cabs to transport some of the arrestees to jail. He ended up spending eight years as sheriff and 12 as county treasurer.

Even though he wasn't quite as big as Musso, Joe Stydahar's nickname was "Jumbo." He is the answer to a pretty good trivia question himself: Who was the first Chicago Bears No. 1 draft pick ever? Joe was the man in 1936 when the National Football League instituted a draft of college players. He was another immovable object on the line, playing on three world championship teams and five Western Division winners between 1936 and 1942 and again for a couple of years after World War II. Stydahar later coached the Los Angeles Rams and the Chicago Cardinals.

As were so many of his teammates in those days, Stydahar was a "60-minute man," a player who went both ways on offense and defense and stayed on the field for the entire game. During his earliest years with the Bears Stydahar did not wear a helmet, though the practice of playing bareheaded faded out during his stint with the team.

Stydahar was George Halas' type of player, rough and tough who gave it his all, who didn't complain, and who was known for his integrity. The two men were close when Stydahar played and remained close. Years later, after Stydahar was a head coach in the league and lost those jobs he rejoined the Bears as an assistant coach under Halas.

"Joe was something special for me," Halas said. "More important than any of the football accomplishments, Joe Stydahar was a man of outstanding character and loyalty. All the things that made Joe a great football player were reflected in his successful business career. (5)

Halas liked Stydahar from the start, giving him more money than the player expected. To some who know of Halas's reputation for being a cheapskate they may have termed some acts as temporary insanity. Stydahar's biggest problem wasn't adapting to the pro game, but first learning how to drink and then learning how to stop. He went cold turkey to sobriety after some challenging times.

Being drafted by the Bears was pretty much the most important thing that ever happened to Stydahar, he said.

"That was the turning point in my life," Stydahar said. "Halas has been like a second father to me. I didn't know anything about football until I had a chance to play for him." (6)

There were a few strange twists in Stydahar's pro career. He was a member of the Bears when Clark Shaughnessy showed up to tutor Chicago in the ways of the T formation before the 1940 game. He succeeded Shaughnessy as coach of the Rams after being his assistant— and was insulted by him as he moved into the office to occupy Shaughnessy's chair. The outgoing coach said, "Stydahar, coach of the Rams? I could take a high school team and beat him." (7)

Maybe, maybe not since Stydahar took the Rams to the 1950 Western Division crown and the 1951 NFL title after Shaughnessy couldn't win it all in 1948 or 1949. Years later, when Stydahar became a Bears assistant – the only team he said he wanted to work for at the time – he replaced Shaughnessy on the staff. He spent two years as defensive line coach before going into private business.

That terminated Stydahar's involvement with football, but he was elected to the West Virginia University Sports Hall of Fame, the College Football Hall of Fame and the Pro Football Hall of Fame.

There probably isn't a 210-pound lineman anywhere in the nation at the top level of college football. Except at small schools, both college and high school, you won't find tackles and guards playing first string at that weight in the 2000s. But Dan Fortmann somehow played the line for the Chicago Bears between 1936 and 1943 and played it well enough to be chosen for the Pro Football Hall of Fame.

The guy lined up next to players with nicknames like "Jumbo" and "Moose," and they were kind enough not to call him "Pipsqueak." As a draft pick Fortmann almost qualified to be called "Mr. Irrelevant," the moniker slapped on the last player chosen in the NFL draft these days. In 1936, he was the Bears' ninth and last selection in the first draft.

"I like that name! I'll take him," Halas bellowed at the draft. (8) Actually, few teams had any type of elaborate scouting system in place beyond word of mouth, so Halas may well have been guessing about Fortmann's fortitude for pro ball beyond the sound of his name.

Somehow it seemed as if Halas saw behind the lack of physical stature to Fortmann's heart and he made All-Pro six times in a career that ended when he entered the Navy during World War II. While playing pro ball was a distinguished part of Fortmann's life, his true accomplishment was becoming a doctor, a general surgeon, after being released from the Navy. By the time Fortmann, who excelled at offensive guard, was selected for the Hall of Fame, he thought it was a case of mistaken identity because so much time had passed since retirement.

From afar, it seemed as if Fortmann would be supremely challenged by attending medical school and Dr. George Halas' practices for the Bears, but he laid his cards on the table, asked for Halas' help in making it work and informed the dean of students at the University of Chicago that he was working his way through college by collecting checks for playing football.

"It really worked quite smoothly, with the cooperation of the dean and the coach," Fortmann said. "Chicago works on a quarter system. So, for all intents and purposes, it was a matter of substituting the summer quarter for the autumn quarter." (9)

He did miss a couple of weeks of summer practice leading up to the start of the season – with Halas's blessing – though he sneaked in some Bears workouts on the weekends. But Fortmann never could have played pro if Halas hadn't been flexible, a trait that few identify with Papa Bear.

Fortmann was only 19 when he graduated from Colgate University and became eligible for the player draft. He had some learning to do to make the transition from college to the pros, and he said he benefited mightily from playing with Joe Stydahar.

"It helped me tremendously to play next to Joe for so many years," Fortmann said. "A true partnership built up. We got to know exactly what to expect from one another." (10)

Halas could be a demanding taskmaster, but Fortmann didn't mind the hard work and he thought Halas was a masterful reader of men who understood how to psyche up a team for a top-notch performance. He particularly marveled at the way Halas boosted the team leading up to the romp over the Redskins.

"For three weeks George kept reminding us of the close loss and what Marshall was saying about us," Fortmann said of the outspoken Redskins owner George Preston Marshall. "I have seen some highly charged teams during my playing days, but the Bears that day were the highest emotionally of any team I ever saw." (11)

One thing that Fortmann got a kick out of on the day of that supreme massacre was claiming that he made a major contribution to the final score. He often joked that without him it would never have been possible because he called the coin toss that gave the ball to the Bears to start the game.

Musso, Stydahar, and Fortmann – any NFL team would have loved to be able to say it owned the rights to just one of them. Yet for all of their talent they ranked behind Turner. The Bulldog was the best of them all up front, a center who was revered in the game for decades, a linebacker who was playing the position almost as a hobby, but still intercepting passes constantly.

As someone who came out of Sweetwater along with Sammy Baugh, it would be worth asking for real just what was in the water in that town that made it so sweet. Others suggest it was not exactly an aptly named place, but more of a hardscrabble environment that demanded a lot of energy put in by its residents for them to make a go of it. Turner was a product of a West Texas that could be harsh and unforgiving. He made it big elsewhere, but like Baugh he also returned to his roots. Unlike Baugh, his later years weren't quite so pleasant.

Young Clyde Turner was a terrific ball player, a magnificent athlete who might well have been the second coming of Bronko Nagurski if he concentrated on playing fullback, but instead became the first Bulldog Turner by ferociously tackling other Bronko wannabes.

Turner was no secret coming out of college, even if he did attend little Hardin-Simmons. He was big and fast and could terrorize other teams. The big dudes who played in the 1940s were not to be confused with Olympic sprinters, but Turner was faster than most of the backs in the

NFL. He once turned in a spectacular play against the Washington Redskins, running back a Sammy Baugh interception 97 yards for a touchdown. Baugh, some 50 pounds lighter, and someone who played quarterback and defensive back, caught up to Turner as he entered the end zone. Turner didn't understand how that was possible.

"How did you ever catch me, Sammy?" Turner said. "I know I can outrun you." (12)

Turner was a rookie in 1940, the season of the Redskins romp, but he almost didn't become a Chicago Bear. As much as George Halas coveted Turner and how clearly he recognized that he could be a special player, Detroit Lions scouts also had spotted him. The Lions made a special visit to Texas to chat with Turner and gave him $200 in illegal advance money, ostensibly to have his teeth fixed by a dentist. It really was walking around money as a bribe so that Turner would think of the Lions fondly. The Bears drafted Turner the legal way and then the dispute over Turner's rights surfaced. Commissioner Bert Bell made the call that Turner belonged to the Bears.

With the University of Chicago dropping football, the Chicago Bears were about to lay claim to the nickname "The Monsters of the Midway." The true monster among monsters was Turner, as good as the gaggle of other Bears surrounding him was.

Turner came from a hard background and he made it hard on those who faced him on the gridiron. Rural West Texas lacked electricity and running water in the homes when Turner was a youth. Turner came of age during the Great Depression of the 1930s, but really, his family lived amidst the same conditions in the years leading up to it. In Turner's neighborhood many families subsisted on the barter system. They grew crops and traded them to other families in the same circumstances that grew other fruits or vegetables. It was one way to keep food on the table during tough times. Of course, in a parched land where rain did not fall in abundance at any time, the Dust Bowl years were brutal on growing anything consistently or with much success. Turner's father was a cowboy, a ranch hand, initially, but then tried farming and had to cope with the lengthy 1930s drought.

As it is now, by the time Turner reached high school, football was a huge form of entertainment in Texas. This is where the phrase "Friday Night Lights" originated. The big game in town featured the local high school team on Friday nights and the whole town turned out to watch. Excelling on the field was certainly one way for a boy from a poor family to get noticed and nobody played the blood sport that was the favorite of the area better than The Bulldog.

The Turners had moved from their dust-buried ranch in Plains, Texas, to the bigger city of Sweetwater and that's where the children were educated and Bulldog earned a name for himself playing football. Jay, an older brother, was a top athlete in football and then as a boxer, but died young, at 27, from a combination of high blood pressure, bloody noses, blackouts and overall no clear diagnosis at all. A younger brother, Virgil, or "Dugie," was a boxing, basketball and track star. Athletic talent ran through the Turner strain. Dugie was a prisoner of war during World War II, but then played football at Hardin-Simmons in Abilene, as did Clyde.

Bulldog's first motivation to succeed at football was to earn a varsity letter after he enrolled at Sweetwater as a junior. By then Sammy Baugh, two years older, had graduated, and they did not meet until later in life. Turner worked at the game.

"I had cleat marks all over my shins," Turner said of his first day of high school football practice, the day he judged his toughest ever in the sport. (13)

Still, Turner was a late bloomer and did not really star in high school. His name was known because he was on the team, but he did not carry the team. He was very much a young, naïve, cloistered teenager when he finished high school and did not assume he would play college football, although the idea appealed to him.

When the Sweetwater coach mentioned Turner's name to the Hardin-Simmons coach as someone with potential, Turner weighed 170 pounds and that was generously spread up and down his 6-foot-2 height. But when coach Frank Kimbrough sought him out Turner recognized this as a special opportunity and he whipped himself into shape before school began, punishing his body with unbelievably challenging workouts.

Turner entered Hardin-Simmons in 1936, ostensibly to study journalism. He so intensely disliked his given name of Clyde that he told everyone to call him Bulldog.

"I was just country and dumb," is the way Turner described his bearing as a freshman. (14) But he learned, in the classroom, how to behave socially, and how to master the plays on the football field.

As the seasons and years passed Turner grew larger and stronger and once viewed as puny for football he morphed into a chiseled 235 pounds while retaining the speed of a dash man. The more he played football, too, the better Turner got, at whatever Kimbrough asked him to do and at whatever he tried. He prided himself on his versatility and he often amazed Kimbrough with that very trait.

"He was a natural-born athlete and could play any position," Kimbrough said. "We played him at center, but made him run with the backs." (15)

Although Turner got so he could overpower just about everyone he faced and Hardin-Simmons compiled a 23-3-2 record during his three varsity seasons, Hardin-Simmons was not on the national map of big-time football schools. In an era without either television coverage or the Internet, it took some digging to learn about the exploits of the Bulldog. But even then, so long ago, if you were good enough, somehow, some way, the NFL would find you.

"Pro ball didn't get into my mind until my senior year at Hardin-Simmons," Turner said. "Then I got to thinking, 'Maybe I can play pro ball.'" (16)

Although the sort of national hype that follows the best college football players while they matriculate has only mushroomed in intensity over the decades, some fast-thinking publicity agents did help win their star players extra attention with their facile minds. In 1924, as nationally known scribe Grantland Rice sang their praises, the members of the Notre Dame backfield were mounted on horses, had their pictures taken, and were forevermore known as "The Four Horsemen Of Notre Dame."

Turner, too, was the beneficiary of a clever public relations man. Hardin-Simmons brought in a Dallas photographer named Jimmy Laughead to create some memorable images of the school's star players. One picture featured Turner and two teammates, wearing their numbered jerseys and football pants on galloping horses as they waved ten-gallon hats. Another photo, which showed off Turner's impressive strength, displayed the Bulldog with a calf draped across his shoulders as he seemed to snarl. It was catchy, fun, stuff that served as eye-openers for those who didn't know who Turner was. Testing to see how this campaign was received, officials at the school were astonished when they received 6,000 newspaper clippings of the calf photo.

Suddenly, Turner was viewed as a strong man, his nickname chanted from the stands during games, and other sportswriters actually called him "Young Hercules" in print. (17)

Craziness ensued. The Detroit Lions owner wined and dined Turner and paid him hush money not to discuss this courting. George Halas of the Bears did not know that the Lions were chasing Turner and when his turn came around on NFL draft day he called Turner's name. This was a surprise because usually first-round picks were reserved for quarterbacks or other offensive weapons.

When Halas' pick was revealed, George Richards, the Lions owner squawked. It was a messy little dispute. The problem was Richards had broken the rules and Halas had played it straight, so Turner became a Bear for the 1940 season by decree of Commissioner Bert Bell. Richards was steamed and it was a costly mistake (he was also fined $5,000 for tampering) and his misjudgment penalized his club on the field for years to come given the way Turner blossomed.

It took almost no time for Turner to adjust to the pros. He became a starter for the Bears right away and began building his reputation as an all-time great during that 1940 season. He was technically a rookie, just turning 21, but Turner played like a seasoned veteran. Even other great football players were impressed by Turner.

"Bulldog Turner was the best football player and smartest player I ever knew in my whole life," said George Connor, who became a Chicago teammate a little bit later. "He knew everybody's position on every play. He could play halfback. He could play center. He could do everything." (18)

As one opponent after another fell before him, Turner began to realize how good he was. He displayed no false modesty about his talent when it came to blocking charging defensive linemen.

"I was such a good blocker," Turner said, "that the men they put in front of me – and some of them were stars who were supposed to be making a lot of tackles – they would have their coaches saying, 'Why aren't you making any tackles?' They'd say, 'That bum Turner is holding.' Well, that wasn't true. I held a few, but I was blocking them, too. I used to think I could (overpower) anybody that they put in front of me." (19)

The Bears-Redskins showdown for the NFL title in 1940 came at the end of Turner's first season with Chicago. He thought Halas was a genius for the way he emphasized George Preston Marshall's insults and felt it did fire up the Bears as they wiped the grass with Washington.

There was only one thing that annoyed Bulldog Turner that day. As the Bears kept piling up the touchdowns and kicking extra points that sailed into the stands, the balls never to be seen again, Halas wanted his center to purposely hike the ball in a sloppy way so that the kicker could not convert.

Turner was appalled by this request, or order, and it went against his nature.

"I told Halas I wasn't going to make a bad snap, not in no championship game," Turner recalled. Turner was a perfectionist who took pride in not making mistakes, though inevitably they were committed even by the best players. Halas was the coach and Turner was a rookie player and finally Halas convinced Turner to simply drop the ball instead of snapping it to the holder. "The next day in the paper they say the point was missed due to a bad pass from center. Hell, I never made a bad pass in my life." (20)

In a give-no-quarter game, that was showing a little bit of kindness to the Redskins, even if that wasn't Halas' motivation. He just wanted to save the cost of a football.

SECOND QUARTER

The man the Redskins were counting on to bring them back after the Bears shot out to their 21-0 lead was back-up quarterback Frank Filchock. Born in the aptly named coal mining town of Crucible, Pennsylvania, Filchock played his college ball at Indiana University.

In 1938 Filchock was drafted by the Pittsburgh Pirates. Few remember that the much better known Pittsburgh Steelers were founded as the Pirates, the owners trying to ride the coat-tails of the already-established baseball franchise. Although Washington already had Sammy Baugh on its roster the Redskins bought Filchock from Pittsburgh.

Filchock stood 5-foot-11 and weighed 193 pounds. He did not have the arm strength of Baugh, but neither did anyone else playing at the time. Being down by three touchdowns was stunning, but not a completely hopeless situation with three quarters of the game remaining. Filchock would later become embroiled in a scandal and his career was checkered. Several years later, when Filchock was playing for the New York Giants, he was approached by gamblers with a bribe to affect the outcome of the 1947 championship game. Eventually, Filchock was caught and banned from the NFL for a few years, though ultimately reinstated. One Filchock claim to fame in a positive manner was that he was on the throwing end of the NFL's first-ever 99-yard touchdown pass. Given the way yardage gains are measured that is a record that can never be broken.

In 1940, however, Filchock was a young prospect trying to make his mark in the league and this circumstance provided a major opportunity. If Filchock could lead a comeback he would be a hero.

Baugh, or no Baugh, the Bears continued to feast on the Redskins. The second period opened with Washington obtaining first possession on its own 20-yard-line. Filchock rolled out to pass and fired the ball downfield to Wilbur Moore. It was not a bad call by coach Ray Flaherty and Filchock. The idea was to strike fast and make quick inroads in the Bears' lead. But the play was poorly executed.

Chicago's Ray McLean filched the pass. McLean was one of the comparatively overlooked mainstays of the Monsters of the Midway, playing in the shadow of several future Hall of Famers, but always a solid contributor. McLean came out of tiny St. Anselm's college in New Hampshire and was a rookie in 1940. He was born in Massachusetts and grew up in Concord, New Hampshire. As someone who played small-college football he rated as a find for George Halas when Papa Bear picked McLean in the 21st round of the 1940 player draft.

McLean played on four Bears title teams in eight seasons and did a little bit of everything – doing all of it well. He caught passes, ran the ball, played on special teams, and during his tenure as a defensive back intercepted 18 passes, none flashier than this one. By the time McLean stopped running with his theft of Filchock's pass Chicago had the ball at the 50-yard-line, halfway to another touchdown, and given the way they were playing something that seemed inevitable.

After three straight running plays, Bears quarterback Sid Luckman called for a pass. For the most part he had been content to go with a conservative game plan because the running game was working fine.

He fired a bullet to Joe Maniaci that gained 24 yards and put Chicago on the Redskins' 16. The march to the end zone continued. Except that ironically on a first and 10 McLean fumbled a Luckman handoff and Washington's defensive end Bob McChesney recovered. For once the Redskins halted a Bears drive. Luckman was not truly fazed, though.

"There were plenty of short, flat passes to (Ken) Kavanaugh and (George) McAfee," he said, followed by sharp jolts at the line which baffled the Redskins. No need for lengthy passes. "Our runners were picking up enough yardage and our line blockers were almost drunk with power. Musso, Stydahar, (Ed) Kolman, they were really playing for keeps, throwing the Redskins' front wall wide open." (1)

Washington was renewed, escaping a major catastrophe, and began its possession from its own 19-yard-line, similar to its usual initial line of scrimmage after kickoff touchbacks. Perhaps Filchock was cold when he first came into the game, but he had warmed up and seemed to have some play-calling rhythm.

On first down Filchock kept the ball and gained three yards. Then he threw to Dick Todd, but the play was broken up by Luckman, who was also playing defensive back this day in addition to running Chicago's offense. Filchock came right back throwing and gained seven yards on pass to Bob Hoffman (able to play after all), giving the Redskins a first down by less than a yard.

Dropping back again from his own 29, Filchock scanned the field for a receiver. This time he found an open Wayne Millner. Millner made a leaping catch. If anyone was going to make such an acrobatic downfield play for the Redskins it would be Millner.

Millner was an all-state high school football player from Massachusetts and excelled as a two-way, two-time All-American end at Notre Dame before joining the Redskins in 1936. He was 6-1 and weighed 190 pounds and had good speed. During his seven-year pro career that was halted by World War II, Millner was one of the finest receivers in the sport. Although he never compiled anywhere near the number of catches or other statistics NFL receivers accumulated later, he was elected to the Pro Football Hall of Fame in 1968.

One of Millner's greatest fans was his coach, Flaherty. On the day the Redskins drafted Millner Flaherty issued a complimentary, if somewhat foolish statement. He said, "With that Yankee playing end, please accept my resignation if the Redskins do not win the championship this year." (2) They did not, settling for a divisional championship, and Flaherty did not resign. But a year later, in 1937, Washington did win that crown.

After his playing career Millner said he was always very close to Flaherty. His best friend among the players was Baugh, who treated him like a favorite receiver. Baugh didn't aim this pass, but Millner still recognized what to do with the ball that came from Filchock.

Millner turned in a 42-yard gain and that was uplifting for Washington morale. Now they had to keep advancing. The next play was an incompletion. Then a heavy Bears pass rush caused another incompletion. The Chicago defender on the play was Dick Plasman. Not regarded as one of the very best players on the Bears defense amidst the crowd of Hall of Famers, Plasman was still a two-time NFL All-Star. He also had one distinction that followed him into retirement as the answer to one of pro football's great trivia questions.

Born in Miami, Plasman was drafted by the Bears in 1937 out of Vanderbilt. He spent eight seasons in the league wrapped around military service competing for the Bears and then the Chicago Cardinals.

Plasman is noted for being the last player in NFL history to play without wearing a helmet. He simply didn't like wearing headgear. The last season Plasman suited up minus a helmet was 1940, the championship massacre season. The practice of going helmetless was fading out anyway and in 1943 the league office made it illegal to play without one. Although his name does not resonate with the average football fan now, at the time he continued as a solo example of hardheadedness Plasman was the object of curiosity.

One teammate, Hugh Gallarneau, said, "I mean, he had a piece of cement for a head." Later, when Plasman was an assistant coach in the league he went hatless on the sidelines, even in frigid weather, and frostbit an ear. Asked to look back with 20-20 hindsight on that decision Plasman admitted if he had to do it all over again in a more modern era of football he would wear ear muffs. (3)

It takes a certain kind of macho guy to keep playing without a helmet to protect his noggin' even after equipment makers created more comfortable and useful protection. Bears teammate Ray Nolting said, "We called him Eric The Red, not because he had red hair, but because of his temper. He was something." (4)

Undeterred, Filchock went back to the air, flinging an 11-yard pass to Millner. But when Filchock tried to take another shot to Todd, Plasman was ready for him and batted down the pass. Sticking with the passing attack, Filchock desperately sought to drive the Redskins to a touchdown. The groaning was loudest amongst Redskins fans when Filchock threw to McChesney on the 5-yard-line and McChesney dropped the ball. McLean broke up a pass to Moore and then Filchock overthrew McChesney in the end zone. Washington stalled out on the Bears 18-yard-line.

A touchdown at that point could have transformed the game – at least in the eyes of Redskins supporters. But Washington controlled the ball and field position on a time-consuming drive, moved from the 19 to the 18, yet didn't add a point. It could have been 21-7, but remained 21-0.

Bears ball. It would be too strong to suggest that Chicago dodged a bullet since the Bears would have had a two touchdown lead anyway if Washington scored. However, the defense shutting down the Redskins that close to the goal line stifled any possible momentum switch. Chicago took over on its own 18-yard-line. Unlike the trend in recent NFL play, at least since 2010, teams did not then rely so heavily on one featured back to make most of the carries coming out of the backfield. Halas spread around the running responsibilities.

The player who got the first carry of the series was Jack Manders. Manders had been with the Bears since 1933 and he was most often used as the place kicker to boot extra points and the occasional field goal, though Halas seemed to juggle kickers with regularity, too. There seemed to be no reason not to stay with Manders for all kicking duties, especially since he was nicknamed "Automatic Jack" for his accuracy. In 1937, Manders led the league in scoring with 69 points. His total included five touchdowns, 15 extra points and a league-high eight field goals.

Manders was ahead of his time as a kicker. Until he started booting field goals and extra points for the Bears all kickers employed the drop kick. Manders really was a "place" kicker, as the action was described. Manders worked out a routine with Carl Brumbaugh, the Bears' quarterback prior to Sid Luckman, as his holder.

Each time the Bears lined up to try a kick Manders wiped off the toe of his shoe. Brumbaugh got busy making a dirt tee on the field roughly eight yards behind the line of scrimmage. Then as part of the ritual Bumbraugh spit on the toe portion of Manders' shoe. This supposedly meant that the ball would fly through the uprights with accuracy.

"There's nothing mysterious about place kicking," Manders said, despite the apparent contradictory superstition he and Bumbraugh engaged in. "It's a matter of timing and following a golf rule – keep your eye on the ball." (5)

Manders, a sturdy 200-pounder, was more than just a kicker on the roster. That season he also averaged 4.4 yards per rush for 319 yards. Manders' run duties were diminishing – he carried just eight times during the regular season – and 1940 was his final year in the NFL.

The Redskins stopped Manders at the line of scrimmage for no gain. Luckman gave it another try, handing the pigskin to Manders on second down and this time he advanced the ball one yard. The Bears had relied on the run all day, but on third down, looking to shake things up, Luckman picked out a fresh target, Bob Swisher, whose moves faked out Filchock in his other role in the defensive backfield, and produced a gain of 36 yards.

It looked as if the Bears were on the move again. McLean skipped around the left side and was not stopped until Washington's Todd bumped him out of bounds after a gain of 19 yards. Bill Osmanski was tackled for no gain and then McLean added two more yards. But after Luckman's pass for Plasman was knocked aside by Todd the Bears attempted a 30-yard field goal. Despite the presence of Automatic Jack, Halas called on Phil Martinovich for the boot, but the kick went awry. No points for Chicago.

The Redskins could well have been energized by keeping Chicago off the scoreboard as they began their possession from their own 20. Those feisty Bears linemen, however, were starting to wear down Filchock's protectors. On first down Filchock was chased by Bulldog Turner, killing any thought of a pass. But he was lucky to scramble for 17 yards. Filchock still had throwing on his mind on the next play, but his pass was so rushed that it floated through the air like a wounded duck and Plasman almost intercepted.

A posse of defenders came after Filchock on a third straight play and this time as Filchock sought to put a pass into Millner's arms Ray Nolting jumped in and intercepted it. Nolting's return went for 10 yards and the Bears had good field position on their own 44-yard-line.

Typical of two-way players at the time, Nolting, the man who made the interception to set up the offensive possession got the call on the first play from scrimmage and raced for nine yards. He was on such a roll that Luckman called Nolting's number again and he gained five more yards for a first down.

Osmanski, who had not been terribly productive following his opening touchdown dash, was tackled for no gain on the next play, but when he got another chance on a pitch-out from Luckman, the fullback sped around left end and collected 11 yards. It was Nolting's turn again after that and he gained three yards. Osmanski was turned back on the next play, losing two yards.

The Bears faced third down and nine at the Washington 30-yard-line and Luckman limbered up. End Ken Kavanaugh streaked into the end zone. Darting and faking he got behind Filchock and Andy Farkas and made the grab for the touchdown.

Before receiving numbers began to pile up like pinball points, Kavanaugh recorded some extraordinary statistics for the Bears. He was 6-3 and weighed about 210 when he arrived in Chicago from Louisiana State University in 1940, drafted in the third round. A member of the College Football Hall of Fame, Kavanaugh ran a recovered fumble 100 yards for a touchdown for the Tigers.

Kavanaugh, who grew up in Little Rock, Arkansas, caught as many as 13 TD passes for Chicago in one season and gathered in 50 in his career, partnering quite comfortably with Luckman. He was a two-time All-Pro.

As a rookie in 1940, Kavanaugh said he began to learn the difference between college play and the pros in the pre-season college All-Star game. Although he played well, he found out he couldn't just use his size to push around opponents.

"In college, it took two blockers to wall me out," he said. "In the All-Star game I was opposite Baby Ray (of the Green Bay Packers), all 265 pounds of him. He just muffled me. He slapped a hand on my headgear, pushed me to the ground, and landed on the middle of my back." (6)

Kavanaugh also learned quickly that George Halas' moods could fluctuate mightily depending on whether the Bears won or lost, played well, or didn't. Chicago bested rival Green Bay by 34 points in the opener, but spaced the following game, losing by 14 points to the Cardinals.

Halas' response to his players? "I'm paying you fellows to play football," he growled, "and you're gonna pay me if you don't play it." Halas' tantrum continued from there as he outlined the kinds of on-field mistakes that he would fine players for. Kavanaugh, a rookie, was still coming to grips with the pro game and thought he was in big trouble. "My heart sank. I said to myself, 'I'm gonna wind up playing for nothing.' George was so tough that he once fined (Lee) Artoe 25 cents for throwing a snowball during practice." (7)

Kavanaugh was one of a cast of outstanding Bears players who were at the peak of their games when World War II put their football careers on hold. Kavanaugh was a pilot who earned the Distinguished Flying Cross and Air Medal with four oak leaf clusters fighting in the war. After retiring as a player Kavanaugh spent decades as a New York

Giants assistant coach and scout.

The savvy of Clark Shaughnessy recognizing Kavanaugh's skills as a receiver and the way he would fit the T formation was the reason why the pass catcher became a Bear, Kavanaugh said.

"They drafted me on his recommendation after Bulldog," Kavanaugh said. "Bulldog was as great at his position as any player who ever lived." (8)

Drafting Kavanaugh and signing him were two different things. His goal was to play Major League baseball and the St. Louis Cardinals' Branch Rickey identified him as a prospect, signed him, and sent him to play in Houston. Halas didn't even make contact until after that. Kavanaugh basically burst out laughing when Halas offered him $50 a game to play pro football. Halas upped the deal to $100 a game. Kavanaugh countered with $300 since he was making that amount as a monthly paycheck from the Cardinals.

"Three hundred dollars a game or I go back to baseball," Kavanaugh said. Halas caved and said, "You're getting paid better than anyone else in the league." (9) Not quite, but the money was good enough to make Kavanaugh into a football player.

Kavanaugh suggested to Luckman in the huddle that the Redskins might be starting to catch on to the running-short passing style and why didn't they take a shot at a long pass. The result was the 30-yard TD.

"I think they're getting onto short passes," Kavanaugh said, "Let's try a few long ones." (10)

One was enough. The catch gave the Bears a four-touchdown lead and even if the game was still in the first half, 99 percent of the time that margin would be enough for a win.

Playing musical kickers, Halas asked Bob Snyder to kick the extra point this time. With slightly more than three minutes to go in the second quarter, the Bears led 28-0. Things were starting to get embarrassing for the Redskins.

Sid Luckman said Halas was not really at ease, though. He wanted more scoring.

"He just wanted us to keep it going," Luckman said. (11)

There was enough time left in the half for the Redskins to obtain at least one more possession. Lee Artoe kicked off. Artoe came to the Bears from the University of California as a tackle-kicker who had been a college All-American. A couple of years later Artoe said he gained his biggest thrill as a player by scoring a touchdown as a lineman, also against the Redskins, also in a championship game.

Artoe was in on a sack of Sammy Baugh and the ball bounced free. He plucked it out of the air and ran it back for a touchdown. George Wilson, the Bears' defensive back, and a faster runner, kept urging Artoe to lateral the ball to him.

"He had about as much chance of getting that ball from me as Khrushchev has of becoming president," Artoe said years later. "Later, we saw movies of the game and I was zig-zagging down the field like a (George) McAfee and giving imaginary stiff arms, even though there wasn't a Washington player near me." (12)

Artoe's toe booted the 1940 kickoff following Chicago's fourth TD to the goal-line. There, Filchock, playing every position, it seemed, fielded the kick and ran it back 25 yards. On first down Filchock attempted a pass to Millner that was incomplete.

Then Baugh returned to the lineup, re-taking the quarterback position. Baugh's rest after being knocked unconscious on a defensive play was not a long one. Baugh was trying to cover one of his punts snared by Luckman and in attempting the tackle was knocked out. This was one of those heat-of-battle returns to play with his team needing him desperately. Given the National Football League's current focus on concussions suffered by players, it is very unlikely that Baugh would have been allowed to return to the field that day. There was not such clear thinking about player health at the time and in the title game, with his Redskins in dire need of a lift, Baugh returned to action.

On his first play back in the lineup, Baugh drifted back to pass. It was second down and 10 to go from the Redskins' 25. Cutting over the middle Andy Farkas was open and Baugh hit him for a 19-yard gain. On the next play Baugh completed a pass to Jimmy Johnston, advancing the ball another seven yards. First down. Baugh went back to pass again, but his completion to Bob Hoffman was worth just one yard.

It was third down and two to go for a first down when Baugh sent Johnston deep, but then overthrew him. On fourth down Baugh zipped a pass to Johnston over the middle for a gain of eight and a first down. Hot to get on the scoreboard before intermission, the Redskins kept moving. The most remarkable play of the drive followed. Baugh was under siege from the Bears rush in the backfield, yet managed to throw deep to Charley Malone. Malone was double-covered by Snyder and McLean, yet hauled the ball in on the Chicago 5-yard-line.

A five-yard Washington penalty shoved the ball back to the 10. The clock was ticking down on the second quarter when Baugh faded back once more. Trying to hit Farkas in the end zone, Baugh missed the mark and Osmanski killed the drive with an interception just as the clock ran out on the first half.

The Bears retreated to their den sitting on that cozy 28-0 lead.

HALFTIME

If ever a team needed a break after 30 minutes of football, it was the Washington Redskins. The halftime intermission after the first two quarters is designed to provide rest for physically straining teams and to allow time to regroup.

This is when the coach takes over again, supposedly exhorting the troops onward. The football halftime pep talk is a thing of great lore, where the coach assembles his sweaty men and usually addresses them at loud decibels if he believes they need to correct their play.

The long list of corrections the Redskins had to fix was probably too long to be analyzed individually by Washington coach Ray Flaherty. Trailing 28-0 and with the Bears manhandling them, it may not have seemed possible to fix enough problems to make a difference. Some games are hopeless and some fans, hopes thoroughly dashed, may have adjourned from Griffith Stadium for the nearest taverns.

There was no way of calculating how many of the 36,000 fans on hand might have been dreaming of a miracle comeback. There is no way to know how many even hoped that the Bears had ceased scoring and that the Redskins could notch a touchdown or two to make the result look halfway respectable.

The one man in the building who needed to keep his head and prevent panic was Flaherty. Although it is a cliché, it behooved him to think "one play at a time," or one possession at a time.

Born in 1903, Flaherty might have been a fairly young head coach in terms of age at 37, but he had been around the pro game for years and spent a lifetime in football. He grew up in Eastern Washington and played college ball for Gonzaga, better known on the national sports scene in the 2000s for its basketball teams than its defunct football program.

Flaherty originally played professionally for the Los Angeles Wildcats and the New York Yankees, teams that competed in the American Football League of the 1920s, not to be confused with the American Football League founded in 1960 that eventually merged with the NFL. The first American Football League was created as a showcase for Red Grange by promoter C.C. Pyle. Pyle, whose first two initials were sometimes claimed to stand for "Cash and Carry," was the first major player agent who transformed Grange from a college football hero into a rich professional football player.

It was Pyle that pulled together the barnstorming tour that featured Grange as he and the Chicago Bears toured the United States. When George Halas failed to meet Grange's contract demands (no surprise there) after the successful tour that helped put pro football on the map, Pyle established the competing league. Flaherty played one year for Los Angeles and two seasons for New York, but the league didn't last long. More significantly, Flaherty spent seven seasons as an end with the New York Giants until 1935.

However, he skipped the 1930 football season to play a year of professional baseball as an infielder with the Providence Grays of the Eastern League. Always harboring the desire to coach, Flaherty's playing days ended conveniently enough for George Preston Marshall to hire him as the Redskins coach in 1936.

Optimistic in outlook and confident in demeanor, Flaherty promised championships when he was hired to lead the Redskins. He delivered in 1937 and believed he could deliver in 1940 until the Bears squashed his team in the first half of the title game.

Flaherty was a man for the times because his offensive philosophy stressed playing the game wide open. He was an adherent of the passing game and being gifted with a quarterback like Sammy Baugh, Flaherty had his greatest personnel need filled before he called a play.

When he was still playing for the Giants, Flaherty was the one that suggested his team use sneakers in the 1934 championship game so his guys could conquer the ice on the field as well as the Bears. New York won 30-13, because the home team's footing was better at the Polo Grounds. As if that didn't make George Halas irritable enough, in 1937, when the Redskins won the NFL crown they beat the Bears, 28-21.

Halas was piecing together his "Monsters of the Midway" defense and he planned to bring the house, as the phrase goes, rushing rookie quarterback Sammy Baugh. Anticipating the strategy, Flaherty called for some innovations within the Washington playbook. Baugh was a master of throwing the long pass, but in the face of a heavy pass rush he might not be able to wait long enough for his receivers to get downfield. So Flaherty devised an alternative passing style. Seen all of the time now, it was a new thing when the Redskins and Baugh began throwing short pass after short pass to men coming out of the backfield behind a squadron of blockers. Essentially, Flaherty invented the screen pass and it killed Chicago.

"It was the first time the screen pass had been used," Flaherty said. "They were breaking their necks trying to rack up Baugh. So we kept screen passing them all day, and they never knew what the hell they were doing." (1)

Ah, but payback is sweet and the 1940 Bears made it seem as if the Redskins didn't know what the hell they were doing in the championship game. Although Baugh needed a break, Flaherty already had a plan in place for using Frank Filchock. In the 1940s coaches had a set lineup and didn't tamper with it much, to the point where the starters on offense were also the starters on defense. Being a second-stringer in those days made you a bench warmer for what seemed like forever. However, Flaherty actually employed two backfields. One was built around Baugh and the passing game. The other was built around Filchock and the running game. Defenses weren't complete dummies, so depending on which quarterback was in the game tended to tip off the Redskins' play choices. It was a matter of execution. So when Filchock got playing time in the first half it didn't matter so much that it was of an emergency nature, he had been there before.

"We made the defense change," is how Flaherty viewed his swapping of backfields. "They'd get all set for Baugh's passing and they'd have to change when we put the running combination in. Filchock was a great ball handler, so we put in a lot of spin plays with this unit. Filchock could also throw, so that made it a pretty effective combination both ways." (2)

Everything Washington tried on this day backfired, whether it was Baugh throwing or Filchock handing off, Baugh handing off or Filchock throwing. That was the frightening prospect that Flaherty had to confront in the locker room in halftime. What could he say to perk up his players' spirits? What could he do to adjust the game plan to catch Chicago off guard? The answer in both cases was nothing.

"The funny thing about that game is we made just as many first downs as they did," Flaherty said. "But they intercepted eight passes and we just kept getting further behind. So we just went ahead and put the ball in the air some more." (3)

Certainly "two yards and a cloud of dust" was not going to allow Washington to eat into the lead so Flaherty's men did have to pass. Flaherty always clung to his comment about the teams having the same amount of first downs. But to even mention it was a delusional thought since it mattered not one bit. Nobody was counting first downs. Nobody cared about first downs. First downs were totally irrelevant. Points mattered.

Strategically, there was really nothing for Washington to do but stick with the passing game in order to swallow large chunks of yardage in a hurry and try to fool the Bears' secondary often enough to score some long-range touchdowns. Besides, owner George Marshall had a standing order to Sammy Baugh – throw and keep on throwing.

It was the Bears who gave the big boost to the use of the T formation with their performance in this title game, but the Redskins were inching their way into using it all of the time, too. Baugh said he took a tremendous beating playing in the single wing, and also going both ways in games. He was lucky he was not hurt more often.

"I had to run the ball once in a while," Baugh said of being in the single wing, "or the opposition would key on the other runner. You also played both ways in those days, so you didn't get a rest. I played safety on defense and I had to take on either the end on either (side) or wingback coming down field. Both of my shoulders had been knocked out and both of my knees were banged up before we went to the T." (4)

Imagine a multi-million-dollar property in the football world of the 2000s being thrown onto the field to make a few tackles. The risk of severe injury would be astronomical and the foolishness of hanging such an investment out to dry would be criticized forever.

For all of Baugh's dispassionate analysis of the battering his body took playing the game, he said he was never truly seriously hurt playing football and the worst injury he incurred was as a cowboy from the horn of a young steer.

Baugh never had the luxury of playing pro ball after so many rules had been instituted to protect the passer from late hits, high hits, and low hits. The roughing-the-passer rule wasn't even ingrained yet and he remembered well for a long time how he was frequently legally creamed by charging defensive linemen who could keep bashing into the quarterback even after he threw the ball, as long as the play was still live downfield and the whistle had not blown.

Marshall, who recognized Baugh as his franchise player, and who saw him as a star in the entertainment world as well as an athlete on the field, once summoned Baugh to his office to discuss a potential rule change that would prohibit those defenders from beating up on the quarterback once the ball was airborne. Naturally, Baugh said he would very much like to see such a rule enacted.

"I told him I probably would live longer if we got a rule like that," Baugh said. (5)

It was a good idea and the rule was implemented. For decades that rule was the main protection offered to quarterbacks as they attempted to sidestep stampeding over-sized linemen. But on this day, with the Bears as ornery as anyone had ever seen them, it didn't seem as if anything would be able to rescue Baugh.

For their part, the Bears were practically gleeful in their dressing room. Even Halas had difficulty focusing on anything to criticize. What could he say? The only warning he could issue was about complacency, not to let down, not to let the giant lead erode. He was as aware of anyone in the stadium that football games last for four 15-minute quarters, not two, but even Halas had to be feeling pretty good.

Certainly, Chicago quarterback Sid Luckman was feeling fine and pleased by what he witnessed and took part in during those two periods of play that to him were as beautiful as any Vincent Van Gogh masterpiece he may have ever seen.

"It was the kind of day when everything seemed to click," Luckman said. "A boner was good for 10 yards. A fumble gave us another 10! From the first quarter on the T took a back seat to something made and indefinable, as the score fattened on intercepted passes and wanton gallops." (6)

What Luckman was really saying was that even when the Bears made mistakes they did themselves no harm. When the Bears screwed up, the Redskins couldn't capitalize.

Luckman never lost sight of the fact that the Redskins were a talented team, one that beat Chicago just three weeks earlier, one that had a roster bursting with All-Star players. That group could come alive and bite back.

"Frustrated, but not asleep," Luckman said of Washington trailing 28-0. "They might have been likened to a fellow chasing a swarm of bees – his head going one way and then another, not sure whether the bees would pass, run, lateral, smash, or just sit down and relax." (7)

This was one day when everyone on the Bears roster would see playing time. It didn't matter who got into the game, Chicago just did its thing and executed called plays to perfection. Although Luckman observed that Halas sent in players at some positions who might have been called fourth string, he wasn't really sure that Halas was trying to ease up and hold down the score. Halas was pretty angry at Marshall and the Redskins and he might well have been inclined to rub it in.

"They were saying the 'Boss' didn't want to make it any tougher on Washington," Luckman said. "But I wouldn't be sure of that. Halas was never one to spare a foe. The rapid substitutions did not lighten the attack one bit." (8)

There were 30 more long minutes of play still scheduled when the Redskins emerged from their locker room at the end of halftime to face the snarling Bears and their own grumbling fans in Griffith Stadium. And yes, the Bears did make it tougher on Washington in the second half.

REDSKINS TRY TO DIG OUT

These were players with pride. The Washington Redskins of 1940 were winners. They owned the National Football League's Eastern Division title. Three weeks earlier they had defeated the hardy Chicago Bears. So even if they fell behind by 28 points in the championship game they would not surrender, they would not write off the last 30 minutes of play.

That was the common-sense thinking. No matter what coach Ray Flaherty said in the locker room at halftime each Redskins player knew that he had to dig deep to make up for the pathetic first-half showing. They could believe, even if it seemed hopeless to others on the outside that they could overcome. If the Bears were capable of scoring four touchdowns in the first half then why couldn't the Redskins score four touchdowns in the second half?

Many of the same Washington players rode to the championship together in 1937, beating the Bears that day, as well. If they could play up to their capabilities then surely they could they rally.

Albert Glen Edwards, better known as "Turk," was one of those players whose capabilities ranked higher than most in the league, but he was unfortunately unavailable. He was a 6-foot-2, 260-pound tackle enshrined in the Pro Football Hall of Fame in 1969. Edwards was an All-American at Washington State, a teammate of the great New York Giant lineman Mel Hein. Edwards starred in the Rose Bowl and signed with the Boston Redskins, before the NFL draft existed, in 1932 for a rate of $150 per game. One of those blocks-of-granite types typical of the era, Edwards played both ways on the Washington line.

"When he got mad, which was rarely, he could play the whole side of the line himself," said teammate and fellow Hall of Famer Wayne Millner. (1)

Edwards looked out for his teammates. He was the enforcer who not only threw a scary look at anyone whom he felt unfairly hit his pals, but delivered payback when he determined it was necessary. Sometimes he did so legally. Once, fullback Andy Farkas was the victim of what Edwards considered to be a cheap shot. When he returned to the

Redskins' huddle he called the next play. He ordered that Farkas be given the next handoff

"Give Andy the ball over me," Edwards said. The play evolved as he envisioned it, Edwards pile-driving the defensive offender backwards with Farkas notching a seven-yard gain. (2)

Edwards was disgusted with what he witnessed in the first half and it was frustrating for him that he could not be out on the field. Washington apologists looking for excuses about why the Redskins were falling apart could always point to the fact that Edwards was not able to play. A multi-time All-Star, before a game against New York during the 1940 season, Edwards twisted a knee. His cleat caught in the ground. He may be the only player in league history to suffer a career-ending injury on the coin toss.

Edwards and Hein, old college buddies, were captains of their teams, so they got to call the heads or tails on the silver dollar as an official flipped it. They shook hands, as those who meet at midfield always do, but because they also knew one another for years they added a personal message. "Good luck, Mel," Edwards said. "Take care of yourself, Turk," Hein responded. "Don't get hurt." (3) Ironically, less than three seconds later Edwards was on the ground, the victim of his knee giving out, right in front of friend Hein.

Nine seasons into his pro career, with four All-Pro honors won, Edwards was at midfield for the usually simple coin toss. After the coin came down Edwards whirled towards his bench and threw his knee out. It made little sense. Playing a style reliant on power and strength, afterwards Edwards could no longer push off on the knee and could no longer overwhelm opponents he was used to running over.

In a sense, Edwards' situation was a metaphor for the Redskins-Bears title game. There was a lot of want in the Redskins' hearts, but the Bears were too strong for them. Edwards, who became an assistant coach and then head coach of the Redskins in mid-decade, could offer nothing more than moral support for his embattled teammates.

Likewise, absent from the Redskins' roster by 1940 was one of their aces from the 1937 season. Running back Cliff Battles, another future Hall of Famer, retired young. Battles came out of West Virginia Wesleyan and played just six seasons in the NFL, gaining 3,511 yards. He was chosen All-Pro in 1932, 1933, 1934, 1936, and 1937.

A combination of the Depression and cheapskate salaries paid by penurious NFL owners drove him out of the sport. Battles was making just $3,000 a year in 1937.

Battles became an assistant coach at Columbia University for $4,000 and his second career revolved around college coaching. After serving in the Marine Corps in World War II Battles went into private industry. The Redskins did not adequately replace Battles during the first few years after his retirement and the lack of his complementary running did not help Sammy Baugh's passing.

Even if finances likely played a larger role in his departure, perhaps Battles merely read the handwriting in the playbook and realized with the arrival of Baugh and his fantastic arm that he would not get the carries he was used to in the games. Owner George Preston Marshall gave Baugh a perpetual green light to throw, and coach Ray Flaherty possessed that clever offensive mind that could maximize Baugh's talent. While Flaherty was cautious about counting on a rookie quarterback too much in 1937, Baugh was relaxed and confident. Flaherty issued some advice to Baugh about professional receivers.

"These receivers up here want their passes to be really accurate," Flaherty told Baugh. "They want you to hit them in the eye." (4) Flaherty was trying to make a point more than being taken literally, but Baugh seemed to bristle.

"Which eye?" Baugh replied. (5) As it so happened, most of the time he was that good.

Neither Baugh nor the Redskins were at their best for the 1940 title game. It was depressing and humiliating for Redskins fans, who are among the most passionate in the league, and who embraced the new Washington team with all their hearts after Marshall moved them to the nation's capital from Boston.

A lifelong fan named Bob Smithwick, whose father worked for the U.S. Treasury department, was one of the luckier boys on his block because his family held season tickets. Smithwick was 13 at the time of the game and he was an avid sandlot player with his friends. Given the blossoming Redskins-Bears rivalry following the 1937 season, Southwick said when they played in the neighborhood one side got to be the Redskins and the other side was the Bears.

He never forgot the sights and sounds of the 1940 championship game, which he attended with his father, sitting on a 40-yard-line.

"I knew all the verses to the fight song," Smithwick said, and he sang the words that day, brimming with confidence before the game that his Redskins would emerge victorious and champs once again over the hated Bears. "We were very confident. The Redskins could do no wrong, especially with Baugh, who played both ways, ran the ball, threw the ball, punted, and even did the place-kicking. I was as excited as you could get seeing that championship game with my dad at Griffith Stadium. No boy could ask for more." (6)

Except, that is, perhaps a better, winning performance from the home team. It was a day of great disappointment for boys like Smithwick who bled Redskins colors of burgundy and gold. Touchdowns aside, a first-half development that made all Washington fans edgy was seeing Baugh hit the ground and stay down. Smithwick said it was a shocking moment.

"When Baugh got hurt I remember the crowd coming to its feet," he said. "There was a big guy sitting in front of me and I couldn't see well. But then I saw No. 33 laying on his left side and everybody saying, 'Sam's down. Sam's down.'" (7) Such are scarring childhood memories made.

Neither Smithwick, nor his father was embittered by bearing witness to the worst defeat in National Football League history, even if their favorite team was on the bad end of the score. They kept up their dual allegiance to the team through 1974 when Smithwick's father passed away. Any time the Redskins lost a game during those next 34 years, the older Smithwick told his son, "Well, at least it wasn't 73-0." (8)

When Battles made it clear that he was retiring, the Redskins delved into the draft to pluck a replacement. With their No. 1 draft pick in 1938 the Redskins chose fullback Andy Farkas out of the University of Detroit Mercy. Farkas was 5-10 and weighed 190 pounds. His season-high rushing total came in 1939 when he gained 547 yards from scrimmage and was on the receiving end of Frank Filchock's record 99-yard pass play.

That time the Redskins were stuck on their own 1-yard-line following a penalty. Filchock called a screen pass to Ed Justice, who dropped the ball. It was just as well because the Pittsburgh Steelers defense was poised to cream Justice. However, when Filchock signaled the play again it was for Farkas.

"He called the play and made such a perfect fake to Justice that Ed started to reach for the ball," Farkas said. "Then he turned and dunked a little pass to me on the other side. It was really about a 104-yard run and I remember the safety man looking for the ball on the other side of the field. All I had to do was run." (9)

Farkas was out of commission most of the 1940 season with a knee injury, but did play in the championship game. He was probably not at his sharpest, yet another problem for Washington. But he was a very solid player (though perhaps not in Battles' class) when he was in shape, twice being named all-league. Besides being the usual top rusher for Washington, Farkas was a skilled receiver with a high of 19 catches one season.

Although he did return for the title game, Farkas was in a sort of forced withdrawal from football for most of the fall. In fact, he returned to Detroit and accepted another job as the boss of a fueling crew at an industrial plant. He had a long commute from and to home each day and he used that time pining away for football, almost as if he was a jilted boyfriend looking for a second chance.

"I had plenty of time to think things over," Farkas said, "especially on those cold mornings driving 26 miles over an icy road to the plant. I began to think pro football wasn't so bad after all. I made up my mind I was going back and I was going to make good. I told myself I'd play football like I never played it before. I'd make that 1939 season seem like a warm-up session, if I could play at all. I got the fever bad, worse than I've ever had it. And the more I thought about it, the more I wanted to play." (10)

Farkas got his name in the play-by-play a few times against the Bears in his return to action. He received a kickoff and went out for a couple of passes. But Farkas had to win back the starting job from his able replacement Dick Todd. Todd rushed for 408 yards, at 5.4 yards per carry, during the 1940 season, and the Texas A&M product saw more activity on championship day.

While Farkas was chosen to specifically replace Battles, Wilbur Moore was an afterthought in the 1939 draft. He was picked in the ninth round out of Minnesota, yet made the team, playing some halfback and defensive back and in 1942 even became an All-Star. Moore was pretty much a little-used back-up in 1940, but developed into a productive receiver a couple of years later. In consecutive years he caught 30 and 33 passes, the 5-11, 185-pounder showing considerable skill as a pass catcher once he got the chance for more playing time.

Moore's advancement had been hindered early because he kept getting injured. Over the first couple of years of his career Moore suffered broken bones just about every time he turned around. He was Edwards times 10 as an injury magnet. At one point someone counted 13 broken bones Moore suffered while playing the sport, though that may have been an estimate more than a specific tally. Earlier in his career, before being a member of the Redskins' 1942 title team, and during a given period when Moore was able to dodge defensive backs better than injury he called a 35-yard game-winning touchdown pass his biggest thrill as a pro. He was not able to duplicate that feat against the Bears.

"What made Wilbur a great football player was his fierce competitive spirit," said Dutch Bergman, a later Redskins coach. "He gave it everything he had every minute." (11)

On the day the Redskins met their comeuppance against the Bears, the left tackle on their side was a 6-5, 265-pound hunk of man whose nickname belied his frame. Wee Willie Wilkin was anything but small and he was much faster afoot than most of the linemen of his time. He came by it naturally since he chose not to work out very hard. In fact, he was famous for breaking team training rules, being fined $25 nine different times in a single season for ignoring the organization's policies. A product of St. Mary's College in California, Wilkin was gifted enough to toss opponents out of the way when the mood struck him – most of the time.

Another of Wilkins' nicknames was "The Frisco Bruiser" since he hailed from the San Francisco Bay area. That moniker was attached to him after he briefly tried to become a professional boxer, mainly for the money. He was promised a $12 purse, but after knocking out his opponent in the third round Wilkins' manager applied a curious series of tax deductions and handled the athlete his $1.87 cut. Wilkins did not accept being short-changed and after knocking down his second foe of the day he got his full pay.

Coach Ray Flaherty knew of Wilkins' gridiron exploits, though, and thought his brute strength would transfer well between sports so he signed him. Wilkins may have been the only Washington guy who played up to his normal standards against the Bears in the title game shellacking. When it was over he was chosen as the lineman of the day – despite the wide margin of the score and despite the Bears featuring so many star linemen.

Yet not even gaining recognition as a three-time NFL all-star changed Wilkins' fun-loving habits and tendency towards laziness in practice. George Preston Marshall once hired a private detective to follow Wilkins and the man came back both exhausted and with a huge expenses bill.

And sure enough, during one pre-season training camp, when the sun beat down strongly and the humidity was high, scorching the Redskins, Wilkin sidled up to his coach, Bergman, and suggested a change of plan for the day's workout.

"C'mon, Dutch," he said. "Let's all go home. Let's not wear out the leather." (12)

Wilkins may have been paid the exceptional courtesy of being termed the game's best lineman in the Bears contest, but nothing he did really made the slightest bit of difference in the final score.

Chicago Bears Hall of Fame running back **George McAfee** (5) runs upfield against the Washington Redskins during the NFL Championship game, Dec. 8, 1940 in Washington. McAfee scored on a 35-yard interception return in the Bears 73-0 win at Griffith Stadium. (AP Photo/Pro Football Hall of Fame)

THIRD QUARTER

The Chicago Bears appeared to be in complete command and it would have been picky, picky, picky for coach George Halas to do much criticizing. What he did instead was to make reference to the George Preston Marshall stupid quote collection, just as he had before the game.

"At the half we were leading 28-0," said Chicago tackle George Musso, "but he brought it (Marshall's insults) up again and we got mad all over." (1)

Halftime of a football game is a respite, a time for regrouping, adjusting strategy. It may be the time to ditch the game plan because it hasn't been working – certainly a consideration for the Washington Redskins trailing 28-0. If a team is behind, it is an important break, hopefully one that will shift the momentum.

In a case like this game coach Ray Flaherty said his piece and hoped it would inspire his troops to rally, to come out of the locker room fresh and determined to make a dent in the huge lead the Chicago Bears spent 30 minutes compiling.

Even better for the Redskins was that they would get the ball first. The Bears had to kick off. That meant Washington could mount an immediate attack, make something spectacular happen when receiving the ball, or get the offense rolling down the field for a touchdown to chop that lead by a little bit right away.

Chicago's Lee Artoe kicked off and Washington's Charley Malone gathered in the boot. It was a short kick and Malone received the ball on his own 25-yard-line. Artoe's failure to kick the ball deep, however, meant that the Bears' coverage team could converge in a hurry. Malone's return lasted only nine yards. But still, Washington had pretty good field position with a first down on its own 34-yard-line.

Flaherty was looking for his men to pull together and drive the ball the length of the field for a TD. Putting six points up on the board might even energize the crowd, which had been virtually shocked into silence by the way their heroes had been completely manhandled.

Instead, just about the worst series of events that Flaherty could imagine occurred. On first down quarterback Sammy Baugh handed the ball off to Jimmy Johnston, who was tackled at the line of scrimmage for no gain. It didn't matter anyway because the officials whistled the Redskins for a holding penalty and that sent the ball backwards 15 yards.

It was second down and 25 to go for a first down when Baugh faded back to pass. The call was for a pass in the flat, with Johnston the receiver four yards behind the line of scrimmage. Only Chicago's Hampton Pool jumped the play, sneaked in, stole the ball and ran the interception into the end zone. In seconds, the Redskins' long-shot hopes were demolished. The 15-yard runback gave the Bears a 35-0 lead. In later years a phrase that would become common when a rout was on was, "One could hear the sound of television sets being turned off all over the nation." Maybe it was radios this time, the clicking eliminating Red Barber's observations.

Pool was a rookie with a checkered college career that involved more bouncing around than a beachball during its lifespan. A native of California, Pool first enrolled at the University of California in Berkeley. Then he transferred to Army, West Point, in New York. When he realized that the military life was not for him, Pool moved back to California and finished his college days at Stanford. He was the Bears' ninth-round draft pick in 1940.

A firmly built 6-foot-3 and 220 pounds, and mainly a wide receiver, Pool experienced a minimum of playing time his first season. A fullback in college, Chicago was rich at that position, so coach George Halas shifted Pool to receiver. He appeared in just five games for the Bears and he did not score a single touchdown during the regular season.

Pool made larger regular-season contributions over the next couple of years, but eventually had his Bears' career truncated by World War II. After the service, where Pool began his coaching career, he played briefly for the All-America Football Conference's Miami Seahawks. However, combining his playing, coach and scouting days, Pool spent 28 years in the pros. The touchdown against the Redskins on that back-breaking interception was probably his biggest moment in uniform.

Pool's swipe spelled doom for a Washington comeback. Indeed, although the Bears were ruled offsides on Artoe's next kickoff and the Redskins were given a do-over, Washington seemed rattled. Continuing the nightmare, Ed Justice fumbled the ball in his own end zone. He recovered for a touchback, averting bigger disaster, and the Redskins began their next series on their own 20-yard-line.

It might safely be assumed that any optimistic thoughts generated in the locker room during the intermission were at best hanging by a fragile thread. The Bears lead had only ballooned. By this stage of the game the best Washington had mustered was making it through a possession without committing a turnover. Not a recipe for success.

From that point on it was almost as if Washington had to play employing a two-minute drill. The description was not yet in vogue, but the reality was that if the Redskins had the slightest dream of catching the Bears they had to score on every possession and they couldn't really afford to give the ball back to Chicago on punts after three downs, but had to utilize a desperation style of taking advantage of all fourth downs.

It was actually Baugh's idea for Washington to throw on almost every play and to play through fourth down instead of kicking the ball back to the Bears. He approached Flaherty on the sideline with the plan and since the situation was so dreary and the prospects so slim, he okay'd the drastic suggestion.

"I remember saying, 'Hell, we may get beat 60-0, but we've got to try it,'" Baugh said. (2)

This was a risky style, depending on how far Washington could advance downfield. If the Redskins were in their own territory going for it on fourth down could well spell fresh problems rather than relying on Baugh's skills as the best punter in the league. But the object of the game was to win a championship, not to keep the score close.

Following Justice's bobble, Baugh came on to lead the offense from the 20. On the first play he fired to Charley Malone for an 11-yard gain and a first down. Ball on the 31. The next play was also a pass. Complete for seven yards to Bob Masterson, it seemed as if Washington might be clicking.

Aimed at Jimmy Johnston the next pass fell incomplete. Chicago was called for pass interference. Bulldog Turner, in his other role as a linebacker, was the one nailed for the infraction. Washington gained four yards, with the ball placed on the Redskin 42. To mix up his play-calling, Baugh handed off to Johnston for a gain of three yards. So far, so good, with the ball on the 45. Baugh went back to the air and found Johnston for four more yards.

The line of scrimmage was the Washington 49, but that was as far as the Redskins got. On the next play, Baugh fumbled the handoff, the ball bounced around and was rescued by Johnston, but Washington lost 16 hard-earned yards on the play. On fourth down and with 19 yards to go for a first down Baugh passed to Malone, but the play was incomplete and Chicago took over on downs at the Washington 33-yard-line.

Given the way the Bears' offense was doing a fine imitation of an avalanche and the Redskins' defense was doing its own sad imitation of a sieve that was gift field possession. One could almost picture Bears quarterback Sid Luckman in the huddle going "eeny meeny miny moe" in choosing a play because to that point in the game anything he called had worked out fine.

The selection arrow stopped on Ray Nolting's name and there was nothing wrong with that. Nolting darted 10 yards around right end, leaving the ball on the Washington 23. One could easily envision Nolting returning to the huddle and begging to be allowed to carry the ball again because he felt invincible. For whatever reason, Luckman obliged him, handing off to Nolting once again.

This time Nolting burst through the middle, zipping past the Washington linemen, only to meet up with Baugh trying to do his defender job, on the 8-yard-line. Just to emphasize with an exclamation point that it was the worst day of Baugh's storied career, Nolting faked out Baugh, side-stepping him and carried the ball into the end zone for another Bears touchdown. Resuming his personal game of alternating kickers, Halas sent Dick Plasman out to boot the extra point and the helmetless wonder did the job, making the score 41-0 Chicago.

For most of his football life, at Texas Christian and with the Washington Redskins, Baugh was a superstar leader of his team. When in doubt, turn the game over to Sammy. When the chips were down, he would come to the rescue. This was one day when Baugh did not have the answers to deflect an overpowering Bears squad.

Since war was raging in Europe and the United States was on the brink of war in many minds, it was not surprising that some of the sportswriters sent to cover the game resorted to war analogies to describe what was happening the Redskins. A Time magazine correspondent suggested that things went downhill immediately after Malone dropped the pass on Washington's first possession. "What happened after that was a waking nightmare to the Washington fans. The Bears began to roll – like the German Army rolling through France. Dazed onlookers waited for the defenders to make a stand – in Belgium, at the Somme, at Dunkirk – but the juggernaut kept rolling, rolling, rolling. Radio fans, tuning in at halftime thought they were listening to a basketball game – or an Atlantic City auction." (3)

With hindsight all of the mixed metaphors about war and wars were pretty much in poor taste, though the point was made: This was a step-by-step bombardment.

Baugh was a handsome, raw-boned man, but he was disheveled, hair tousled, face long and depressed. After the score hit 41-0 Flaherty waved the white flag of surrender and took Baugh out of the game. He had already employed Filchock, but this time turned to back-up to the back-up Roy Zimmerman. Basically Flaherty told Baugh to take a seat on the bench because the game was out of reach and there was no reason to expose him further to a ferocious Bears pass rush that could result in a serious injury to him.

"That was the most humiliating thing I've ever gone through in my life," Baugh said. (4)

Not being relegated to the bench, but being slaughtered by an unstoppable Bears team.

Zimmerman was a rookie, a seventh-round draft pick of the Redskins' in 1940, even though with a young Baugh at the controls and the handy Frank Filchock around there really was no need for another quarterback. Zimmerman was 6-2 and weighed 200 pounds. In 1939, he led San Jose State to a 13-0 record, so that mark on his resume may have made him an appealing candidate for the draft. Even if the Redskins took Zimmerman with the idea of transferring his athleticism to another position it must have seemed worth taking a shot on him.

It is very unlikely that when he woke up on the morning of December 8, 1940 that Zimmerman expected to see action at quarterback in that day's championship game against the Bears. He probably could not have envisioned a game scenario where Flaherty would have called upon him to replace Baugh and to be thrust into action instead of Filchock.

During Washington's 9-3 regular season Zimmerman made cameo appearances at quarterback in six games, but his entire season stats consisted of attempting 12 passes and completing four. None of his tosses went for a touchdown. As a 22-year-old newcomer when Flaherty shouted his name on the sideline, it would have been remarkable for Zimmerman not to be nervous. He had been watching his All-Star teammates get bulldozed. He had seen the All-World Sammy Baugh beaten into submission.

There is no telling what Flaherty really hoped to get out of Zimmerman's participation other than a sneak preview of a rookie's career and someone who might be able to help the clock tick down faster. That might have been the thinking of the optimistic side of his brain. What Flaherty got was pretty much a continuation of the horror show.

After the Nolting touchdown Lee Artoe kicked off into the end zone, giving Washington the ball on its own 20-yard-line once more. Zimmerman's first down in charge followed and he safely handed the ball off to Bob Seymour who attempted to squirm over left tackle, but was halted for no gain at the line.

On the next play Zimmerman settled on variety and called a pass play. He stepped back, fired, and the ball went right into the arms of Chicago's George McAfee at the 35-yard-line. McAfee gripped the pigskin, tucked it under his arm and dashed for the end zone, producing another Bears' touchdown. Almost as if willing his kickers to miss extra points, Halas chose someone fresh to kick. Almost humorously, as if one point less would seem like cutting the Redskins some slack, lineman Joe Stydahar came in and made the kick. Chicago led 48-0.

It was simply McAfee's turn to put six points on the scoreboard, something which seemed inevitable given McAfee's all-around talents. George McAfee was another rookie in 1940, a highly regarded draft pick out of Duke University where he distinguished himself on the gridiron well enough to later be inducted into the College Football Hall of Fame.

During an NFL era where versatility was not only prized, but necessary, McAfee was one of those do-everything players who could be effective on offense and defense, running the ball, catching the ball, basically just saluting and saying "Yes, sir" whenever George Halas requested that he perform some task that would help ruin the other team.

It took a little bit of persuasion for Halas to sign McAfee, though. Halas, known for his Scrooge-like approach to salaries, thought highly enough of McAfee to make what he considered a fair offer to an untested rookie. McAfee thought more of his abilities.

"The first contract the Bears offered me," McAfee said years later of his 1940 negotiation, "called for $165 a game. But I held out and got $170. Salaries are a little better now." (5)

McAfee stood 6 feet tall and weighed just under 180 pounds. He was a swift runner, but also possessed Red Grange-style shiftiness. The average pro football fan of the 2000s doesn't know McAfee's name unless he is a true student of the game, but McAfee was one of the best all-around players of his era and was inducted into the Pro Football Hall of Fame, too.

In fact, before McAfee made his mark with the Bears, Grange had a chance to see him play and predicted greatness for him.

"This boy is one of the finest backs I've ever seen," said Grange, the back who essentially made pro football. "He's got everything, and I don't see how he can miss being a sensation. He runs with such ease and such high knee action that he gives no indication of his tremendous speed unless you note the manner in which he separates himself from players who try to catch him." (6)

One thing that McAfee established pretty early in his career was that he was a brilliant punt returner. In 1941 he tried out that new role, returning five kicks for an average of 31.6 yards per return. His lifetime return average was 12.8 yards. Jock Sutherland became famous for coaching the University of Pittsburgh, but in 1940 he became head coach of the NFL's Brooklyn Dodgers. He watched with dismay when McAfee beat his club with a 70-yard touchdown return of a punt.

"When I became coach of the Brooklyn Dodgers in 1940, the first player I tried to land was McAfee," Sutherland said. "Remember our game with the Bears a few seasons ago? We had the Bears 9-7 with only 25 seconds to play. It was fourth down in our own territory. We thought time would run out before the Bears could run a play from scrimmage so we kicked. McAfee caught the punt and ran it back... for the winning touchdown. I think all my boys had a shot at him. He's Frank Merriwell come to life." (7)

McAfee, who was one of 12 children from Ironton, Ohio, might catch 32 passes in a season, or rush for 474 yards in a year.

"It is positively amazing to see defensive backs try to keep up with him when he goes out for a pass," Grange added. And that hadn't yet addressed McAfee's prowess on the defensive side of the ball. "He's a terrific tackler and how he can punt and pass. You just can't build a defense for a player like that." (8)

Having Grange, with his supreme reputation, say that about you was the type of commentary any young player would die for -- and could put on a resume for a lifetime.

McAfee developed the habit of wearing lightweight, sneaker-type shoes rather than clunky cleats during his days with the Bears because it made him feel as if he was winged afoot with nothing weighing him down. Chicago Cardinals' coach Jimmy Conzelman said of McAfee that, "He puts the defense off-balance and fakes with his head as well as his arms and body." (9)

The player could run the 100-yard dash in 9.7 seconds, a much more respected time in the 1940s than now, but still cooking. When McAfee reported for duty at the Bears' training camp in the summer leading up to the 1940 season he was coming off an All-American season at Duke. What impressed him the most, though, was the behemoths, the George Mussos, Clyde Turners, and Joe Stydahars, on Chicago's line. That was one difference between college and the pros he quickly realized.

"I never saw so many big men in my life," McAfee said. "I remember clearly, on one of the first scrimmage plays, that a rookie halfback was knocked cold trying to bring down Bill Osmanski. That play served as a valuable lesson for me. Whenever I ran with the ball, I had that picture in my mind of that back there on the ground, cold as a stone. I would run as fast as I could if there was any daylight." (10)

Supposedly, McAfee weighed only 165 pounds when he reported to training camp and he looked the part of a skinny lad in over his head. Halas was said to fear for his draft pick's life going up against the league strongmen, then watched with awe and pleasure when McAfee danced around tacklers and broke free into the open field.

"The kid's gonna get killed," was Halas' first impression, one that changed instantly when he saw McAfee change direction to avert defenders. "I think we've got something there." (11)

Although McAfee forfeited that original salary tug-of-war with Halas, after World War II, when he had lost 1942, 1943, 1944 and most of 1945 at his peak, the news that Halas signed McAfee to a three-year contract stunned the football universe. Given Halas' penny-pinching ways and making his players justify every dime he shelled out, that seemed to indicate Halas loved McAfee as much as he did his blood relatives.

Part of it may have been vindicating Halas' initial judgment of McAfee's talents in 1940. Through his own recruiting network, naturally far less sophisticated than scouting is today, he was on to McAfee before just about anyone else, beating not only Sutherland, but other NFL coaches to the player with his wise draft pick.

One owner who was extremely jealous of Halas' capture of McAfee was Washington's George Preston Marshall, who saw up close how much damage McAfee could do. When World War II ended and the new All-America Football Conference started up to compete with the NFL, some players whose contracts were up invariably signed with the upstart league. One of those was Chicago kicker Lee Artoe. When Marshall heard Halas complaining about the loss of his man, Marshall left his feelings unguarded.

"Artoe?" Marshall bellowed. "Who cares about Artoe? What is Halas crying about? I wish someone would steal McAfee away from him. Then we'd really be getting somewhere." (12)

In the everybody-scores-game, McAfee was just taking his turn to up the score to 48-0 in that ugly third period for Washington. Just about every series seemed to play out in a kind of slow-motion instant replay even though that technology was years in the future. It was Groundhog Day for the Redskins, as in the Bill Murray movie where events unfold repeatedly without much time passing.

McAfee's TD painfully earned the Redskins another opportunity with the football, even though they did not appear safe even when the Bears were without the ball. Artoe, whose toe was probably tiring from kickoffs, sent the ball into the end zone. Of all people, Zimmerman, was back to receive. He did as well as anyone in a Washington uniform had all day, carrying the ball out to the Redskins' 33-yard-line.

At that point of the demolition nobody would have blamed the Redskins too much if the only thing on their minds was trying to advance the 15 minutes of the third period as quickly as possible.

Right after Zimmerman caught his breath from the runback he assumed his more critical role, stepping back in at quarterback. On first down from the 33 he handed the ball to Seymour, who gained one yard over left guard. On second down Zimmerman tried a pass and although it was incomplete that result was better than an interception. Perhaps he was getting comfortable and maybe not feeling so much pressure after all since the score was out of hand, but Zimmerman's next pass went to Masterson for 15 years.

That was not only Zimmerman's most productive play at that point from the offensive set, but Washington's biggest gainer of the second half. Rookie Ray Hare (Flaherty figured he might as well clear the bench and let everyone play some) got his first attempt and even though he gained seven yards, when the Bears were called for an offside penalty, Washington accepted the five-yard penalty instead of the run gain.

Washington had possession with a first-and-five at the 46-yard-line and Seymour's number was called again. He took the handoff and scampered around right end for a 16-yard gain. All of a sudden the Redskins were moving the ball. But if the last few gains indicated any loss of concentration by the Bears, or a sign of relaxation, that was dispelled on the next play.

Zimmerman faded back to pass from the Bears' 30, but tough George Musso came crashing through the line to pin him for a 12-yard loss. However, when he body slammed Zimmerman to the turf, the officials felt he hit the quarterback too hard and whistled a roughing penalty. Washington had a first down on the Chicago 28 and the way the Redskins were marching forward there were hints they may be able to score.

The thought apparently occurred to the Redskins, as well as their supporters, and Zimmerman took the hike, backed up and fired into the end zone trying to hit Hare. McAfee loomed up and batted down the pass. Still, Zimmerman liked the plan of attack and went to the air again on second-and-10 at the 28. The throw was a little short, but Masterson bent over and scooped up the ball inches above the ground for a 12-yard gain to Chicago's 16-yard-line. Could Washington break through? Could the Redskins at least escape without being shut out?

Washington tried a run. Seymour carried, but Jumbo Joe Stydahar and Dick Plasman reared up at the line of scrimmage and road-blocked him for no gain. On second down from the 16, Zimmerman tried a pass. But before he could get set, Bears defenders rushed in on him forcing a quick throw that was incomplete. Zimmerman tried another pass, to Masterson, but even though Masterson dropped the ball it didn't really matter because both teams were offsides and no play registered.

It was third-and-10 at the 16 when Zimmerman took the snap and scanned the field for an open receiver. He didn't have very much time, though, because the Bears' rush put serious pressure on him. Zimmerman threw, but the ball fell harmlessly to the turf. It was fourth down and Washington called a clever play. Dick Farman was in the game, but not somebody the Bears were likely to pay much attention to since he was an offensive lineman. He was 6 feet tall and weighed 220 pounds and was a very fine blocker who won NFL all-star honors more than once. He hardly ever touched the ball, however, during his entire five-year career.

Yet Farman was a tackle eligible receiver on the play and dashed into the end zone. Zimmerman saw his open pass catcher, but he misjudged the distance and threw the ball over Farman's head. The drive halted on Chicago's 16. End of threat. It seemed to be a now-or-never play for a Washington touchdown and things seemed to be shaping up as never.

Chicago took over on downs on the 20-yard-line and McAfee took the first down handoff and gained four yards over right tackle. Fullback Bill Osmanski rushed on the next play and gained two yards before Zimmerman, starting to show up everywhere, ended the play by shoving him out of bounds.

If it seemed the Bears were content to merely run out the clock against the Redskins, they gave Washington even more to think about on the next play. Following the snap the ball went to McAfee, but instead of running, he rolled out for a halfback option. The play worked because it drew the defense in and fooled the Redskins. Dick Plasman was wide open downfield, and McAfee threw a strike, but Plasman dropped the ball.

That left Chicago with a fourth down and a strange circumstance arose – at least for this day – the smart play was for the Bears to punt the ball to Washington. McAfee did the kicking and the ball rolled out of bounds on the Washington 36-yard-line. The Bears actually went through a series without scoring a touchdown.

Since the Redskins had just produced a respectable offensive series, threatening to score, they probably thought they could do it again, especially with decent field position. Zimmerman wanted to pass on first down, but was chased and had to hang onto the ball. He gained two yards before Plasman drove him out of bounds.

Just to show that Redskins follies were not over for the day, on the next play the hike sailed over Zimmerman's head and he had to turn on the afterburners to retreat and catch up to the bounding ball before a Bears player could fall on it. The sloppy play cost Washington 21 humiliating yards. That was pretty much a reminder of which team was boss.

That made it third down and 25 yards for a first down for Washington. The only choice was to pass and Zimmerman did his best. He had the right idea and the wrong execution. The ball was caught not by a Redskin, but by Bulldog Turner, who ran the interception in for a 24-yard touchdown. Right about then, Zimmerman, who likely never contemplated seeing so much action, was probably wishing he had awakened with the flu that day. The Bears were making him look sick, anyway.

The point after, this one attempted by running back Joe Maniaci, was blocked by Washington's Clyde Shugart. That effort might well have earned Shugart Redskin defensive player of the game honors if such a thing existed. Of course, given the doings on the field that would have been regarded as sarcasm.

After that major miscue, the Bears led by the mind-boggling score of 54-0.

That still did not kill the clock in the third period. Although it ordinarily would have been regarded as a privilege, or at least an opportunity, that meant the Redskins had to come back out and play one more series in the third quarter.

Even Artoe's toe got a rest after the last touchdown. Tackle Jack Torrance kicked off to Washington. It was a short kick and Redskin Ernie Pinckert fielded the ball on his own 21 and returned it 10 yards. Once more Washington's field position wasn't bad, but it had been demonstrated that it hardly mattered where the Redskins started drives, often enough the ball ended up back in the hands of Chicago Bears.

First-and-10 from the 31 and Zimmerman threw over the middle to Hare. Alas, Hare dropped the pass. Even when Zimmerman had time to pass by dodging the Bears' rush, his receivers didn't always help him out.

What looked like a very successful and slick play followed. Zimmerman retreated to throw to Masterson at the line of scrimmage and Washington swiftly formed a four-man wedge of blockers for protection. Masterson galloped 19 yards before the Bears hauled him down. Only the entire play went for naught because the Redskins were ruled offsides. If the Bears didn't overwhelm Washington with their superior play, the Redskins killed themselves with ill-timed, foolish mistakes. This mistake was one of nadirs of the game for Washington. It couldn't be declared the worst of the worst because there were so many bad ones to choose from and certainly an interception run back for a touchdown was going to be a top contender.

Instead of a first half, the Redskins had to regroup on their own 26. Zimmerman completed a seven-yard pass to Seymour and then went long to Sandy Sanford, but the throw was inaccurate and went incomplete. After all of the back-and-forth Washington had a fourth down on its own 33-yard-line, just two yards further upfield than where the series began.

No longer harboring any fantasy of a comeback, the Redskins punted. Zimmerman boomed a 62-yarder, certainly one of the big pluses of the day for Washington. Chicago took over on its own 15 and had time to run one play before the clock mercifully ran out on the third quarter. Harry Clark got his name in the box score with an 11-yard run.

For onlookers, the score was surreal. Chicago led 54-0 after three quarters. If the score is run up in that manner in a high school football game the coaches often agree to play running time for the fourth period. There is no such option in the pros. The Redskins were stuck on that field to live out the nightmare with another 15 minutes of play.

Halas' only indication that he was lessening the heat on the Redskins was his liberal use of players who were not starters. For his part, Luckman couldn't believe what he was seeing. McAfee had a phenomenal third quarter and the Bears had their way with Washington. Despite the evidence and the mounting score, Luckman had difficulty assimilating it.

"McAfee, with the long legs and the trim hips of the perfect runner, made yardage almost at will," Luckman said, "eight or nine at a crack. Once he leaped right over the heads of two crouched linemen. His 34-yard dash to the goal with an intercepted pass was one of the masterpieces of the massacre, as he cut his field, retraced his steps, twisted about like a hula dancer to shake off tacklers. George tried to convince me, just as Nolting did, that the Redskins 'were going to sleep out there,' but I couldn't believe it. They still had Wilkin, Malone, (Jim) Barber, (Steve) Slivinski, and Farman with them – big boys all." (13)

THE BEARS' SIDELINE

During most professional football games, especially if they are at all close, the sidelines are businesslike. The coaches keep their eyes on the ball and they talk to their assistants for advice, as needed. Players who are not on the field watch the action, ready to be inserted into the game if a coach calls, or merely just ready to run in when the ball changes hands, the need to punt or kickoff comes along.

After three quarters of play the Bears really couldn't believe what was taking place. The biggest problem may have been to maintain a serious demeanor. This was an all-out slaughter, they led by 54 points, and there was more of a chance of an unscheduled eclipse than a Redskins comeback.

Twenty years into his tenure as boss of the Chicago Bears, George Halas had an established image. He harangued officials as he patrolled the sidelines, looking for every edge in an unfolding game. He brought a killer instinct to every game, trying to squeeze the maximum effort out of his players. He had been motivated by revenge for that regular-season loss going into this championship game and he used the ploy of George Preston Marshall's badmouthing to psyche up his players.

Halas wanted his guys focused and angry, anxious to take out their emotions on the Redskins. He felt that was the best strategy to prepare them. At no time, not even as many years passed in his long life, did Halas ever admit that he thought the Bears could run up the largest plurality in the history of pro football. He would have been content just to win the game and the championship by something as unremarkable as a 10-3 score. Not even Halas would be so greedy as to think his team might be leading by 54 points with one period remaining. Preposterous.

It was nearly impossible to believe that this was reality. Had Halas fallen asleep and dreamt this wipeout, his team playing the perfect game, his enemy playing its worst game? This was almost like "The Wizard of Oz" of football.

After Luckman was taken out of the game at quarterback in favor of Bernie Masterson, the regular signal caller watched Halas on the Bears' sideline.

"I found Halas almost delirious with joy," Luckman said. "In two full seasons I never saw him in this condition. After we had rung up our 50th point or so, he began to murmur, 'Wonder what Mr. George Preston Marshall is doing at this stage?' (I was sure Mr. Marshall couldn't be doing anything sensible.)" (1)

Marshall had probably fainted on the ground by his seat. Or perhaps he was contemplating his escape route. Or just maybe he was paralyzed with disbelief. For a guy who thought he would be celebrating that day, this was one long, drawn-out, painful display of ineptitude.

Whether Halas was thinking sincerely or sarcastically about his counterpart, Luckman never knew, but he heard assistant coach Hunk Anderson comment, "It's hardly a thing to laugh at George, getting beaten like this. A shameful thing for a pro boss." (2) Anderson gave off a hint of sympathy, but Halas definitely did not feel any. As far as he was concerned the Bears could keep on scoring until Doomsday and if they cracked 100 points, so be it.

It would not disturb Halas in the slightest if Chicago recorded the biggest victory in the history of the sport. He loved watching his men beat the Redskins to a pulp, fooling them with pass plays and end-arounds, squashing them with tackles. If Halas owned a sympathy gene it only showed itself on the occasion of more serious matters, such as when a player of his had a family health problem. On the field? No charity was to be shown during a game. Never.

One thing the Bears were not going to accomplish was setting a point differential that would surpass the worst slaughter in college football history. That record dated to 1916 when Georgia Tech, coached by John Heisman (the man for whom the Heisman Trophy is named) defeated Cumberland College, (coached by someone named George Allen, thought not the George Allen who later coached with Halas on the Bears), 222-0.

That game made Bears-Redskins look like a nail-biter. Georgia Tech scored 63 points in the first quarter, and 63 in the second quarter. Remarkably, in an upset of sorts in its own way, Cumberland came out to actually play the second half. In the third quarter, Georgia Tech scored 54 points. Then Georgia Tech eased up in the fourth period, scoring only 42 points.

The lopsided score had some strange facts behind it. Cumberland, located in Lebanon, Tennessee, had dropped football as an intercollegiate sport, but Georgia Tech refused to allow the team out of the schedule commitment. That doesn't sound as if it makes much sense, but it is what occurred. Apparently, Tech really wanted that home game at Grant Field.

Cumberland may not have been mentioned much on the national sporting landscape since that infamous day, but the school must have had a pretty decent baseball team because it notched a 22-0 shellacking of Tech the previous season. Some theorized that's why – revenge -- Heisman took it out on the football team.

The biggest margin of victory in college basketball history was recorded on November 26, 1997 when NCAA Division I Long Island University beat Division III Medgar Evers 179-62. On December 31, 2013, a recent New Year's Eve, Southern University manhandled Champion Baptist College, 116-12. The Jaguars must have been playing terrific defense. Southern led 44-0 before Champion Baptist scored on a free throw.

"I still hate it," said Long Island athletic director John Suarez 15 years after the Blackbirds pummeled Medgar Evers. He takes no pride in the record. "I hope someone is as stupid as we are and beats us. It is never going to happen again. I hate it. I hate it that we're in the record book for that." (3) And that's a voice from the winner's side.

From the start it was a scheduled mismatch in the sense that it was a large-school program meeting a small-school program. But those types of games are scheduled every season without results approaching the spread of 117 points.

"We knew we were going to get punched in the face," said Medgar Evers coach Bryan Mariner. "Obviously, I never thought it would be that magnitude." (2)

Every once in a while a score that no one sees coming breaks out and that's what happened on December 17, 1991 when the Cleveland Cavaliers clobbered the Miami Heat, 148-80, in an NBA game. The plurality of 68 points is the league record for margin of victory.

The Cavaliers, whose record was 13-8 after the victory, put eight players in double figures, no doubt because playing time was widely distributed. The Cavs shot 60.2 percent from the field. Cleveland's high scorers were Mark Price and John Battle with 18 points apiece. The Heat in the pre-LeBron James days, were 11-12 after the debacle. Miami shrugged off the devastating loss and won its next game over the Indiana Pacers.

Each major sport has its own game of infamy where one club was belted around like the speed bag in a gym, helplessly enduring the onslaught of another team for one horrible day.

On January 23, 1944, the Detroit Red Wings ripped the New York Rangers, 15-0, in a National Hockey League game. Even though it seems as if Gordie Howe, Mr. Hockey, has been around forever, he was not old enough to be in the Red Wings' lineup yet. He didn't miss by much, though. Playing junior in Saskatoon that season Howe made his NHL debut for the 1946-47 season.

Syd Howe scored a hat trick for Detroit, but in all 10 Red Wings scored goals. It was a slow-forming blowout, too, with Detroit firing in eight goals in the third period. The final score could have been 16-0 because Detroit unleashed one final puck at the net as the buzzer sounded. It went in, but was a second too late on the clock. The Rangers were used to being body-checked hard into the boards just about every night that season, finishing last with a record of 6-39-5.

Those were the Original Six days of the NHL when there were only six franchises spread around North America, so those teams had to meet one another quite often. It was not as if the Rangers could duck the Red Wings until the next season.

In 2007, the Texas Rangers blasted the Baltimore Orioles 30-3 in a Major League baseball game which stands as the record for most one-sided contest. One might say that the Orioles' pitching was off that night, but such a margin in a baseball game when teams play series day after day looms even more inexplicable. This stunning score was recorded as part of the middle game of a three-game series in August in Baltimore. The Rangers lost the opener 6-2 and the day after the brutal wipeout the Rangers won 9-7.

The game sandwiched in the middle made history as the biggest plurality in the modern era (starting in 1900). Texas cracked 29 hits and the Orioles used just four pitchers to absorb the damage. It was equal-opportunity-destroy-earned-run-average night at Camden Yards. Daniel Cabrera gave up the first six runs in five innings. Not distinctively horrible, just a bad game.

Cabrera was relieved by Brian Burres whose outing was probably the most nightmarish of his life. He lasted two-thirds of an inning and surrendered eight runs. Baltimore manager Dave Tremblay couldn't sprint to the mound fast enough to get Burres out. The third Orioles pitcher was Rob Bell. He gave up seven runs in one and one-third innings.

By this time Tremblay could probably identify with the tribulations of Ray Flaherty. It was clear that no matter what he did, no matter who he called upon to throw, the Orioles weren't going to get too many Rangers out in a timely manner. Even worse, unlike football, where a clock was running, the Orioles had to get Ranger batters out if they wanted to go home on the same day.

Once again Tremblay signaled to the bullpen for his fourth hurler of the game. He had to think the law of averages was with him. But it wasn't. Paul Shuey entered the picture and he had nothing either. Shuey allowed nine runs in two innings. It was almost impossible for a succession of pitchers to be so bad on the same night, but the Orioles did it.

Meanwhile the Rangers partied on. Just as the Bears seemed unable to stop scoring touchdowns, Texas players seemed unable not to hit safely each time they stepped into the batters' box. For them it was a little bit like hitting a pitching machine where they set the speed to their own preference. Left-fielder David Murphy swatted five hits. Catcher Jarrod Saltalamacchia stroked four and so did infielder Ramon Vazquez. Six other Rangers collected two or three hits.

While there has never been a pro football game to rival the Bears-Redskins gridiron carnage, every big-time sport has seen a result where one unsuspecting team showed up for a contest feeling it could win only to be battered mercilessly. None of those milestone plurality games took place in a championship setting, however. In the NBA, NHL and Major League Baseball the winning team barely had enough time to sleep on its fabulous performance and the losing team didn't even have enough time to develop amnesia because it had to take the court or field again so quickly.

During Bears-Redskins, Chicago players recognized they were in the midst of doing something historic. The only concession to the point margin by Halas was that he took out starters and let lesser used players have some fun with extra playing time. Some Bears kept clamoring for more time on the field. They realized that Chicago was likely to keep on scoring and they wanted to be part of the cannibalization of Washington.

Running back Joe Maniaci complained when Halas took him out of the game in favor of another sub. Maniciai wanted more yards and more touchdowns. Luckman observed that scene unfolding and had to laugh.

"Maniaci squawked when Halas sent in another alternate for him," Luckman said. "Joe had already had two chances at the Redskins so far. 'I don't get a chance to run wild every day, chief,' he said. 'Neither does anyone else,' said Halas. Then he rose and took a stroll in front of the bench to warm himself. Maniaci slid behind him and began to shadow the Boss, a comically grim look on his face as Halas tried to shrug him off." (5)

Meanwhile, the Bears scored again and Halas jumped up in the air to celebrate once more. As soon as things calmed down Maniaci continued lobbying for more time in the game.

"Halas desperately turned to the bench and said, 'Won't somebody get this character out of my hair?'" Luckman said. (6)

It was almost as if someone was giving away free lunches and Maniaci didn't want to miss out. The Bears were feasting on Washington and he recognized that such an opportunity as this, where every play on offense seemed to lead to a touchdown, might never come along again.

Some of the Bears were beginning to sound a little bit like Anderson, wondering if it was proper to pile it on. Others were like Maniaci, gluttonous in their desire to score more, more. They didn't want to turn off the faucet.

"This is ridiculous, beating them so bad," Luckman recalled hearing one teammate say. "Let's not score any more." (7)

To whatever degree any debate ensued, other players were definitely in Maniaci's corner. They wanted to get theirs and they wanted to rub the result in the faces of the Redskins.

"The other players were so hopped up about the game even with this one-sided score they all jumped on him (the one that pondered the piling on issue) for having the nerve to talk that way," Luckman said. (8)

After all, this wasn't high school football, and there was no room for fragile egos in the pro game.

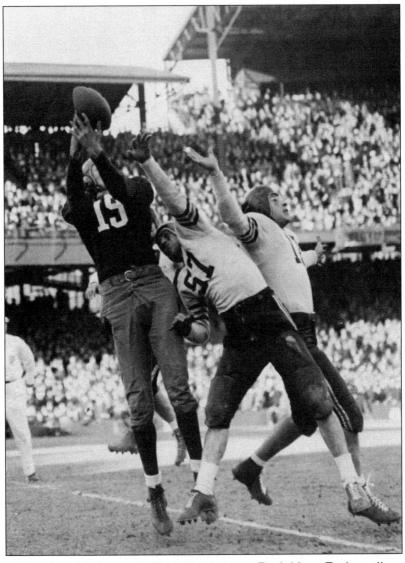

Charley Malone, (19), Washington Redskins End, pulls down a 42 yard pass from Sammy Baugh in the closing minutes of the first half of National Professional Football League Championship game with the Chicago Bears in Washington, D.C., Dec. 18, 1940. The Bears won 73 to 0. **Ray McLean** (57) and **Bob Snyder** (17) of the Bears are on the play. (AP Photo)

FOURTH QUARTER

Sammy Baugh was a spectator before the start of the fourth quarter. It was one of those days that it would be really nice to forget the moment his head hit the pillow that night, but it was going to be one of those games that always lingered in the background, in memory, a scarring that would not heal easily, if at all.

"They came out with fire in their eye," Baugh said of the Bears. (1)

Chicago players' eyes were still glowing hot in the fourth period. At least they played with that kind of emotion, whether it was starters or back-ups, whoever lined up for Chicago. There was no minimizing the thoroughness of the beating. Sportswriters didn't have to wait until the gun sounded to determine the victor. There was no suspense other than how high the final score would climb.

What began as a partisan crowd of more than 36,000 in Griffith Stadium began to shrink as time passed and the score mounted. Some fans may well have realized that they were witnessing an historic contest, even if they couldn't enjoy it because they were rooting for the wrong side.

Indeed, reviewing the situation on the field in 1940 and carrying straight through to the end of its run as a stadium in 1965, it made for amusing chatter to try and figure out if there had ever been a more unique sporting event contested at Griffith. Named after a baseball figure and more in use as a baseball stadium during the six months of spring and summer into fall, baseball was much more often played within the confines of the building. However, during the lifespan of the stadium, there were only rare years when the Washington Senators gave their fans something to remember them by.

Opening day of the 1911 season was pretty special because the previous wooden ball park on the site had burned down and it took an extraordinary labor effort for the then-named National Park to be ready for play in time. National Park was one of the earliest in a new generation of steel structure ball fields that was sparked by the erection of Shibe Park in Philadelphia in 1909.

In 1912, behind the magnificent Walter Johnson, who recorded a 32-12 record with a 1.39 earned run average, the Senators had their first winning season since their founding 12 seasons earlier. Maybe it was the glow of the new park as well as the whiplash in Johnson's right arm.

The 1924 season was the one that produced the grandest memories at Griffith Stadium. The baseball team won the American League pennant and then captured the World Series. D.C. threw a parade to honor the team, cavorting down Pennsylvania Avenue to the White House. Once there the team was feted by President Calvin Coolidge, who had thrown out the first pitch to start the season.

A year later the Senators made it back to the World Series, but lost in seven games to the Pittsburgh Pirates.

In the latter years of the stadium, when the Senators were consistently the worst team in the AL, the phrase was coined, "Washington, first in war, first in peace, and last in the American League." In May of 1921 Babe Ruth hit two home runs out of the park that each traveled approximately 500 feet. In 1953 Mickey Mantle blasted a home run that was figured to be the longest in baseball history, carrying 565 feet. In the 1930s and 1940s, various Negro Leagues clubs called Griffth Stadium home, including the Homestead Grays. Slugging legend Josh Gibson also belted a 500-foot homer at the park.

Home to the Redskins from the time when the team moved to town from Boston until the stadium was shuttered, Griffith hosted the NFL title game in 1937, 1940, and 1942, one of the best stretches of play for the Redskins in team history. On December 7, 1941, Washington was playing the Philadelphia Eagles. On that morning in Hawaii, Pearl Harbor was bombed, plunging the United States into World War II. But no announcement was made over the public address system, so the fans attending the game were essentially in a news blackout.

One day after Pearl Harbor was destroyed by Japanese attack, President Franklin D. Roosevelt addressed a joint session of Congress to ask for a declaration of war. This was his famous speech in which FDR described the horror in Hawaii as "a day that will live in infamy." That memorable phrase has long been identified with the start of hostilities embroiling the U.S. in the war that lasted until 1945.

However, some snarky sportswriters, despite the questionable taste, in future years sometimes referred to the Bears-Redskins football championship of 1940 as "a football game that will live in infamy."

The other two NFL championship games of the period that Washington hosted, as well as the two World Series the Senators played, were all more fondly remembered by Washington sports fans than the 1940 tilt. So was Joe Louis' heavyweight title defense of 1941 when he stopped Buddy Baer in front of 35,000 witnesses. The Redskins took a harsher beating from the Bears than Baer did from Louis.

Sid Luckman didn't mind at all when Bernie Masterson got the nod to start the fourth quarter, signaling that his work day was over at quarterback and that it was a job well done. There was no other way to read a 54-0 lead.

Despite Maniaci nagging Halas to distraction, the Bears coach gave running back Gary Famiglietti a chance to tote the pigskin on Chicago's first play of the fourth quarter. The Bears started their series from their own 15-yard-line and Famiglietti ran for three yards over left tackle.

Famiglietti was from Medford, Massachusetts, a suburb of Boston and attended Boston University. After his eligibility for the Terriers was up, the rugged 6-foot, 225-pound fullback heard from representatives of the Cleveland Rams, Philadelphia Eagles, and the Bears inquiring as to his interest in playing pro ball. He answered in the affirmative and it was the Bears who grabbed him with their third-round choice.

His bulk and the results he produced bashing through the offensive line impressed those who watched Famiglietti play in college and a local newspaper tried to keep tabs on him for the fan base long before the draft rolled around. Famiglietti did not know how things would turn out, but only a few weeks after the end of the Boston U. season he was working out trying to stay in shape.

"I think I'll go over to the gym and knock off a few pounds," he told a sportswriter, "just in case something does turn up." (2)

Famiglietti moved into the Bears' starting lineup to replace retiring Bronko Nagurski, then, in turn was superseded by Bill Osmanski. However, he was a two-time All-Pro and played on three Chicago championship clubs.

On second down Familietti grasped another handoff and again gained three yards to give the Bears a third-and-four on their 32-yard-line. Harry Clark's turn came next. Masterson's call was for a fake reverse and Clark executed beautifully, gaining 10 yards. Clark was still another rookie, a 13th-round draft pick out of West Virginia. That season Clark rushed for 258 yards, showing he had the right stuff whenever he got the opportunity by averaging 4.6 yards a carry. His defensive backfield performance was more eye-catching. Clark intercepted four passes and his all-around work earned him a slot in the Pro Bowl.

The reverse gave Chicago a first down on the 42. Bob Nowaskey had been drafted by the Rams that season, but ended up with the Bears. He churned out seven yards on the play. However, the man handing him the ball was the back-up to the back-up at QB. Solly Sherman was at the controls. Sherman played his college ball at the University of Chicago, one of the last of the Maroons as the school dropped football. He joined the Bears in 1939.

One of Sherman's key attributes was his knowledge of the T formation and although he wasn't as talented as Luckman, Sherman had a firm grasp of the offense and helped instruct the newcomer in the intricacies of the style. The 6-1, 190-pound Sherman was the 166th player selected in the 1939 draft, in the 18th round by the Bears.

Sherman lasted just two seasons with Chicago and he did not play much, and he threw even less. Sherman was a mop-up man making his cameo appearances, but he did earn the right to call himself a champion in 1940. When World War II started Sherman wanted to fight, but an old knee injury disqualified him. He joined the family business as a manufacturer of machine tools and did not return to football after the war ended.

When Sherman passed away at the age of 93 in 2010, the Chicago Tribune speculated that Sherman and his good friend Luckman – who remained pals for the rest of their lives – "may have been the only Jewish quarterback tandem in NFL history." (3)

Sherman kept the ball for his own carry on the next play from scrimmage, but didn't get beyond the line of scrimmage seeking to turn the corner of the left end. But officials sniffed out a sinister infraction and nailed the Redskins, as it reads on the official play-by-play, for "slugging." That was a 15-yard mistake which would probably be classified as fighting in the modern era, or unsportsmanlike conduct.

On the next down Sherman was hit legally, decked by Washington's Wayne Millner for an eight-yard loss. That dropped the Bears back to the Redskin 44. Sticking to the ground, Sherman handed off to Clark, but it was a busted play all around. He was shut down for no gain and the Bears were whistled for a penalty. Washington refused the penalty, setting up a Chicago third down and 18 to go on the 44. This looked like one of the rare occasions in the game when the Washington defense would hold and force a Bears punt.

Showing no quarter, the next play the Bears called was the type of thing that one might expect of a desperate-for-offense Redskins club. Sherman took the handoff and gave the ball to Famiglietti, who headed towards the left side. Clark passed him running right and completed a double reverse by gathering in the ball and sprinting around the corner. Clark was on his way to a 44-yard touchdown. Frank Filchock was back at the 15 and had a shot at Clark, but the Bears' interference was downfield already, Frank Bausch and George Wilson knocking Filchock out of the way.

In this one-sided game it seemed as if everyone on the Bears could point to a special moment where he contributed to the fabulous win. Bausch, who played college ball at the University of Kansas, had spent three seasons as a member of the Boston Redskins during the days when empty seats dominated the stadium prompting Marshall's irate evacuation of the city. With the Bears, Bausch had the rather thankless job of backing up Clyde Turner at center. Turner practically never missed a minute of a game.

Wilson's involvement in the block was probably best-remembered by Clark and Bausch, but he got more credit from his big block made on the Bears' first touchdown when Osmanski scampered into the end zone. The score was 0-0 at the time, so it was more important. Many years later, when Wilson was coaching the Miami Dolphins, a feature story about him in a game program said that Wilson and his block on Osmanski's behalf were "still remembered…in one of the most famous games in pro history." Then Halas was quoted as relishing the play vividly 27 years after the fact. "The greatest block I ever saw," he said. (4)

On this touchdown the extra point was attempted by Famiglietti, who missed. The score was 60-0 with plenty of time left for more.

Although the exact timing of the discussion between officials and

Halas seems difficult to pin down, it was around this time when it was pointed out that Chicago was scoring so many touchdowns, setting up the opportunity to kick extra points, that the game administrators were running out of footballs. Indications were that the Bears would keep scoring touchdowns and officials feared they would run out of pigskins and prevent the appropriate conclusion of the contest.

After the officials met in their own huddle, referee Red Friesell walked over to the Bears' sideline for a little confab. He appealed to Halas by saying, "We're running out of footballs, George. Would you mind asking the boys to run or pass for the point after?" Halas replied, "Only too happy to oblige." (5)

That would have been a very embarrassing moment for a league striving to be considered big-league. The finite number of balls in reserve was running short because no one envisioned a game where so many TDs would be rung up. This is likely the only time in history the NFL was ill-equipped to cope with this situation. No one even asks the question in the modern era. It is assumed there are plenty of footballs to go around. One big difference was that extra points were booted into the stands in 1940 and fans claimed them. Now the NFL raises nets behind the goal-posts so there is no threat of the balls being swiped.

This was truly one of the most humorous aspects of this crushing win by the Bears. A team could score so many touchdowns the officials would run out of footballs? Unreal. That development became one of the symbols of the extremely one-sided nature of the title game.

It is easy to picture Halas being approached with the request from the referee not to kick more extra points. He must have chortled, unleashing a self-satisfying sound. Even the officials, in their own way, were asking him to take it easy on the poor Redskins. Heh, heh, heh.

By then Halas had already miffed Turner by asking him to make a bad snap the next touchdown around. No thanks, the Bulldog said. He had too much pride to make a mistake on purpose. Not even snapping for a kick, now that seemed to be a better idea.

An absence of more Bears extra points presumably also managed to snuff out whatever joy the remaining fans seated in the end zone might glean from the game. They had long before begun booing the hometown team and its pathetic performance. Some could have hoped for a souvenir football – if they even wanted to be reminded of this game.

Flaherty decided that Zimmerman had had enough experience for the day and put Filchock back in at quarterback after he fielded the Jack Torrance kickoff on the 12-yard-line and returned it to the 24.

It didn't look like that bad an idea when Filchock flung a first-down pass to Millner for a 12-yard gain. But the play was erased by a Redskins penalty. Even when things appeared to go well for the Redskins they turned sour. On the next play Filchock heaved a pass to Bob McChesney for a seven-yard gain, but Torrance was called for pass interference, so the line of scrimmage ended up on the 19, not quite where Washington had started the drive from.

On second down Filchock seemed to want to pass, but he had no time to duck onrushing Bears tackle Joe Mihal, who leveled him. Filchock fumbled and Torrance recovered the ball. Just what the Redskins needed. Just when the Redskins believed it was impossible for things to get worse. Torrance fell on the ball on the two-yard-line. Everyone knew what was going to happen next. Washington's defense hadn't been able to stop the Bears' offense from anywhere on the field all day, so no one was radical enough to suggest that the Redskins would prevent Chicago from making another visit to the end zone.

Sure enough, there was no suspense. On first down Gary Famiglietti had his number called and he erupted into the end zone for a two-yard TD run. Politely complying with the referee's request Halas did not bother to send out a kicker to try the point after. Instead, the Bears lined up to run a normal style play. Solly Sherman was at quarterback and lofted a little pass to Maniaci (who got his wish for more action) and the score was up to 67-0.

The simple rule of football was that whenever a team scored it had to kick the ball back to the opposition. It was almost pointless (which is what Washington was, too) since the Redskins contrived to give the ball right back to the Bears one mortifying way or another.

Jack Torrance, who set up the most recent Chicago touchdown, kicked off. Flaherty sent Andy Farkas back to receive. The ball nestled into his arms on the five-yard-line and he took off upfield. It was one of the better Washington runs of the day of any kind. Farkas sped 35 yards before being pushed out of bounds.

Once again the Redskins' dispirited players trotted out to take possession of the ball, this time on their own 40-yard-line, which ordinarily would not be a bad place to be. Filchock was behind center and on first down he tossed a completion to Millner. The play gained eight yards and advanced the ball to the 48.

Next time Filchock faded back and looked deep. Whatever he saw was apparently misleading because the ball did not reach any Redskin receiver. Instead, Maniaci, on a hot streak now that he was back in the lineup, picked the ball off on the Bears' 32. Seeing some open territory, Maniaci returned the ball to the Redskins' 42-yard-line. Unbelievably, it was Chicago's seventh interception of the game. Baugh had to be happy to sit out the latter stages of the game. He was responsible for just two of those turnovers.

Actually, as the game wore on and the scope of the disaster grew and grew in the fourth quarter, Baugh's counterpart, Sid Luckman, felt a twinge of pity for the man he so highly respected as a great quarterback. Luckman tried to imagine how Baugh was feeling across the field.

"Whatever we had done couldn't be pinned on Sam," Luckman said. "And yet he was part of that badly beaten gang, and the raucous noises (hometown fan insults and booing) behind him must have been hammering at his ears. Think about Sam – the plaudits he had earned over the years with his incomparable passing – and now, on a dismal afternoon, he seemed alone, as all the Redskin boys did – without a single booster in Washington." (6)

Luckman wondered whether Washington's fans would forsake the Redskins completely because of this horrible showing in the title game and he actually mentioned that thought aloud to Bill Osmanski. Osmanksi appeared to be a harsh realist.

"You can't tell about grid fans," Osmanski said. "But why bring that up after we've just taken the world title?" (7) Osmanski wanted to enjoy the victory, not worry about the vanquished.

Luckman was more thoughtful.

"Shucks, we clinched it an hour ago," he said. "What I'm getting at is, what does a man have to do to keep the loyalty of fans in this town? It's not as if the Redskins had a weak team or didn't try their damned best to produce." (8)

Osmanksi came across as more cynic than realist, saying winning by such a huge amount would gain a team fan loyalty for at least one more day. Actually, as the game neared its end Washington fans applauded the Bears. They were either being cynical or they were tipping their hats to the excellence on the field Chicago displayed.

So the latest Maniaci initiative gave Chicago the ball once more, first down on the Washington 42. As a reward for the interception, Halas inserted Maniaci at running back and he carried on first down, rushing for five yards over left tackle. But the play was negated because the Bears were offsides.

Chicago had a new face at quarterback. Bob Snyder took a turn. Snyder, who played for Ohio University, had his finest moments for the Bears as a place kicker, once booting a record 39 conversions in a season and three field goals in one championship game. He also later coached the Los Angeles Rams for a season and between competing in a second old American Football League, spending four years with the Bears, coaching and scouting, he spent the better part of three decades in football, including college and minor league football.

Snyder was 6 feet tall and weighed 200 pounds. He was athletic, but except for his kicking skill, his only position was quarterback. That marooned him behind Luckman on the Bears' roster and he was just 30 when he retired from the field. Still, for experience's sake, his time spent with Chicago was timely. The Bears won four Western Division crowns and three NFL titles during his stay on the team. If Chicago had had a need for a kicker, or booted extra points after every touchdown in the championship encounter with the Redskins Snyder likely would have set records never to be broken. There were 11 chances.

After Maniaci's carry, Snyder was buried behind the line by Washington's Wayne Millner for a loss of 10 yards. The Bears were looking at second-and-25 from the 43 to obtain a first down, so Snyder dropped back to pass. He tossed a short pass to Ken Kavanaugh and it gained just two yards. The next play worked much better. Snyder passed to Joe Mihal for a 14-yard gain.

It was fourth and nine at the Redskins' 41-yard-line when Snyder loosed a shaky pass to Maniaci. The ball was not a tight spiral and was a dead ringer for the wounded duck description, but wobbly or not the ball reached its destination. Maniaci made Snyder look good on the play, producing 21 yards.

Whether they wanted to or not, once again Chicago was threatening. No matter who played, Washington couldn't stop anyone wearing a Bears uniform. The Bears had a first down on the Redskins' 20. Chicago could have stopped trying altogether, just falling on the ball enough downs until it was returned to Washington, but taking a knee wasn't really in vogue during that era of NFL play and the clock still had some minutes to run.

Harry Clark scooted around right end for an eight-yard gain, putting the ball on the Washington 12. Once again the Redskin defense had its back to the end zone, uncomfortably nearby. Maniaci ran next, recording a seven-yard burst over right guard. Chicago had the ball first-and-goal at the Redskins' five-yard-line, allowing for four cracks at the goal line from the five if the Bears needed them. If the public address announcer had asked the fans remaining in Griffith Stadium to raise their hands how many believed the Redskins would stop the Bears here, he would have been greeted by a passel of folded arms across the chest.

Maniaci, aching to put his name on another touchdown, got the call and bulled his way most of the distance to the end zone. He was brought down after gaining about four-and-a-half yards, but officially the ball was placed at the one. On second down Chicago was really at the half-yard-line so pretty much all Clark had to do was fall down to score. He powered into the end zone off right tackle. Touchdown! It was Chicago's 11th touchdown of the game. Snyder might well have kicked the extra point blindfolded, but since he was being prohibited from kicking at that stage he tried to pass to Maniaci. The ball fell incomplete, leaving the score at 73-0.

73-0! It was an unheard of score in the NFL. It was a number that was stamped into the consciousness of pro football fans forevermore.

If there was an ounce of spirit left in the Washington players it was not visible. Famiglietti kicked off to Filchock. It wasn't a long boot. Filchock received at his own 12 and brought the ball out 28 yards to the Redskin 40-yard-line.

There really was nothing for Washington to do other than go for a single touchdown in the most efficient manner possible. That meant passing. Filchock threw on first down to Millner and gained 12 yards. The play penetrated Bears territory at the 48. Filchock went to Millner again and the future Hall of Famer made the catch for nine yards.

As long as the connection seemed to be working, Filchock sent Millner long on second down from the Chicago 39. Good old Joe Maniaci, proving to Halas that it was worthwhile to put him back in the game after his earlier rest, intercepted the ball on the 20-yard-line. As greedy for more points as ever, Maniaci lateraled to Clark, hoping he might out-run the would-be tacklers. Only he misjudged the angle and the play was stopped and Chicago penalized because it was an illegal lateral.

Now, at last, as the Redskins must have been thinking, there was little time left in the fourth period. The Bears had the ball on their own 20 and Snyder pitched to Famiglietti dashing around left end for 11 yards. On the final play of the historic contest, Snyder kept the ball for a quarterback sneak over center, and gained two yards.

The long game was officially over, long after the scoreboard had announced realistically that it was over. Washington had played out a very painful second half. Even at that very moment it was possible those involved realized there would never be anything like this title game again. 73-0 was a unique score and the dazed losers couldn't begin to clear-headedly figure out how it had happened.

Well before the final seconds ticked off, George Preston Marshall had begun a long trudge out of the stands, demoralized, angry, beaten, and with the impending result leaving a bitter taste in his mouth. One of the very first things he said when he probably should have kept his mouth shut, was that his team had quit. Marshall was good at making blanket, ill-advised statements and he would have been better served by making himself unavailable for comment for a little while, maybe even a long while, like days or weeks.

The scene in the Washington locker room was morgue-like, as befitting the funeral it felt as if the players had just attended. It was one of those post-mortem scenes where the loudest noise in the dressing area is the sound of shower water pelting the floor, or steam hissing from hot water.

As expected, the circumstances in the Bears' locker room were much different. It was Mardi Gras and New Year's Eve rolled together. The party was just beginning when the locker room door closed. Players, with George Wilson playing a key role in the hoisting, lifted Halas off his feet onto their shoulders, homage paid to the coach who planned the attack and who psyched them up in just the right way.

Luckman etched the exuberant yellers and screamers in his mind, a picture that he would call upon for fun whenever the mood struck in the following years.

"Our quarters had become a wild scene of football players hugging and kissing one another," he said, "while frenzied intruders poured in on them, and photographers tried to pull them apart to take pictures. I understood then what victory can do to a fixed tradition, a well-mannered club. There was absolutely no control in that dressing room. The Bears had pulled the most amazing finale ever witnessed in a football season. Scarcely a man there had failed to participate in the orgy." (9)

Irv Kupcinet, who had played for the Philadelphia Eagles, was the head linesman that day in D.C. before embarking on a career as a Chicago newspaper columnist legend telling pithy tales of the city. He assessed the final score in the context of the Bears' regular-season loss to the Redskins in November.

"Today the Bears unleashed the fury that had been pent up," he said. (10)

Even in the pleasure of the championship – after all, the main goal achieved that day – the Bears realized that to some extent the 73-0 spread was a fluke, though they may not have thought much about how long the record plurality would last. So far it is going on three-quarters of a century. The result was so overwhelming, so surreal the numbers became imprinted into lore.

Looked at in a vacuum, because it was a season-ending championship game, the score stood out all the more. The Bears were not playing a team of amateurs. They played a team felt to be as good as they were. It is also rarely noted that the Bears were a very young team. Sid Luckman was just completing his second season.

But the astuteness of Halas's ability to evaluate talent was an undercurrent theme in the game. Bulldog Turner was a rookie in 1940. So was Ken Kavanaugh. As was Ed Kolman out of Temple, Hampton Pool, Lee Artoe, Harry Clark, and Ray McLean. There was every reason to believe that this super team would be able to return to the championship again in 1941 and with so much talent might be building a dynasty for the 1940s.

And really, the destruction of the Redskins did not mark an endpoint, except as the wrap-up to the 1940 season. The Bears were feted and complimented, praised and celebrated. Sportswriters searched their vocabularies, dictionaries and the thesauruses for the right words in seeking to describe Chicago's exalted status and to tell the world just how great they were at Griffith Stadium.

For a little while, though, Halas and his men wanted to savor the moment, not think ahead to the future, to another season. By all accounts they had accomplished the impossible with the massacre of a good Washington team. Even they had to shake their heads and remind themselves that what transpired over the preceding few hours was real.

Luckman offered a cool assessment. In baseball, there was such a thing as a perfect game. If a pitcher set down all 27 batters in a nine-inning game it earned the label of a perfect game. No one had considered that a football team could accomplish the equivalent and there was no strict definition.

But the Bears scored a record 11 touchdowns. They won by the largest margin ever in an NFL game, never mind in a championship game. The defense had pitched a shutout, not allowing the foe a single point.

"Whatever we did, we did right and whatever they did, they did wrong," Luckman said. (11)

The NFL rulebook may not address the concept of a perfect game, but until anyone can come up with a clearer definition, the Bears' 73-0 trouncing of Washington will do. Even from a vantage point of close to 75 years later it still stands as the closest thing to a perfect game that any pro football team has ever played.

CHICAGO - SEPTEMBER 7: 1940 Chicago Bears team photo shot in Chicago, Illinois. The team went 9-3, winning the World Championship with a 73-0 victory over the Washington Redskins in the 1940 NFL Championship Game. (AP Photo/NFL Photos)

POST GAME

George Halas was stingy both with his bank account and his compliments. But what he saw on the field at Griffith Stadium on December 8, 1940 made him gush with tributes, if not rush to the vault and hand out bonuses to his men who produced such a stunning victory.

It would have been sufficient for the Bears to triumph over the Washington Redskins, good enough to rub George Preston Marshall's silly pre-game remarks in his face. But never could Halas have possibly imagined that his charges would put such a whuppin' on the Redskins. Man, he could lord this over Marshall for the rest of their lives.

In the euphoria of the championship locker room, with his players hoisting him on their shoulders, with his players bellowing and shouting and emitting all types of noises, including the typical growl of grizzly bears, the first thing that came to Halas' mind was a sentence that would rise to the occasion.

Although when Halas spoke the Bears quieted down, he still spoke loudly when he announced to the assembled that this Chicago Bears team was the greatest football team of all time.

In the glow of the moment, in the face of the results, who was to dispute him? Certainly not the sportswriters who witnessed the carnage. Their game reports echoed the theme.

"At this moment, the Bears are the greatest football team of all time," is how the New York Times put it. "Greatness came to the Chicago Bears today," is how the Chicago Tribune said it. (1)

The Tribune's description was a bit misleading. Greatness did not just happen by, the Bears made it happen. The Bears seized greatness. Offensively, Chicago totaled 501 yards, 382 of them on the ground. Defensively, the Bears prevented Washington from scoring a touchdown or a field goal and more humiliatingly intercepted eight passes. That was amateur hour for Washington, a series of quarterbacks steadily throwing the ball to players wearing the wrong-colored jerseys. In all, the offense and the defense accounted for those 11 touchdowns.

Fullback Bill Osmanski led the Bears in rushing with 109 yards. Harry Clark gained 73 yards, Ray Nolting 68, and Joe Maniaci 60. There was little need for Sid Luckman to air it out. He attempted just four passes, completing three for 88 yards. The only player who scored two touchdowns was Clark. Three TDs came on interception returns.

Washington, which couldn't waste much time running, gained just 57 yards rushing. Forced to throw, as they sought to come from behind, the Redskins gained 223 yards through the air.

Probably the most absurd post-game commentary – though the gullible were willing to swallow it whole – was an observation penned by a Washington sportswriter. It read, "Halas would not confirm reports that the Bears had been on a diet of raw meat all week." (2)

Oh, what a delight it would have been for the reading public if members of the Bears stepped up and began chatting about the raw, bloody meat they ate in preparation for devouring the Redskins, if a butcher discussed how he supplied the meat for the training table on the Q-T. Alas, no such outpouring followed because the story was not true. Or if it was, it went to the grave with all of the participants.

Either because he was too gentlemanly to rub it in to start with, or because he was at ground zero of the reaction when the Bears read Marshall's taunting comments, Chicago quarterback Sid Luckman was very gracious in victory, particularly complimentary towards his vanquished counterpart Sammy Baugh.

"We beat a great football team," Luckman said. "We beat one of the greatest football players who ever lived in Sammy Baugh. Nobody dreamed that could happen to the Redskins. He was probably one of the greatest athletes we ever had in our country." (3)

Normally, if a player speaks in such a manner after a game like this it is dismissed as a simple platitude. But the thing that did set this amazing slaughter apart from all other sports mismatches is that it occurred in a championship game. The Redskins DID have to be good to get there. Over a months-long season the Redskins had proven themselves. It was not idle chatter on Luckman's part.

Both then and now it remains accurate to say that the Redskins were a good team. While more attention was focused on what the Bears' offense did than what the Bears' defense did, Washington had scored

245 points in 11 regular-season games, more than the Bears' 238. The Redskins' defense allowed just 142 points all season. So yes, Washington was a good team, just not on that day. And no team before or since has so thoroughly been crushed when it mattered most.

Reporters did pay a visit to Baugh in the Washington locker room. They wanted to hear what he thought about the grim day and why it so happened that for this championship game the Redskins looked like the worst football team in the universe. The context for the most memorable question posed to Baugh is never discussed, but only the question and answer. Perhaps the gentleman of the press was trying to break the ice and not tick off Baugh immediately so he stomped away.

When a team batters another by a score of 73-0, it is difficult and too facile to claim a singular turning point. A coach is not going to take the game film home, study it, and say, "Aha, that's where we went wrong." Essentially, the loser must admit that where things went wrong was showing up. But a sportswriter gave it the good old college try with Baugh. He was asked if things might not have been different, if way back in the first quarter, on that first Washington possession, if Malone had hung onto the ball at the goal-line and the Redskins scored first.

It was never reported that Baugh rolled his eyes while listening to the question, but his words were the equivalent. What would have happened if Washington scored then?

"Yeah, it would have been different," Baugh said. "It wouldn't have ended 73-0. It would have ended 73-7." (4)

That pungent observation was the most memorable quote that came out of the afternoon's event, the one that stuck in people's minds, and seemingly so neatly summarized the action. For Baugh, it was a polite way of saying to the questioner, "What were you watching?" What did the guy, think, that the Redskins might have pulled it out 76-73?

Standing nearby, stripping off his dirty uniform, was Washington tackle Jim Barber. Baugh's reply seemed right on to him since that was the way it was.

"Damn good answer, Sam," Barber said of what he thought when he overheard Baugh's comment. "We stunk it up pretty bad." Barber's memory of what followed, though, was a bit surprising. He did not recall being skewered by fans that had every reason to feel let down. "But then everybody in town had an excuse for us. Walking downtown nobody said, 'Hey, you bums.' They were all for us. 'You just had a bad day.'" (5)

Barber did not walk a mile in Marshall's shoes, though. Throughout the proceedings Marshall watched from high above the field in his own box. No doubt if he had been wired for sound his utterances would have made for a priceless recording. There was about two minutes left in the fourth quarter when Marshall emerged from his cocoon and began his trudge through the Griffith Stadium stands, weaving past the fans who stuck around.

There were not a lot of attaboys sent his way, no back slapping, no congratulations on a great season. Fans were boiling and at least once Marshall nearly came to blows with a spectactor. "Get 'em out of here, you Lug," one man shouted. "Take 'em back to Boston." Marshall was hot himself, so he did not let the remarks sail through the air and fade of their own accord. He shouted back: "You come down here and say that, you Lug." (6)

The boss of the Redskins did not end up fighting it out with a disgruntled fan of his team, although he probably felt like letting off some steam. Later, Corinne, Marshall's wife, who was with him, admitted that she was very worried about what would happen. She did not even say, "Now, George," to hold him back. "I didn't even turn my head," she said, "just leaned on the rail and prayed." (7)

One of the other famous remembrances that came out of the game was something that could have been – and should have been – avoided. Only a short time was left on the clock when the Redskins' public address announcer informed the fans that season tickets for 1941 would soon go on sale. Although the speaker was just doing his job, and most likely just had the announcement on a list he was obligated to say, Marshall probably would have punched him in the mouth then if he was within reach.

Sports columnist Bob Considine wrote that it was "the most ill-advised announcement in the history of sport." It is hard to argue with that analysis. (8)

During that era sportswriters were less likely to spend time in the locker room asking questions about how players felt about what they did rather than only report "just the facts, m'am," like the phrase Sergeant Joe Friday used in the television show "Dragnet." But this time they wanted to hear anything anybody said. Everyone was groping for answers for how this type of plurality could be registered.

"We were just fired up and we went out there to kick the pants off them," said Bears tackle George Musso. (9) That, of course, really said nothing of the how because winning teams bring that attitude into games all the time without being able to accomplish the goal.

At a time when there was no television to speak of, it was the responsibility of the press box gang to provide more play-by-play information than analysis. Their readers had not seen the action unfold, so it was relevant to tell them just how touchdowns came to be. There was less of a tendency to be interpretative. Again, though, this was different. The magnitude of the championship combined with the magnitude of the result sent people scurrying for answers. It is instructive to review how some contemporary accounts handled the game report, especially given that the writers in no way anticipated what they were about to see.

"Never in the history of the National Professional Football League was there anything so thorough as the beating the Chicago Bears gave to the Washington Redskins in the playoff for the Ed Thorp Memorial Trophy emblematic of the national championship," read one newspaper lead. The crowd, it was noted, "gathered on Sunday, Dec. 8 to watch what figured to be a titanic struggle..." It was added, "The crowd was ready for anything except what happened." Also, "On this day the Bears were the greatest team that ever handled a football." (10) Oh yes, the case of the football shortage was also mentioned.

Naturally, nowhere was the runaway bigger news than in Chicago. If they hadn't by then heard the news, sports page readers must have been astounded about the events of the day before when they picked up the paper on December 9. One Chicago newspaper summary of the game read, "Ten Bears scored 11 touchdowns and five others contributed points to an all-time National league scoring high, as an alert, relentless, band of white-jerseyed gridiron giants crushed a struggling Washington Redskins eleven, 73-0." (11)

What did the Bears do to the Redskins? The story said, "They overpowered the Redskins, out-smarted them, defied them, and charged on mercilessly to three touchdowns in the first period, one in the second, four in the third, and three more in the fourth." (12)

A glance was thrown Baugh's way. "Baugh had a miserable time and played very little after the Bears had taken a three-touchdown lead in the early minutes of play. Stars in the Chicago ranks were as numerous as the players who came into the game to the din of continual booing. But Sid Luckman, with a superb exhibition of generalship, probably is most deserving of praise for his play before the issue was definitely decided in the first quarter." (13)

That was a phrase rarely used in seriousness, as compared to the cynicism of a suffering fan because games are virtually never "definitely decided" in the first period. Sometimes that is said in jest. This was one time there was no doubt that the result was settled after one, 15-minute period.

Since he was being asked, Halas sought to narrow down a decisive point and picked the Bears' first touchdown, the long run by Bill Osmanski, as being important.

"The turning point of the game was the second play after the opening kickoff when Bill Osmanski got away for 68 yards and our first touchdown," Halas said. "On the first play, on a quick opener from a man in motion to the right, we learned four things about their defense – four things this play was supposed to tell us and four that were important to our success. Thereafter I felt confident we would get enough points to win."(14)

The Bears had practiced based on the assumption that the Redskins would employ a defense that had been successful for them all season. The playbook for the game was designed to pick holes in it and create opportunities. That was the responsibility of Luckman.

Harkening back to the 7-3 loss to the Redskins three weeks earlier, Luckman kept wondering how the "W" got away that day. The Bears had played very good offense – between the 20s – but made ill-timed mistakes in the red zone (even though that description was not in use at the time). Every time Chicago closed in on the goal-line it committed a turnover. The way Luckman viewed it the Bears were the ones who had saved the Redskins' butts, not that the Redskins had truly beaten Chicago.

"Some days, those things happen in football," Luckman said. "We knew we had moved the ball at will, and we vowed if we got back to Washington to play them again we would not make the same mistakes." Washington's defense was a 5-3-3 and Chicago drilled expecting to come up against that formation again. "We had practiced against other things, but we'd built the whole offense hoping they'd use that defense." (15) That's what Halas meant when he said the Bears wanted to check out the Redskins with that probing first play.

Not only did the Bears not make the same mistakes as they made in the first game, they made almost no mistakes at all. Chicago throttled the Redskins' fans almost as thoroughly as they did the players – they had nothing to cheer for. After the Bears ran up several touchdowns, with no apparent end in sight, Griffith spectators began taunting their own team by mimicking the public address announcer's routine informational statement, "Artoe will kick off for the Bears." It was a broken record announcement. Artoe will kick off for the Bears. Artoe will kick off for the Bears. That simple comment was probably enough to drive fans nuts.

Marshall was probably close to having a stroke, but rather than compound his previous blabbermouth error, at least at first, he was reasonably restrained in his critique. Reasonably. "It looked as if some of our lads had their fountain pens in their pockets trying to figure out who was going to get what share of the playoff money." This time he insulted the Redskins, not the Bears.

The winner's share of the $112,508 pot was $873 per man, at the time a record amount. The loser's share was $606 each. For the 2014 Super Bowl, the players on the winning Seattle Seahawks received $92,000 per man. The losing Denver Broncos received $46,000 per man. Seattle, like Chicago, had the additional pleasure of being anointed an NFL champion. Seattle, like Chicago, clobbered its foe, 43-8. One difference: A few months after the February, 2014 Super Bowl few pro football fans could name the score. Many of those same fans might well be able to name the margin by which the Bears beat the Redskins in 1940.

In a newspaper story written 47 years after the massacre, the game was described as "The Perfect Murder." And that very point, that everyone remembers the 73-0 score, was emphasized. "The Perfect Murder…words are not necessary to describe what happened on that long-ago Sunday. All you need is a number. 73-0. Just say 73-0 to any football fan – even those who were yet unborn on December 8, 1940 – and recognition will be instantaneous. 73-0. What happened that day could not happen again if they replayed the game every Sunday until eternity." (16)

Bears end-of-game quarterback Bob Snyder said the final score really should have been 77-0. He was thinking of those extra points not taken because of the impending shortage of footballs. Someone did note there was one more football in reserve than commonly thought, but the Redskins' mascot chewed it up. If the score had been 77-0 it would have been just as catchy as 73-0.

Snyder remembered, accurately or not, or a mere broadening of the pre-game theme, that when players checked into their hotel rooms there was a newspaper laying on the beds showing the headline, "Gutless Bears Hit Capitol." (17) No one else mentioned that, even if many Bears mentioned Halas pointing out Marshall's harsh assessment of them.

The first thing the Bears did when they hit the capitol, actually, was practice at Griffith Stadium. What was different, the way Luckman recalled it, was the mood and attitude of the team on the trip from Chicago to Washington.

"Usually, we'd play cards and have fun," Luckman said. "But there was none of that hilarity or fooling around. This game meant so much. For many of us, it was the first championship game we'd played in. The boys all studied their playbooks, which was unusual. Everything was building up. The adrenal glands were pumping as they never had before. We had a tremendous practice in Griffith Stadium when we arrived the next morning." (18)

The feeling amongst the Bears was that this was a business trip – and boy, did they take care of business. There was little doubt in Halas' mind that his team would have no privacy at Griffith Stadium, and that it may well have been spied on in Chicago as it prepared. He was going to spring the T formation emphasis on the Redskins, so he incorporated it cautiously and quietly into routines.

"We knew they probably had people watching us," Luckman said. "Halas was always fearful, so we put in some new formations, called them 'Dummy formation, Dummy formation 2.'" (19)

In the world of the 2000s, a 73-0 final score would set off alarms all across the land. The Bears would be vilified for piling on in so many forums in print, radio, TV and on the Internet, that their heads would spin. The plurality would be hard to defend. If one follows the play by play carefully, yes, there are places where one might question if it was necessary to throw a pass rather than call a running play. But the Redskins made so many major mistakes, gave the ball away so often and carelessly, they also made it easy for Chicago to score. Luckman insisted the Bears weren't trying to run up the score.

"We were only ahead 28-0 at the half and they had Sammy Baugh," he said. (20)

That was true, but the lead ballooned from there and except for the diplomatic cooperation about the extra points and preserving the footballs, the Bears showed no other hints of mercy. They kept on playing hard and they kept on scoring. Washington was inept on offense and helpless on defenses. When the score was 60-0, one unidentified player on the Bears' sideline suggested that enough was enough.

"On our bench," Halas said, "a player said, 'This is ridiculous, making them look so bad. Take it easy.' He was shouted down." (21)

That was no doubt the same incident Luckman had described. Whether it was the disappointing defeat of November, the insults of Marshall gnawing at them, or their own power running amok, the Bears really did want to kill the Redskins on this day once they sank their teeth into them.

"We didn't hold back, which wouldn't have been right either," said George McAfee. (22) They definitely didn't do that.

Perhaps back Ray Nolting was more candid and spoke for more players than would say such a thing out loud, but he said, "We wanted to put it down their throat and twist it." (23)

If the Bears wanted to destroy the Redskins' morale as well as blow up the scoreboard, they succeeded. This was the worst game of Baugh's career. Willie Wilkin was so frustrated that his emotions began to fray before the final gun.

"One of their guys, Wee Willie Wilkin, about 270 pounds and playing his heart out, started to cry," said Solly Sherman. (24) You know you have whipped your opponent not only physically, but mentally, when something like that occurs. The temptation, of course, if one were cruel, given Marshall's insult of the Bears as crybabies, would be to say, "Look who's crying now." As far as is known, no one said that.

As the Bears stacked up the touchdowns, at one point Sherman was startled to hear a big bang coming from the stands. The players joked about it.

"Something exploded in the stands," he said, "and everybody said it was Marshall shooting himself." (25) Not true, but it was gallows humor believable.

Although hyperbole was easy enough to apply to such a monstrous clobbering, there didn't seem to be much writing about the slaughter of Indians or the like. That would have been in awful taste, but not necessarily unusual during that age. One Chicago writer did make an historical comparison. He wrote, "Not since the British sacked this city more than 100 years ago has the Washington area seen such a rout." (26)

Really, the Bears' individual statistics were not that overwhelming because so many players shared the opportunities. Halas did spread the wealth, did rest starters after they compiled an unsurmountable lead. That was the real indicator he did not ruthlessly chase after every point available.

"Everybody scored, as I recall," said end Ken Kavanaugh. It only seemed that way. "No matter what they did, we would have beaten them." Kavanaugh definitely believed that the number of available footballs was dwindling. Some of the game-used balls were not shiny new, but scuffed up and well-worn. (27)

From an X's and O's standpoint, the game was remarkably simple to break down. The Bears' behemoth linemen created big holes on offense and the Bears' backs ran through them. The Bears' swift and opportunistic defense sealed holes and prevented the Redskins from running past or the receivers from getting open.

"Hard to believe," said two-touchdown Harry Clark. "Everything just seemed to work for us and nothing worked for them." (28)

Not a single, blessed thing.

Ordinarily, Halas did not want his players to get too high in victory, not even celebrating major wins. He had a two-beer rule for partying (though it is not clear if anyone actually stuck to that rule). This time he waved it. It was champagne all around for everyone and the train ride back to Chicago was one raucous time, one even sanctioned by the boss.

Still, Halas was worried about too much celebrating. That's because at that time the National Football League champion became the representative to face the All-Star squad put together from the league's other teams. The game was set for December 29, three weeks hence. By winning the NFL crown the Bears had clinched the opportunity to be the league's team in the game – and it was regarded as a prestigious reward.

Halas wanted the Bears to show a certain amount of restraint until that obligation was cleared and then a big bash celebrating the season would be held, he promised.

"When we have whipped the All-Stars, we'll really have a time," Halas said. He urged the players to stay in shape and announced a team luncheon for the following Wednesday at the Palmer House in Chicago. Halas would work out practice plans for the All-Star game and decide whether the players would get a few days off in-between. (29)

Almost incomprehensible to the modern-day fan was the emphasis placed on a different All-Star game scheduled for the following August leading up to the 1941 season. This, too, was considered to be a prestigious assignment. The charity game in Chicago that began in the 1930s pitted the NFL champion against incoming rookies fresh out of college. It is difficult to imagine such a pro-college matchup these days, or anyone really caring about such a contest now, but it was a big enough deal in 1940 that the topic was raised the very day of the 73-0 win and discussed on the scene.

"We've been trying to get back into the Chicago All-Star game since 1935," Halas said after the Redskins' trouncing. "Qualifying to meet the collegians in Soldier's field really was our objective. We want to get at those collegians." (30)

Although meeting the All-Stars was a perk that came with the championship, Halas' comment seemed to be a patently ridiculous statement. It was far more important to Halas and the Bears to beat the Redskins and win the NFL crown. They really wanted the Redskins – and they got them good.

After issuing his more oblique snide remark about how his Redskins were just counting the dollars that would appear in their bank accounts following their horrible play against the Bears, owner George Preston Marshall really let loose to reporters in the losing locker room. He trained the big guns on his players.

"Those guys out there quit," Marshall said. "(Frank) Filchock's quarterbacking was awful. Two of the highest salaried backs in the league, Dick Todd and Andy Farkas, stood in that backfield and not once carried the ball. Boys, that's one on Ripley." (31)

Marshall, who was really marshalling his thoughts by then, was referring to the popular "Ripley's Believe It Or Not" newspaper feature. Of course, he failed to take note of the fact that his backs weren't carrying the ball because the quarterbacks had to keep throwing in an effort to play catch-up. No one was about to interrupt him to debate fine points of the game, though.

Marshall said he was sorry the Redskins' fans had to witness such a debacle and he promised that the team would be better in the future.

"It'll show up in next year's salaries," he said. "We've got some good rookies and we'll get some more. There'll be some changes." Marshall paused and thought about the players that took the Griffith Stadium field that day. "Maybe they didn't lack courage, but they lost their heads." (32)

After venting a bit, Marshall's talk tamed down, although word spread about his confrontation with the fan in the stands as he hustled to the locker room. He admitted that the comment that raised his ire was the taunt to take the team back to Boston. Marshall apologized to fans on the post-game radio show, and indicated the Redskins were going to be staying in Washington. Later, Marshall tracked down the name of the seat-holder, found out he was a season ticket-holder, yanked his tickets and banned him from the park. So much for freedom of speech in the Marshall realm.

Coach Ray Flaherty was button-holed and actually said he thought the Malone pass might have made a difference because "it would have put us in the ball game." But he quickly confronted reality. "The Bears couldn't miss today. They did everything right and we were completely demoralized." (33)

Working their way down through the hierarchy of the Redskins, reporters went from Marshall to Flaherty to Baugh. Besides issuing his observation about the potential for the score change from 73-0 to 73-7 if Washington did just one thing right all game, Baugh had some heartfelt thoughts about what he and his teammates had just gone through. It was as if they had suffered a thousand little cuts that all drew blood and now were faced with reflecting on it for their rest of their lives.

"That was the most humiliating thing I've ever gone through in my life," Baugh said. (34)

Halas smiled broader and longer than he had about anything he had ever experienced during his long career with the Bears as player, coach and owner. Perhaps it gave him more pleasure to beat Washington and Marshall in such a decisive manner than watching a Marx Brothers comedy.

Yet even Halas recognized the rarity of the moment. He understood that his team had played a once-in-a-lifetime game and produced a once-in-a-lifetime result. It was not as if that detracted from his enjoyment of being on top 73-0, but as a few months passed and the Bears began preparing for another season with the welcome exhibition game against the college All-Stars, Halas penned an opinion piece for a Chicago newspaper. In it he basically told Bears fans not to expect a repeat. He concluded that any football observer should realize that as good as the Bears were that they would not be duplicating that shining performance against Washington.

"In weighing the chances of the Chicago Bears against the All-Stars," Halas said, "or vice versa, you can throw out the 73 to 0 victory of the Bears over the Washington Redskins for the National league championship last December. You can discount it on the basis that it was purely a dream game in which a combination of luck and skill enabled the Bears to achieve perfection for one full game, something which I never expect to see again. The Bears were virtually 100 percent efficient that afternoon in the nation's capital." (35)

So many elements went into that 73-0 result and a long season of play and practice were some of them. Facing the All-Stars before the 1941 regular season meant the Bears were not at their peak.

"It is my honest belief that in the short period of training before the All-Star contest the Bears will do well to attain 20 percent efficiency," Halas said. "If the Bears were 100 percent efficiency (versus Washington)…then 20 percent efficiency should give us about 14 points the night of August 28 in Soldiers' field. I have an idea we must do a little better than that." (36)

The Bears got off to a slow start against the All-Stars, a team that included such notables as Michigan's Tom Harmon, Boston College's Charley O'Rourke, and UCLA's Jackie Robinson, but Chicago closed hard, showing quite a bit of offensive pep, even if Halas was perhaps worried about a letdown in his team's first game since the 73-0 victory.

Chicago beat the All-Stars, 37-13 and 98,203 fans watched.

The real reason Halas pooh-poohed the overwhelming result of a game that meant a lot to him was a natural fear that the Bears could not match the 73-0 score no matter who they were playing, and even worse, especially coming off summer training camp instead of a game test for months, could actually lose. In the end, the result was satisfactory to him and Chicago could set about preparing for a fresh season and a defense of the 1940 NFL title.

1941

One of the Bears who did not score a touchdown against the Redskins in the 1940 championship game – because it was not his job and no accidental bounces came his way – was lineman Danny Fortmann.

The future Hall of Famer was celebrating the grand triumph on the train back to Chicago – Halas managed to have a club car added for the Bears – when a civilian passenger commented on the bright colors surrounding Fortmann's left eye. Bruises around the eye are always referred to as part of a black eye, but Fortmann's injury featured the colors of the rainbow.

"My, my," the observer said. "That's a terrible black eye you have there." Fortmann, was no doubt too busy sipping champagne to stare into the mirror, said, "Yes, but it will disappear in a day or two. Think of the Redskins – that 73-0 score is in the record books for all time." (1)

What Fortmann realized instinctively, as fresh as the game was in his mind, was that no one was ever going to forget it. The bruise on the Redskins' reputation would never fade.

Whether George Halas was just musing, serious, or joking, he had taken the trouble to review the entire game film from the title game and came to one fresh conclusion – the final score should have been higher.

"Looking at films," Halas said, "I saw where we could have scored another touchdown." (2)

Maybe 80-0 would have sounded better to him.

The victors had accomplished something so monumental that no one would ever forget. However, a strange thing occurred. Rather than serving as a period at the end of a season, or era, the incredible game really was more of a beginning for the Bears. The 1940s is remembered in Chicago as the finest decade in the history of the team. It is unfortunate that the time period overlapped with World War II, but the aptly and freshly named Monsters of the Midway earned that nickname by regularly fielding championship teams.

Players on the 1940 team reached perfection in the championship game, but players on the 1941 team also took the Bears on a very special ride. It was the 1941 club that many believe was the greatest football team of all time, the team coming off the 73-0 game, not culminating a season with a 73-0 game.

George Halas called his 1940 champions the best football team of all time, but a year later, even though he was the first to announce that the 73-0 score would never be repeated, he had presided over a more dominant season. Most of the players were the same ones, but those who had just a year under their belts in 1940, or who were rookies in 1940, were more seasoned.

At that time, the NFL draft was conducted in December, shortly after the conclusion of the regular season. The 1939 draft brought Sid Luckman. The 1940 draft delivered Bulldog Turner. Several other young guys were added to the roster in those years. The drafting of rookies for the 1941 season took place on December 19, 1940. Chicago's number one draft pick was Michigan quarterback Tom Harmon, winner of the Heisman Trophy as the best player in the college game. Only Harmon never played a minute for the Bears. He signed with the New York Americans, who competed in the second American Football League. Harmon then fought in World War II and briefly played in the All-America Football Conference before becoming a well-known broadcaster.

Harmon was viewed as a great talent. Although he would not have supplanted Luckman at quarterback he might well have been a valuable defensive backfield addition and punt returner. In the second round the Bears took Norm Standlee, a back from Stanford, who was a useful contributor, and in the fourth round they grabbed another back, Hugh Gallarneau, also from Stanford.

Although the 73-0 game was a tough act to follow, the Bears added something fresh and new to their repertoire for the 1941 season. Just as the Redskins had, the Bears introduced a fight song to involve and entertain the multitudes at Wrigley Field. Written by Al Hoffman, the tune captivated fans that year, particularly when they performed sing-alongs.

The lyrics go:

> "Bear down, Chicago Bears, make every play clear the way to victory.
> Bear down, Chicago Bears, put up a fight with a might so fearlessly.
> We'll never forget the way you thrilled the nation with your T formation.
> Bear down, Chicago Bears, and let them know why you're wearing the crown.
> You're the pride and joy of Illinois, Chicago Bears, Bear down."

Bears fans still sing the words at home games.

There wasn't much room for rookies on the roster of the 1941 Bears team. The scary thing was that the club that had administered a 73-0 beating in the previous season's NFL title game was still peaking.

Meanwhile, the battered Sammy Baugh, his ego needing as much recovery time as his body once he stripped off his number 33 Redskins jersey, found a respite from football during the spring of 1941, taking his life in a direction far removed from the gridiron, but in one that could soothe him before the start of the next season.

Baugh, who looked the part as much as other cowboys of the general period such as Tom Mix, Hoot Gibson, or William S. Boyd, got an offer from Hollywood to make a western serial called "King of the Texas Rangers." The pay, $4,500, was excellent for those days. Baugh was a celebrity athlete, not an actor, and he didn't pretend to be. He was leery of taking on something he knew nothing about, but the appeal of the money was strong and he hoped he could master what was being thrown at him.

He definitely was not a professional actor, but Baugh spent football down time filming and the down-to-earth Texan was not taken in by the bright lights of Hollywood. It was more a case of wondering how anyone could live in what seemed like a tin-foil type of place to him. Baugh did not film "King of the Texas Rangers" to explore a career change, but for a change-of-pace experience and the cash. After six weeks, his mind somewhat cleansed by the embarrassing loss to the Bears, and with enough time on the West Coast, he jumped in his car and drove back to Texas.

"This is the silliest business I ever got in," Baugh said. "Remember how we used to play cowboy and Indian? Well, that's all this is, except we get paid for doin' it." (3)

Including the playoff win over the Redskins, the Bears ended the 1940 season with a three-game winning streak. The 1941 season began with a five-game winning streak. One thing the 73-0 mashing of Washington did was provide confidence for the 1941 bunch. Who could stop them? At the beginning of the season no one.

Chicago opened with a 25-17 win over the Green Bay Packers. Next came a 48-21 triumph over the Detroit Lions. In the third week of the season the Bears blasted the Chicago Cardinals, 53-7. In week four the Bears manhandled the Detroit Lions, 49-0, and a week later Chicago knocked off the Pittsburgh Steelers, 34-7.

Proving they were human, however, the Bears stumbled in the season's sixth week, falling 16-14 to arch-rival Green Bay. There were no lingering ill effects, though. Chicago immediately righted itself with a 31-13 win over the Cleveland Rams. Chicago was 6-1 leading up to a match-up with the next team on the schedule, November 16, the Washington Redskins.

Under most circumstances, the Redskins would never want to see the Bears again. But schedule makers rule and the Redskins had to face their demons. It was important to see if the Bears owned Washington so thoroughly the Redskins couldn't play a decent game against them. The Redskins were also angry. Eleven months had passed and the wound was still open. Not even Halas counted on the Redskins rolling over – no matter what George Preston Marshall had said during the aftermath of the title game.

Washington was on its way to a 6-5 season, not nearly as strong as it had been in 1940. New faces were on both rosters. And no, the game did not really resemble the massacre of the championship contest. It was not nearly so one-sided. The game remained close most of the way, though the Bears pretty much maintained control.

The score was 7-0 Chicago after the first quarter on a touchdown by newcomer Hugh Gallarneau on a six-yard run. It was 21-7 at the half. Norm Standlee scored on a two-yard run and George McAfee scored on a 12-yard pass from Bob Snyder. Snyder kicked extra points following all three touchdowns. Apparently no one suggested the officials were going to run out of footballs. Washington got its lone touchdown on a 59-yard punt return by Andy Farkas.

Washington did pull to within 21-14 in the third quarter when fresh face Ed Cifers grabbed a 14-yard scoring pass from Sammy Baugh. The big mistake killed Washington again after that. Chicago's Bob Nowaskey returned a fumble three yards for a TD. McAfee caught a second touchdown pass from Snyder of 33 yards, leading to a 35-14 Bears lead before the Redskins recorded one more touchdown on a four-yard run by Bob Seymour. So the final score was 35-21, not to be confused with 73-0, but thorough nonetheless.

The Bears went on from there, compiling a few more wins and taking a 9-1 record into the last game of the regular season and on their way to compiling 396 offensive points while yielding just 147. December 7, 1941 was an NFL Sunday. The Chicago Bears were scheduled to play the Chicago Cardinals. Some 4,250 miles to the west, terrifying events were unfolding that changed the course of the nation's destiny, altered the world landscape, and affected Americans' lifestyles for years and years.

That morning the Japanese air force sprang a surprise attack on the American naval ships docked at Pearl Harbor, decimating the fleet, killing and wounding thousands, and propelling the United States into World War II. Across the country word spread, primarily via radio reports, as three NFL games got underway. The New York Giants and Brooklyn Dodgers were playing at the Polo Grounds and celebrating Tuffy Leemans Day. As the ceremony honoring the future Hall of Famer began, it was announced over the public address system that all military personnel should return to their units.

In Washington, where the Redskins were hosting the Philadelphia Eagles at Griffith Stadium, the hostilities taken against the fleet were not revealed, but individual officers and government leaders were paged. Newspaper reporters were told to call their offices.

The Bears-Cardinals showdown was being played at Comiskey Park, the home of the Chicago White Sox, as well as the Cardinals. The public address announcer began sending messages into the stands.

"They announced it over the loudspeaker," Sid Luckman recalled. "It was a tremendous shock to everyone in the stadium. The teams just didn't have the same emotions knowing our country had just been attacked." (4)

The Bears topped the Cardinals, 34-24, and then wondered what would happen next in their world, the football world, and the real world.

That win concluded the Bears' the regular season with a 10-1 mark. But that was only good for a tie for first in the Western Division. The Green Bay Packers also finished 10-1. The league tie-breaker for such circumstances was head-to-head play. However, Chicago and Green Bay split their season series. Instead of the league office employing any other arcane methods to determine the division champ, a playoff game was scheduled.

By then the Bears were cooking, pretty much breezing past all opposition, and they polished off the Packers, 33-14, to earn a place in a second straight NFL title game, this one against the New York Giants. The Giants won the Eastern Division, finishing 8-3. The two teams did not meet during the regular season, though the Giants did play Washington, and won 20-13.

By the time the regular season ended, some observers rated the Bears as the finest outfit of all time. That was saying something since after the 73-0 triumph, Halas and others called the 1940 Bears the best. That would make the 1941 edition pretty darned good.

Since the title game had been played in Washington, home of the eastern champ, the year before, the 1941 game was scheduled for the home of the western champ. The Bears were the home team, at Wrigley Field, for the December 21 game. For once, though, not much excitement was generated by the showdown. The country was preoccupied.

In a speech, President Franklin D. Roosevelt, termed the sneak attack bombing on Pearl Harbor "a day that will live in infamy" in U.S. history. On December 9, Congress passed a declaration of war. There were no cheap-shot comments made by New York owners for Halas to use as bulletin board fodder. This was not a time for complaining, but for worrying. What was next for the country? War was the only topic. Football had dropped way down the list in importance, even for most fans.

The game was still on, but the anticipation was tepid. Chicago had nothing to prove and the players were all distracted, concerned about their own futures and about the future of their country. George Halas had served as an ensign during World War I. He fully expected, even as he neared his 47th birthday, to serve again in this new war.

For the time being, though, Halas could focus on football and add to the lore of the greatest team of all time. Halas was a rare enough bird who could compartmentalize his thoughts. He may have been ready to play ball, as usual, but the fan base wasn't quite so involved, championship game or not. Attendance at Wrigley Field reached just 13,341. That was at the time, and remains, the smallest crowd to witness an NFL championship game in person. The game was on radio again and Red Barber and Bob Elson constituted the Mutual Radio broadcast crew.

Snyder, who had developed into a solid, clutch field-goal kicker, gave the Bears the early lead with a 14-yard field goal. But unlike the Redskins, the Giants would not be shut out. New York rookie back George Franck scored on a 31-yard pass from quarterback Tuffy Leemans. New York missed the extra point, but led 6-3 after one period.

It had been quite some time since the Bears trailed in a championship game and Snyder remedied that situation early in the second quarter with a 39-yard field goal for a 6-6 tie. Snyder booted a third field goal, this one a 37-yarder, also in the second period for a 9-6 Chicago lead at halftime. For a team that had scored touchdowns at will against Washington and did so against most of the league in 1941, this settling for field goals at the end of drives was unsettling. The Bears were getting close to the end zone, but not crossing the goal line. That type of thing can cost a team at the end of a game and find players looking back at squandered opportunities.

There was not as great a sense of moment in this championship game as there had been a year earlier because of the much more important world news. Nor was there any particular grudge between Bears and Giants players. But the Bears did want to win another championship.

New York wasn't going away easily. The third quarter opened with the Giants adding another field goal to their point total, a 16-yarder by Ward Cuff. At 9-9 it was obvious that this wasn't going to be nearly as high a scoring game as its predecessor either. Heck, the Bears were in danger of not even winning after their excellent season and the publicity that was touting how great they were.

And then everything turned. The offense that was sputtering began running smoothly, as if it had undergone an oil change. The defense decided "no more" and shut down New York's offense, not even permitting the Giants to get within kicking range. Soon enough, although they had taken their time, the Bears turned this title game into a rout, too.

In the second half Norm Standlee scored twice, first on a two-yard run and then on a seven-yard run. In the fourth quarter George McAfee scored on a five-yard run. Three different players kicked extra points and the score grew to 30-9. It was all over, but the Bears added a bonus touchdown on a 42-yard fumble return by Ken Kavanaugh.

This time when Halas inserted Ray McLean to boot the extra point, McLean came out on his own, without a holder. He made the final point in the 37-9 victory. That was also the last time in NFL history that a player hit an extra point on a drop kick. Although little noted in the big picture, that represented the end of an era in pro football.

Many rate the 1941 Bears as a better team than the 1940 team because the 1940 team lost three games during the regular season. Many years later, an enthusiastic sports analyst who produced such compelling work that he was tabbed for a while by college basketball to come up with power rankings for that sport, ran several top-flight NFL teams through his computer. The aim was to pick out the best team of all time. The work was done by Jeff Sagarin in 1979 in Bloomington, Indiana.

Feeding tons of information into an inanimate object without fan prejudice or emotional bias, Sagarin gave special ratings mention to the 1968 Baltimore Colts, the 1962 Green Bay Packers and the 1949 Philadelphia Eagles, in order – all behind the No. 1 ranked team, the 1941 Chicago Bears.

Categories examined included organization, intelligence, power, youth, size, balance, and the T formation.

"Halas' drafting and scouting systems were a decade ahead of some teams," Sagarin said. (5)

Of 39 players who saw PT for the Bears in 1941, 30 played only for the Bears, and were chosen in the draft or signed as free agents. In addition to the Pro Football Hall of Fame inductees on the roster, eight players advanced to the College Football Hall of Fame.

Sagarin rated the Bears as a highly intelligent team since it took some smarts to run the T formation in a more sophisticated fashion than other teams. He cited six members of the 1941 Bears becoming professional coaches, Fortmann becoming a doctor and Bill Osmanski becoming a dentist as evidence that Chicago was an intelligent club.

NFL players were much smaller in the 1940s than they are in the 2000s, but compared to other teams, the Bears had several big boys weighing from 230 to the 260s. And all of the stars played both ways, as regulars on offense and defense instead of resting between possessions. Sagarin was also struck by the team's youth, with all of those two- and three-year men and rookies the Bears had become championship caliber without maturing over time.

There was a suggestion made in the analysis and article that if World War II had not interceded that the Bears might have won NFL titles every year from 1940 through 1946. George McAfee said that he once asked Halas to speculate on that very question. "I asked George, 'Supposing the war hadn't come along? How many championships would we have won?'" (6)

McAfee said that Halas did not respond, that he only sighed.

"Coaches have frequently argued about what contributed most to the Bears' great clubs of 1940 and 1941," Luckman said. "Method? Power? Personnel? Probably a combination of all three, but men on the field would have laid it to experience gained in working together Sunday after Sunday. We made the T formation appear almost simple, which was one of the illusions produced by success. Our chief trouble was the notion, at times, that we produced 100 percent perfect football. (Of course there never was such a critter.) Whenever this attitude developed we played a brazen, overconfident game, usually playing right into the hands of our opponents. Normally, though, we didn't underrate other clubs, from the strongest on down." (7)

Normally, though, the Bears beat just about every team that challenged them.

While analyzed in other ways, perhaps the Bears of that team weren't the brightest light bulbs of all time. Although the days of playing without a helmet had passed, perhaps preserving a few extra brain cells per man per season, hard shell helmets had not yet come into vogue and almost no one wore a face bar to protect his nose, his eyes or mouth in the trenches.

"If you broke your nose, you'd put on a bar," said the Bears' Bob

Snyder. "They had a picture of us in the Chicago Tribune in 1941 before the championship game. We were smiling, and I think most of us had front teeth missing." (8)

1942 & 1943

The bombing of Pearl Harbor sent Americans into shock, the government into action and the military into scramble mode. Isolationists who were determined to keep the United States out of World War II had slowed military production enough that the American armed forces were way behind the capability they needed to combat Japan in the Pacific and Germany in Europe.

This wake-up call erased opposition to U.S. involvement in the war, but the early months were hard on morale. It was difficult to point to many successes as the country enlisted men and put the economy on a war footing, transferring the mission of many manufacturing plants from machinery such as automobiles to machinery such as airplanes.

Many professional athletes sprinted to their home enlistment stations and many others were drafted. The notion of suspending sports play for the duration of the war was discussed. Baseball Commissioner Kenesaw Mountain Landis wrote to President Franklin D. Roosevelt to ask for advice. Roosevelt responded with his so-called "green light" letter, a response that indicated the games should go on, though athletes would not be given special treatment or exemption from service. Roosevelt said that entertainment like baseball would be good for the morale of the public.

As long as baseball did the heavy lifting and committed to continued play during the war, the other professional sports did likewise. Yet just as baseball stars such as Bob Feller, Hank Greenberg and Ted Williams spent several of their prime playing years in war zones rather than on playing fields, numerous pro football players joined them.

Soon after the Chicago Bears defended their NFL title by besting the Giants, capturing the crown for the second straight year, members of the championship roster began disappearing. One by one players checked on their draft status and started exchanging Bears uniforms for U.S.-issued uniforms. It didn't take long for that to occur and soon after the end of the football season 15 members of the Bears were headed off to basic training with the Army or to sea with the Navy, many of them enlisting. A few were trying the Marines.

Those about to depart for an unknown period of time included Ken Kavanaugh, George McAfee, Ray Bray, Dick Plasman, Joe Mihal, Ed Kolman, Joe Maniaci, Al Baisi, Aldo Forte, Billy Hughes, Hugh Gallarneau, Young Bussey and Joe Stydahar. Lee Artoe was exploring military service, but stayed with the Bears through the 1942 season. The 15th player trying to join up was Norm Standlee, who had been rejected by the Air Force because he was color blind.

They were embarking for a war that was not going well for the United States. As the military revved up as swiftly as it could to obtain and train as many men as possible and to obtain and ship out as many munitions and big guns as it could, the enemies reaped victories, unleashed destruction, and advanced through friendly territories.

Japan captured Manila in the Philippines and invaded the Solomon Islands. German General Erwin Rommel began his tank campaign in North Africa. The Japanese bombed New Guinea and captured Singapore. American and Filipino troops were trapped on the Bataan Peninsula.

A piece of uplifting news was the desperate and risky bombing raid made on Japan by American B-25s led by General Jimmy Doolittle.

Japan overran Asia as Germany overran much of Europe, taking control of France and Belgium. The first half of the year was disastrous for the Allies and by the time the football season began, Americans were far more concerned about the fate of other likeminded nations and their own loved ones fighting thousands of miles from home.

The Japanese made their way to Alaska and the Battle of Dutch Harbor in the Aleutian Islands was underway, with a forced evacuation for their safety of Alaska Natives. Japanese soldiers landed at Attu and Kiska, the first time foreign troops set foot on American soil in 128 years.

By late summer the United States was fighting back with some success, invading Guadalcanal Island and launching the first air attacks on German occupying forces in Europe.

This list of Bears players putting aside football for arms did not yet include the patriotic George Halas, coach and owner, then in his 40s. Halas had served in the U.S. Navy during World War I, but was never sent into combat. He spent the duration of the war at the Great Lakes

Naval Training Center north of Chicago, involved with the football team.

For this second world war Halas did not want to be tied up with football. If he wanted to deal with football he could stay home in Chicago and keep coaching the Bears. He wanted to return to the navy as an officer and he also wanted to see combat activity.

The NFL season began on September 27, with the Bears' traditional opener against the Green Bay Packers. It was a road game for Chicago, in Wisconsin, but the Bears won 44-28. Despite the loss of a significant amount of talent (after all, the rest of the league was in the same situation), the Bears swept their first five games under Halas's tutelage. After that, the summons came. Halas had personally sought the attention of officers he knew to rejoin the service.

George Halas was back in the navy. His status had been retired lieutenant commander, but he was activated and ordered to report to the Naval Air Technical Training Center in Norman, Oklahoma on November 2. It was a peculiar location for a navy man. Norman, best-known as the home of the University of Oklahoma, is land-locked, more than a thousand miles from the closest ocean.

For the first time in more than two decades, Halas was not going to be involved in the day-to-day operations of his Chicago Bears. The coaching role was turned over to two assistants. Hunk Anderson and Luke Johnsos became co-coaches. Paddy Driscoll served as their assistant. The front office was turned over to team secretary Ralph Brizzolara, to handle the business affairs. And then Halas was off to Oklahoma.

The NFL season continued without Halas, although being in the country he could still keep up with his team's fortunes. There was nothing to get unduly upset about because the duo of Anderson and Johnsos ran the show admirably. The Bears ran off six more wins and finished the regular season 11-0. Counting the 1941 playoffs the Bears owned a winning streak of 18 straight games.

By blitzing the Western Division Chicago qualified for the championship game for the third straight season. Going through some roster upheaval of its own Washington still managed to emerge as the best of the east, so once again the Bears and Redskins would face one another in the NFL title game. The contest was set for December

13 back at Griffith Stadium. The Redskins had dominated the East in similar fashion, finishing 10-1.

This time George Preston Marshall uttered no inflammatory remarks to tick off the Bears. But in the mind of Chicago quarterback Sid Luckman, the Bears were ripe for a fall. They were getting too swell-headed, too full of themselves, and playing Washington was probably not the best thing for them. The last time the Bears met the Redskins with something major at stake the result was the 73-0 score.

"We were beginning to think of ourselves as unbeatable," Luckman said. "We did not work as before." (1)

Waiting in the weeds were Sammy Baugh and the Redskins. They were so hungry to avenge the 1940 thrashing that they didn't even mind being labeled underdogs. They just wanted another opportunity with the big trophy at stake. They probably realized that nothing would ever completely erase the stigma of the 73-0 defeat, but capturing an NFL title at the expense of the same Bears would serve as the best possible balm.

Before the 1940 title game, Chicago coach George Halas used Marshall's insulting words to inflame his players. Before the 1942 title game Washington coach Ray Flaherty got his message across to his players by writing "73-0" on a blackboard in the locker room. Same effect.

The games played out in a totally different manner. The same 36,000-plus crowd attended in D.C., but the favored and powerful Bears did not bring their offense this time. It was not as if Chicago did not have ample motivation. With a victory, the Bears would record a third straight league title. With a victory, the Bears would record a perfect season.

The placid nature of the first quarter was a partial victory for the Redskins. The score was 0-0 after one. Chicago scored first, though, in the second period and the touchdown was a result of a major Redskins miscue. Shades of 1940 in that. Chicago's Lee Artoe picked up a Dick Todd fumble and rambled 50 yards for a touchdown and a 6-0 lead. The Bears did miss the extra point, however.

A difference this time was that the Redskins retaliated quickly, within the second period. Baugh threw a 38-yard touchdown pass to Wilbur

Moore and Washington did convert the extra point for a 7-6 lead at halftime. For Washington, coach Ray Flaherty, and Baugh, it was a refreshing change to be ahead at the intermission, though a one-point margin was definitely shaky and not really reassuring against the Bears.

This time, though, the Redskins' defense was ready for Luckman and his coterie of backs. Chicago couldn't get rolling. In the third quarter the Redskins scored again on an Andy Farkas one-yard run, and converted the extra point, too, for a 14-6 lead. Once, the Bears marched to the Washington 12-yard-line, but an interception ended the drive. It was Baugh who picked the ball off. The Bears never scored again. Revenge tasted so sweet for the Redskins.

The lead on the Washington Post game story provided the facts, even if the emotion seemed a bit too strong and the impact of the victory seemed a bit exaggerated. It read, "The once mighty football empire of the Chicago Bears was forever crushed and ground beneath the feet of the disbelieving Washington Redskins yesterday in one of the super upsets of all time." (2)

Wow. The Bears lost a close game and were disappointed by the outcome, but it was more than a stretch to say that Chicago was crushed and the empire had collapsed. It was just one game, not necessarily the end of the world as the Bears knew it. The prose was a stretch, too, to say "If ever a team reached the peak of football perfection the Redskins did yesterday." (3) Well...the only game anyone ever suggested approached perfection was the Bears' 73-0 triumph. A 14-6 game?

One important backdrop angle, however, was that the win was a going-away present for coach Ray Flaherty. Flaherty had accepted a lieutenant's commission in the navy and would leave that very night to join the war effort. Some 17 Washington players were also going into the service following the championship game.

There had never been any doubt that the 73-0 game was a one-time affair, but the Bears did loom as the stronger team, a squad that based on performance might be a 10-point winner. But Washington played superior defense and also put to rest any mental qualms that fans might worry lingered from the smashing beating of two years earlier. If the Bears were going to steamroll Washington again, the signs were expected to appear early, after Artoe's first-quarter touchdown.

"The panic, recalling football's famous massacre of 1940, which was feared would strike the Redskins at the first Bear touchdown was nowhere in sight," the Post story said. (4)

Certainly some concern had to remain in the back of Redskins' players minds before the game about what they faced. The loss of 1940 was scarring. But Washington players put it aside and were determined to write their own history. The joy ran deep and the volume ran loud in the Washington locker room after the victory was notched.

"We beat their pants off," yelled Washington kicker Charles "Ki" Aldrich, who had been playing for the Chicago Cardinals at the time of the other championship game. "We beat their pants off." (5)

Aldrich had every reason to feel good. Early in the game Chicago's Ray Nolting intercepted a Sammy Baugh pass and the Bears gained possession on the Washington 27-yard-line. But on the next play Nolting fumbled and Aldrich recovered, critically reacquiring the ball. To escape being stuck deep in their own end, on the next play Baugh dropped back and quick-kicked. Not only did the play catch the Bears off-guard, the ball traveled an astounding 85 yards, moving Washington out of danger.

Fighting for attention amidst the bedlam, Flaherty stole a few minutes addressing the Redskins, for the last time in what surely would be for quite some time, if not forever.

"(I'm) proud of every one of you guys," Flaherty said. "Half of us are going into the service in a couple of weeks. Hit the enemy half as hard as you hit the Bears today. Do that and this war won't take long to finish and we can get back here pretty quick." (6)

In a game with the defense in control, no Washington player scored a bunch of touchdowns or gained a huge number of yards. The sportswriters were trying to figure a way to single out a couple of heroes and asked Flaherty whom he thought played the best game. He chose the cliché instead of singling out individuals.

"Best game?" Flaherty said. "Hell, every one of those guys played brilliant games. Nobody played the best game except the Redskin team." (7) In a game of that style, Flaherty was right.

A couple of Bears players, Bulldog Turner and George Musso, made their way into the Redskins' dressing room and showing class shook hands with players that beat them.

As always, as the team's leader and best player, Baugh was surrounded and asked for his thoughts. After the 1940 loss Baugh had delivered the quote everyone remembered about the score. This time he was nearly as succinct. "Guess that kinda makes up for 'that thing' in 1940, don't it?" (8)

Maybe.

For two years straight, at the end of the 1940 season and at the end of the 1941 season, George Halas and others had proclaimed the Chicago Bears the greatest team of all time. Only minutes after Washington pulled off this 14-6 upset, end Charley Malone put in a pitch for Redskin consideration.

"It's an honor to be even a bench-warmer on this club," Malone said. "This is the greatest team of all time." (9)

It was all in the mind. If the Chicago Bears were the greatest team of all time and the Washington Redskins beat them, then the Redskins were the greatest team of all time. The rosters were not the same, the circumstances, with players departing for the war effort, were not the same, but it was accurate to say that in late afternoon of December 13, 1942, the Redskins were the greatest team of the year.

Although his prediction a couple of weeks before the game did not gain the publicity that a certain guarantee issued by Joe Namath in Super Bowl III did before his New York Jets met the heavily favored Baltimore Colts in January of 1969, Washington's Ed Justice had prophesied that the Redskins would tame the Bears.

"I knew all the time we could take these Bears," Justice said when the win was in the bank. "I wasn't kidding when I offered to play them all or nothing. I knew we could stop their attack, and we did. Boy, oh boy, what a line we had in there today. They were terrific." (10)

The Bears, who were showering and changing their clothes in a much quieter locker room, and also had two coaches to speak up about the contest, all agreed that on this day the Redskins were definitely that. There comments were brief as their thoughts turned inward on just why this title game came out the other way.

"The Redskins won fairly and squarely," said Chicago fullback Bill Osmanski. "They stopped us and we congratulate them." (11)

Whether it was better effort, strategy or preparedness, Chicago co-coach Hunk Anderson said Washington demonstrated superior execution.

"They played their game today," Anderson said. "When a team does what Washington did today, when every man is in his place, and tackling the way they tackled, they're hard to lick." (12)

Luke Johnsos, Anderson's partner filling in for Halas, seemed perplexed by how readily the Redskins stopped the Bears' attack, one that had carried Chicago to its long winning streak.

"We never failed before," Johnsos said. "Anytime we got inside we went to town. We just couldn't do it today. The Redskins were a better team." (13)

No one, not even George Preston Marshall, could say that the Bears were crybabies after falling in this title game. Chicago players and coaches gave Washington its due.

Washington didn't exactly run up a big edge in yardage on the way to the win. Both teams recorded 10 first downs. Chicago out-gained the Redskins 139 to 65 through the air while Washington out-gained the Bears 101 to 69 on the ground. Not gaudy numbers, but it was enough.

Marshall didn't waste much energy or breath denigrating the Bears. He wore a look of satisfaction on his face and sprayed compliments around the locker room the way some of the Redskins were spraying champagne. He praised the players, but Flaherty rated highest on his compliment meter. Marshall had always been a fan of Flaherty. He brought him into the organization to win championships and Flaherty had delivered. Now Flaherty was leaving the Redskins, at least temporarily, not for a fancy job or higher salary, but because the United States was in a war and he was going to fight the enemy on a real battlefield. Marshall had to feel a little melancholy about that.

"Ray," Marshall said, "you ought to be an admiral in the navy. If they let you coach the team when you join the colors, you'll be in Yokohama in 10 days. There's nothing you can't do." Marshall, the man who found it easy enough to complain when things went wrong, felt there was nothing his team couldn't do that day either. "It was terrific. Yes, it was terrific. We really out-played them." (14)

Griffith Stadium fans who booed their home players in 1940 and fled the park early, stayed around long after the final gun to cheer and listen go the Redskins' band play "Hail to the Redskins" repeatedly.

Probably no one was happier with the result than Flaherty. His men had rebounded from ignominious defeat and he faced an uncertain future. But he was part of something special on this cold afternoon in the nation's capital, a result that no one could ever take away from him no matter what came next.

"Give me these same boys," Flaherty said of tackling his next assignment for the navy, "and I'll be alright. They could have licked the world today. They beat a fine football team, and brother, they beat them." (15)

This was one time – one of the few – in the early 1940s, that a team got the best of a Sid Luckman-quarterbacked Bears team. He had little time to pass because of the Redskins pass rush and his receivers did not find it easy to get open. Washington's hungry front line stifled the run game and Washington's secondary bottled up the passing game. No one on offense made the big plays, the end-arounds, or the deep catches.

If Washington had seemed baffled by Luckman's signal calling in 1940, in 1942 the Redskins seemed to know what he was going to call and prevented Chicago from ripping off the big yards. More importantly from the Redskins' standpoint, they did not make the big mistake. With the exception of the ill-timed bobble returned for a TD by Artoe in the early going, Washington protected the ball much better. The eight interceptions the trio of Redskin quarterbacks threw were a big factor in the humiliating 73-0 game. No team can overcome that.

Ordinarily, teams build for the future when they make up their rosters, try to create a balanced club that will stay together and improve over time. During war-time that was not possible. Teams tried to hang onto what they had and when players departed they wished them well. The Bears roster was markedly different by 1942 than it was in 1940. By the time of the 1942 title game, however, the Redskins had lost just five players to military service, the lowest number in the league to that point.

Among those who were serving their country instead of wearing Washington uniforms for the second Bears-Redskins title tilt of the '40s was future Hall of Famer Wayne Millner and back-up quarterback Frank Filchock. But Washington still had Sammy Baugh for that big game.

Baugh was married and the sole support of two children. But he also provided an essential service like those who worked in munitions plants. His job, when not playing football, was raising beef on his ranch in Texas. The cattle sacrificed their lives for American troops. The combination of factors meant that Baugh was not drafted and he did not enlist. There never seemed to be any controversy in the Washington media about Sam not suiting up for Uncle Sam. He did spend Monday through Friday on his ranch and he spent Saturday flying to the site of the Redskins' game. He played on Sunday and returned to the ranch.

Baugh didn't do much practicing with his teammates, but was able to compete throughout the autumn and be present when the Redskins played the Bears for the crown. Baugh was the field general and the leader who never got ruffled in facing pressure in the big game. Washington did not move the ball easily on the Bears and did not pile up passing yardage from Baugh's arm.

But people tend to forget that Baugh was actually a three-way performer. He was Washington's quarterback, a safety on defense, and the squad's punter. This was one of those days that Baugh's foot was more impressive than his arm. He punted six times in the championship game and averaged 52.5 yards per boot. The quick kick that surprised the Bears and flew, bounced and rolled 85 yards, was a potential difference maker.

"That kick turned out to be a big play," Baugh said. "When I quick-kicked I had the wind to my back, and that's why I did it. If the quarter had run out and we had to punt, we would have had to do it against the wind." (16)

Sometimes the littlest of things are turning points in the biggest of games.

Papa Bear Halas had been away from his brood for some time, but when the Bears qualified for the NFL championship game he had been able to wangle leave from the service and catch a plane that brought him to Washington so he could watch the game. A man with little patience, the gruff Halas despised what he saw. The Redskins' payback stuck in his craw and a day later when he attended the NFL owners' meetings, in military garb, he was in a foul mood.

That mood did not improve when he bumped into his nemesis, George Preston Marshall. Still glowing from the victory, Marshall did not even choose to spend much time insulting Halas about the way his team had played and lost the championship. Rather, Marshall found a different way to get under the thin-skinned Halas' skin. He took one look at him and said, "Why don't you take off the uniform and let a younger guy do the job?"

Halas was enraged. "I went through the roof," he said. Pittsburgh owner Art Rooney was present at this friendly exchange and said, "I thought Halas would kill Marshall." (17)

The owners adjourned, Halas returned to his naval work, and the Redskins basked in the pleasure of being champions of the NFL for the next year.

The Bears were not exactly crushed, demoralized and as ruined as one of those game stories about the 14-6 loss portrayed. In 1937, the Redskins beat the Bears for the title. In 1940, the Bears beat the Redskins for the title. In 1942, the Redskins topped the Bears for the title. In 1943, once again the Eastern Division winner was Washington and once again the Western Division winner was Chicago. For the fourth time in seven seasons the same two teams would meet for the NFL crown.

Chicago was still without its head coach, being led by the tandem of Johnsos and Anderson. With Flaherty in the service, Washington had a new coach in Dutch Bergman. The Bears finished their season 8-1-1 and the Redskins finished with a 6-3-1 record. Overall, the Bears were better, but on November 21 in Washington the Redskins had an easier time disposing of Chicago – 21-7 – than they had in the 1942 title game.

Despite falling to Washington again, in 1943 the Bears had some spectacular moments that might worry anyone game-planning for a one-game showdown. Just a week before Chicago lost to Washington the Bears had marched into New York and vaporized the Giants.

Sid Luckman was a native New Yorker and had attended Columbia. In a rare gesture, his hometown fans wanted to honor him although he played for the opposition. So it was Sid Luckman Day at the Polo Grounds. And November 14 really was Sid Luckman Day. Before the game, Luckman was given the gift of a $1,000 war bond. During the game, Luckman played like a million bucks. Playing the greatest game of his career, Luckman led the Bears to a 56-7 mauling of the Giants. Luckman threw a record seven touchdown passes that game, a record that has been equaled, but never broken in the following 70-plus years of NFL competition.

"Before this game the guys got together and said they were going to make sure I had a day to remember," Luckman said. "I remember one pass I threw to Jim Benton. He stretched out parallel to the ground and caught the ball on the very edge of his finger tips. It was the most spectacular catch I've ever seen. Then, after I'd thrown six touchdowns, I didn't want to go back into the game. I didn't see any need to humiliate the Giants. But Sammy Baugh had thrown six a couple of weeks before and the guys all said, 'C'mon, Sid, one more, what difference will it make?'" (18)

That season Luckman completed 110 passes in 202 attempts for a 54.5 percent completion average and a league-leading 2,194 yards. He led the league with 28 TD tosses. Baugh, who did have a six-touchdown game, completed 133 passes in 239 attempts for a league-leading 55.6 completion average. Those three numbers all led the league. Baugh threw for 1,754 yards and 23 touchdowns.

And, of course, they once again met on the field to decide the NFL championship. This time the game was in Chicago, but the Redskins were feeling pretty good about themselves after topping the Bears in the 1942 battle and then besting them during the 1943 regular season. None of that mattered. This time the Bears won 41-21.

It's not likely that any game-day experience would ever be as depressing, shocking, and flat-out irritating for George Preston Marshall as the 1940 championship. But this day probably ranked No. 2 in the worst football experiences of his life for a couple of reasons. First of all, Marshall was dead certain that his Redskins would win. Secondly, as his team trailed the hated Bears going into halftime, Marshall became entangled in a dispute with Ralph Brizzolara, Halas' stand-in as top Chicago chief executive, and was forcibly escorted away from the field.

Attendance at Wrigley Field was 34,320 on December 26, 1943 and while the teams struggled through a 0-0 first quarter there was one momentous development. Sammy Baugh was knocked unconscious in the first period and had to leave the game. Early in the game Baugh boomed a 44-yard punt and was running downfield trying to tackle the receiver, Luckman. Contact was made and Baugh was hit in the head by a knee or foot. Under current NFL rules he would not have been allowed to return, but as soon as the wooziness subsided and he felt better that day in the third quarter Baugh was reinserted into the game. He missed about 35 minutes of time on the game clock.

Washington actually scored first in the second period when Andy Farkas tallied a touchdown on a one-yard run and Bob Masterson kicked the extra point. That was pretty much the high point of the day for the Redskins. Before halftime Luckman drove Chicago to two touchdowns, the first on a 31-yard pass to Harry Clark (Bob Snyder kicked the extra point) and the second coming on a three-yard blast by fullback Bronko Nagurski (Snyder kicked again).

Bronko Nagurski is one of the most famous players in NFL history. He joined the Bears in 1930 as a two-way fullback and linebacker and it was never completely clear if Nagurski hit foes harder when he was tackling them or when he was running them over with the ball tucked under his arm. Once, Nagurski bulled across the goal-line at Wrigley Field and head down plowed straight ahead, through the end zone, until crashing head first into a wall. Afterwards, he said that last tackler packed a pretty good punch.

At 6-foot-2 and 226 pounds Nagurski was conceded to be the strongest man in the sport, one whose big-boned frame belied even his size. He was an unstoppable force who decided after the 1937 season he had had enough football and so he retired to his farm in Minnesota.

However, as key Bears players one by one entered military service and the caliber of available subs was reduced, Halas made a personal appeal from afar asking Nagurski to come out of retirement. The future Hall of Famer came back for one bonus season and won a championship ring. He also made a major impression on Luckman, who had missed Nagurski's act in his heyday.

"He was devastating, the biggest man I'd ever seen," Luckman said.

"He broke more collar bones than any fullback in history. Nagurski was all muscle, an outstanding football player, the kind you dream about." (19)

Luckman, who was on his way to passing for five touchdowns in the title game, hit Dante Magnani for a 36-yard TD to open the third period scoring and then hit him again on a 66-yard strike. The score was 27-7 before Washington scored again. Baugh came back into the game and connected with Farkas on a 17-yard touchdown strike. But Luckman added two more scores through the air on a 28-yarder to Jim Benton and a 10-yarder to Harry Clark. When it was too late Baugh completed one more TD toss to Joe Aguirre.

As had been the case in recent years, once the NFL season concluded, more and more young men from the rosters of the championship game teams would join the military and head off to war. Luckman had remained with the Bears during the early years of World War II, but immediately after this game he became a member of the U.S. Merchant Marine.

It wasn't 100 percent clear exactly where Marshall was at the end of the game. Just before halftime, Marshall, who had been watching high above the field in the grandstand, tried to make his way onto the field and presumably to his team's locker room. He exited from his box and chose to walk down the stadium runway which brought him out behind the Bears' bench. Marshall may well have been innocently standing there waiting for the clock to run out, but Brizzolara saw him hovering close to the Bears players and much in the manner that his boss and mentor George Halas would have reacted, he began shouting at Marshall.

Marshall, Brizzolara, said, was trying to steal the Bears' signals. Accompanied by ushers and police reinforcements, Brizzolara had Marshall removed from the field by way of an exit near Wrigley's home plate. The ushers acted as if they didn't know Marshall from General Dwight Eisenhower and asked to see his ticket stub in order to determine his proper seat. Police officers were more sympathetic when Marshall explained that he was the owner of the Redskins, but as he hurried away to catch up with his team Marshall stopped to berate the officials now coming off the field about their so-called bad calls.

Brizzolara was still hot after the game and accused Marshall of being unsportsmanlike for trying to swipe the signals. Marshall said Brizzolara was no gentleman and he would never speak to him again. (20)

Somewhere George Halas was laughing his head off – and he got the last laugh, too, when the Bears prevailed.

GEORGE PRESTON MARSHALL

Football to George Preston Marshall was always just a form of show business. If he put on a show people would come. Between 1937 and 1945, the Washington Redskins put on a very good show. Led by quarterback Sammy Baugh the Redskins were one of the fiercest and most successful teams in the National Football League.

The Redskins won their first championship in 1937 and surprised the Chicago Bears for their second in 1941. Washington also competed for the title in the famous 1940 loss, in 1942, and in 1945.

While Marshall owned the Redskins from 1932 to 1969, the heyday of his tenure spanned that mid-1930s to mid-1940s period when Baugh was at the helm of the offense.

During that stretch Washington and Chicago were essentially the league powerhouses, with another team sneaking into the title game here and there.

In 1932, Bears owner George Halas lobbied NFL owners to change the rules and open up the game in order for the passing game to flourish. Marshall was later given considerable credit for being on the right side of the issue, but he voted in favor mainly because he thought football would draw more fans. The rules change allowed quarterbacks to run around behind the line of scrimmage before throwing a pass.

It was a rare occasion when Marshall and Halas were in agreement on something. Most of the time they engaged in cats and dogs scraps. Often, they needled one another. Halas took advantage of Marshall's badmouthing before the 73-0 thrashing. Marshall insulted Halas for being in uniform in his 40s during World War II.

They got on one another's nerves, competed for the same rewards, but didn't hate one another.

Marshall was a dictator by nature, but did allow his coaches, particularly Ray Flaherty, pretty much a free hand in running the games. He loved the Redskins fight song and when his second wife, Corinne, wrote a book about her life with the team, Marshall handed copies of the words to the song and the book to Redskins rookies when they showed up to training camp.

Marshall was always careless with words. Over his decades as owner of the Redskins, making him a very visible business-owning figure in Washington, D.C., Marshall offended a selection of religious and ethnic groups.

"I have been accused of being anti-everything," Marshall said. "Anti-Jewish. Anti-Catholic. Oh, I don't know, maybe I'm just anti-people." (1)

Although surely Marshall realized he had something special in Baugh at quarterback he probably did not recognize that after World War II his Redskins teams would never again be serious players in the NFL under his ownership. Nor did a man who had no governor on the transmission of his thoughts realize he would become a lightning rod for the Civil Rights movement in the 1950s and 1960s.

While from a distance many viewed him as a curmudgeon, Marshall prided himself on being well-dressed, cultured, and a gentleman. He loved his moments in the spotlight, but he somehow, whether it was with those legendarily haunting insults of the Bears, or getting escorted off the field during a championship game, managed to botch them.

Marshall hob-nobbed with political leaders and society folk in the nation's capital and was comfortable with whatever old boys network ran football, though several of those team bosses like Halas and Pittsburgh Art Rooney, were not the sort to gallivant on the high seas on a yacht, or hang out with starlets. As a group, much like the American society they reflected, this was not a bunch of liberal politicos.

Baseball team owners may have been even more conservative, yet the Brooklyn Dodgers' Branch Rickey worked his way around their racial intolerance and hired Jackie Robinson to play ball and become the first African-American Major League player in the 20th century. Bill Veeck joined him by inking Larry Doby for the Cleveland Indians only a few months later and soon several teams, understanding that the barriers were down and that they had a whole new talent pool to choose from began signing African-Americans. It took more than a decade for every team to integrate. Robinson broke in at the start of the 1947 season. The Boston Red Sox were last to integrate with Pumpsie Green in 1959.

Some African-American players competed in the early days of the NFL in the 1920s, but during the Depression a lockout of sorts took effect with some using the excuse that black men did not deserve the jobs white men could get. Marshall was new to the league in 1932 and stridently campaigned against employing African-American players.

This ugly boycott period began fading away in 1946. The Cleveland Rams moved to Los Angeles and sought to play their home games in the Los Angeles Coliseum and sportswriters pointed out to the stadium commission that the Coliseum was publicly owned and it would be a violation of federal law to discriminate in the use of a public facility. The new Rams signed former UCLA stars Kenny Washington and Woody Strode.

Meanwhile, just after the end of World War II, a new pro football league sprung up to challenge the NFL. The All-America Football Conference signed numerous black players. Notably, the Cleveland Browns, the most dominant team of that era, introduced fans to African-American stars Marion Motley and Bill Willis. Both men were eventually elected to the Pro Football Hall of Fame.

Inroads were slow, but steady, until all NFL teams, and in 1960, the new American Football League, were populated with African-American stars. That is, all teams except the Washington Redskins. Marshall did not draft African-Americans and he did not sign African-American free agents. Gradually, but steadily, the Redskins slipped into mediocrity. Theirs was once a definitive era fighting it out with the Bears, but the rest of the league had passed them by.

For decades, the Redskins made their home in Griffith Stadium.Griffith Stadium was the site of some of the epic contests with the Bears. It was also home to the Washington Senators baseball team. However, the Senators moved to the Midwest and became the Minnesota Twins and Griffith was growing antiquated and dilapidated. In addition, with the growing popularity of the NFL the league wanted each team to play its games in a stadium that held at least 50,000 fans. What began as encouragement later became a rule when the NFL ultimately merged with the AFL. That same policy resulted in the Bears moving out of Wrigley Field and to Soldier Field in 1970.

Ground was broken for District of Columbia Stadium in July of 1960 and even though it was designed to hold just 45,000 fans, there was no problem about size at that time. The Redskins fully expected to make the new stadium their new home. In 1960, John F. Kennedy was elected president of the United States and neither JFK nor his officials, was deaf to the controversy raging in the capital city.

The people wanted the government to put pressure on the hometown Redskins to sign African-American players. It soon became obvious that the president did, too, and he had the power to make it happen. Officials in the Kennedy administration – with Secretary of the Interior Stuart Udall as front man – informed Marshall that if he didn't start using black players then the Redskins could not play their games in the new taxpayer-funded stadium. Marshall knew when he was outflanked, but he didn't go down without a showy fight.

Marshall called a press conference to respond to Udall's ultimatum and in front of the crowd of reporters ordered his secretary to call Joseph Kennedy, the former U.S. Ambassador to England, and JFK's father – Marshall and the older Kennedy were old friends. "I want to tell Joe Kennedy, an old pal of mine, what a creep I think his son is," Marshall said. (2)

For years, Marshall was not fond of many of the sports columnists in the local papers because it was their job to say what they thought and often what they thought was opposed to what Marshall did. Yet in a moment of weakness, after considerable back and forth between Marshall and Washington sportswriter Morris Siegel, Marshall agreed to allow Siegel to make a Redskins' draft choice just to prove to him that he didn't know what he was talking about.

This is what Siegel wrote sometime later: "Finally, about the 17th round, he said, 'Go ahead.' I checked and saw what was available and then drafted a Texas A&I back named Flavius Smith. The announcement was made, then George came up to me and said, 'Siegel, you've just become the first sportswriter to draft a player.' And I looked at him and said, 'George, you've just integrated the Redskins.' But shortly after that he traded Smith to the Packers." (3)

That all makes for a fabulous story, but no record could be found of a Flavius Smith being drafted by the Redskins in any round of any draft under Marshall's ownership. And no information turned up on a player by that name at Texas A&I.

Bobby Mitchell was born in Hot Springs, Arkansas and became a star at the University of Illinois. When he came out of college, the halfback formed what may have been the greatest running back duo in history with the Cleveland Browns' Jimmy Brown. Mitchell was already All-Pro when the Browns traded him (and another African-American running back Leroy Jackson) to the Redskins in 1961 so Cleveland could draft Heisman Trophy winner Ernie Davis.

Davis died of leukemia without ever playing a down in the pros. Mitchell produced a Hall of Fame career as a skilled runner and dazzling pass catcher. From 1969 to 2003 he continued to work for the Redskins off the field.

Marshall did not deserve the break he got in swapping the draft pick Davis for the superstar Mitchell, but he wiggled out of his predicament, ending the prolonged boycott of African-Americans on the Redskins' roster. Nor, many might argue, did he deserve the bust and plaque of him installed at the District of Columbia Stadium (later changed to Robert F. Kennedy Memorial Stadium after the presidential candidate was assassinated in 1968 while campaigning). There was most definitely a certain irony in Marshall being honored at that stadium.

Marshall would probably have preferred to produce Broadway shows than produce football extravaganzas, but he did love football. He perhaps would have enjoyed a life in politics, but not in anybody's legislature where he would have been one of many representatives or senators. Becoming a dictator most likely would have pleased him, but not even holding high political office where someone, like millions of voters, could have told him he was wrong.

It would have been tremendously difficult for Marshall to get elected to any position because he would almost surely have put his foot in his mouth on the campaign trail. An opponent would have calculatingly provoked him and then, uh, oh.

There was the time that for some reason, by some twist of logic, Marshall announced to the world that all Rhodes Scholars had to be Communists. Someone countered with the example of Supreme Court Justice Byron "Whizzer" White, who among other career distinctions played in the NFL.

"He couldn't have been a Communist," Marshall said. "Because he played football." (4)

There were some times that he thought his foe Halas was a Communist, however. Like the occasion when Marshall, who changed coaches the way some men changed their ties, announced the hiring of Bears assistant Hunk Anderson as his head coach. Halas said not so fast. It was fine if Marshall wanted to make Anderson a head coach – who was he to stand in his way – but Marshall would have to fork over a player in payment. Halas requested tackle Paul Lipscomb.

Capitalist that he was, Marshall was affronted by this example of interference in the free marketplace and began swearing at Halas in the middle of the Anderson press conference and walking away from the deal. Marshall refused to pay and Anderson lost out on the job.

Maybe after Marshall was spoiled by Flaherty he thought the coaching business was a snap, so he injected himself a bit more into that aspect of the game, welcome or not. When it came to showmanship, Marshall had a clear field and the Redskins' band was like an extension of his personality.

Although the Redskins had been a great team during the Baugh years, won their two championships, and appeared in three other title games, they never quite escaped the shadow of that 73-0 massacre. Marshall owned his team for 37 years, but some people never overlooked that glaring number.

In 1963, a vote of sportswriters was taken to choose the best pro football team in NFL history. The team voted as the winner was the 1940 Bears and some writers thought the electorate was influenced by the 73-0 score. The result annoyed Marshall.

"Those sports editors are nuts," Marshall said. "We beat that 1940 team." (5). He was right, going back to that regular-season game, and the Bears did lose three games that season. But that 73-0 score was such a beaut it overrode everything.

As perhaps additional insult to Marshall's sensibilities, the Philadelphia Bulletin noted in its headline on the story of the pro team rankings that "Redskins' Owner Helped Make Bears Football's No. 1 Team." (6) That was a reference to Marshall's bulletin-board material clipped and shown to his players by Halas.

Marshall was seen in public wearing a fur coat and an Indian headdress – though not at the same time. The more recent controversy in the 2000s whereupon many accuse the Washington football franchise of promoting racist stereotypes because of the Redskins' nickname, would have irritated Marshall. He would have fought to the death to preserve the nickname rather than give in. He would not have believed the Redskins were offending anyone and he probably would have said he didn't care if they did.

In 1963, the Pro Football Hall of Fame opened in Canton, Ohio and on September 7 inducted its first class of members. The inaugural class consisted of 17 individuals and Marshall was one of them, listed for his contributions as a team owner. One of those other 17 was George Halas. Joining them was Marshall's greatest star, Sammy Baugh.

There was no doubt that Marshall made major contributions as an owner, bringing the Redskins to Washington, supervising the building of championship teams, playing a role in changing rules that brought more excitement to the sport through passing and also by favoring splitting the league into two divisions to set up a natural championship game, and by adding a touch of flavor here and there with things like the Redskins' band and the halftime show.

He was certainly not without flaws, though. At a later date his firm and wrong-headed stance on race might have kept him out of the Hall of Fame altogether, though it apparently was not an issue at all when Marshall was selected as a member of the first class. The mini-biography that the Hall of Fame has on its web site uses the word "controversial" in passing to describe Marshall, but there are no hints about his racist outlook.

Marshall bluntly stated that he maintained the Redskins roster with all-white players "as a concession for Southern fans who watched the football team over a widespread radio-television network." (7)

Marshall was born in 1896 and he was 72 years old in 1969 when he died August 9, still the owner of the Redskins. Marshall passed away at home in the Georgetown section of the District of Columbia. He had been partially incapacitated by a stroke.

When Marshall died, it was nationwide news and sports columnists in cities all over the country wrote about his career and lengthy supervision of the Redskins. Most of the articles included the word "stormy" in them. One Washington Star story used that word both in the headline and in the lead.

One columnist said it was inappropriate that Marshall would rest in peace, as the saying goes at funerals. Bob August in Cleveland said Marshall would likely have preferred "baton twirlers and a brass band playing The Redskins' March." (8) August was probably right, though most people consider funerals to be somber occasions, not football game halftime shows. The headline on August's column did include the words "Stormy Giant" about Marshall. One might think the guy was a human weather report.

To some, Marshall was an enigma, and to many an anachronism. He was a stalwart builder of the NFL, but a stubborn relic of the antebellum South. One Los Angeles newspaperman knew Marshall for years, recognized his many achievements on behalf of the league, but reported on pickets that appeared outside of the Los Angeles Coliseum when the Redskins came West during the height of the controversy over desegregating the team. That author noted that in his last years of life Marshall suffered "from hardening of the brain arteries." (9)

Another columnist, this one stationed in Baltimore, took note that throughout his tenure in charge of the Redskins that Marshall had an ironclad rule that no one in the organization was to wish him happy birthday because he didn't pay attention to age. "...in his world he was going to live forever," the writer observed. "He was also a strong-willed, unbending, non-compromising man with the strength of his convictions in all matters, be it in the area of politics, sports, religion or racial relations. (Marshall) was not a hypocrite. Whether you liked him or found him repulsive, you knew the stand he had taken because he let the world know it." (10)

Although it was not widely reported, and it seemed contradictory to his personality, at least one sportswriter, the syndicated columnist Bob Considine, indicated that when the Bears bested the Redskins by that 73-0 score in 1940, Marshall said rather calmly, "Well, can't win 'em all." (11)

That just doesn't sound authentic and it is certainly not a phrase that trailed Marshall around for decades the way the score did. There was little hint that Marshall was Mr. Nonchalant any day of the week and definitely not while absorbing a shocking result like that.

While Marshall may have seemed small-minded about human beings with dark skin, he did have a visionary side about football as entertainment. Long before it became reality, he predicted, "You'll see the time when having good seats to a pro football game becomes a status symbol," Marshall said, "when almost every stadium in the land is sold out before the season begins. You'll see it become the game of the country club set, every game a dinner party and a cocktail party for the well-to-do and packed busloads of fans leaving from the clubs and your top restaurants. Going to football will be the thing to do in the social fabric of the nation." (12)

The memorial service for Marshall in Washington attracted many luminaries from the world of pro football, including Commissioner Pete Rozelle, who delivered a eulogy. Marshall was then buried in West Virginia, where he was born.

Rozelle called Marshall "a man of imagination, style, zest, dedication, openness, dry humor, brashness, strength, and courage." (13)

The Washington Daily News used space on its editorial page, headlined simply, "George Preston Marshall" to discuss the Redskins' owner's life. Above all, it read, Marshall was a showman and it was fitting that his memorial service in that city was conducted within the vast walls of the Washington National Cathedral.

In general summary, the commentary read, "…for good or ill George Marshall was always more than a bit larger than life." (14)

GEORGE HALAS

In 1979, nearly 40 years after the Chicago Bears beat up on the Washington Redskins by that 73-0 score, esteemed sports columnist Red Smith wrote a story in which the headline referred to the "sacking of Washington." (1)

Smith discussed a comment made by a fellow named Garry Schumacher, who had begun his professional life as a sportswriter and then gone to work for the New York and San Francisco Giants.

Schumacher told Smith that one of his imaginings had placed him on the train back to Chicago that the Bears rode following the pummeling of the Redskins that December day in 1940.

"I wish I coulda been in George Halas' stateroom on the train to Chicago that night," Schumacher said. "After they'd had their highballs and their laughs, I have to think that when George turned out the light he allowed himself one little private chuckle." (2)

There really was every chance that the word "chuckle" underplayed the private treat of a reaction that Halas granted himself. Something much louder and more uninhibited would have been likely and nobody could blame the man if he guffawed, chortled or let out a scream of pure pleasure.

Granite jawed George Halas never forgot that 73-0 blowout and never quite got over his enjoyment of it. But Halas, who was present at the conception of the league and who like Marshall probably thought he would live forever, spent 63 years running the Bears, from 1920 to 1983, so much of his career stretched ahead of him in the years and decades following the wonderfully satisfying victory.

The late 1930s through the mid-1940s was the apex of the Bears-Redskins rivalry and the Halas-Marshall rivalry. The rest of the NFL caught up and surpassed those two teams after a while, but both strong men owners remained in position at the head of their franchises' organizational charts for many years. Halas retained a more robust health, though, and Marshall began fending off illnesses in the early 1960s, several years before he died.

Halas and Marshall never became great buddies, but they were icons in their sport, institutions, and they had shared a lot and worked hard for the betterment of the league for years. In August of 1963, Marshall was a fairly long-term inmate at Georgetown Hospital in Washington when Halas stopped in for a visit before an exhibition game.

He had previously sent flowers.

"Hello, Dynamite," Halas greeted his frequent antagonist. "Good to see you again." Halas was accompanied by Commissioner Pete Rozelle. Marshall perked up and said, "Sit down, Georgie. You brought the Commish, eh? You never change, Georgie. Still tryin' to get the edge." (3) Marshall may have been a party of one who ever called Halas "Georgie" without his face turning several shades of red.

The men chit-chatted about football – not Marshall's health – and at one point Marshall asked Halas how he thought his team would be that season.

"Good," Halas said. "All right, but maybe not good enough." (4)

Halas was wrong about that. The Bears were good enough to interrupt the Green Bay Packers' early-Sixties dynasty that season and went all of the way. The 1963 season brought the Bears their first title since 1946 and it was Halas' last championship on the sidelines before he retired as coach.

His fedora as much of a trademark as his pugnacious manner, Halas long out-lasted Marshall as owner of his NFL team and in age. Even after stepping down as head coach with a then-record 325 victories, Halas had his hands in Bears' daily operations and remained active in league matters. Through longevity, passion, devotion to the game he practically helped invent, and always looking at the big picture of what was good for the NFL, Halas the player, coach and owner became a singular institution during his lifetime.

One of the press releases and biographical summaries produced by the Pro Football Hall of Fame referred to Halas as "Mr. Everything" of pro football.

It is a mixed sport metaphor to say that Halas really touched all of the bases, but outside of the generalities that Halas filled several roles in NFL history, he was a pioneer and creative thinking inventor whose mark was felt on the sport in numerous ways. When the NFL was organized pro football was growing out of its semi-pro origins. Halas was a true believer who knew that the pro game featured better players than the college game, and he was intent on proving it to skeptics.

Halas was the first coach to schedule daily practices between games. He was the first to allow his team's games to be broadcast on radio. Halas was the first to make sure a grounds crew put down a tarp over the field to protect it from inclement weather. He -- and on this one he was partnering with Marshall – argued for rules changes to open the way to more offense, was in favor of splitting the league into two divisions, and helped create the initial NFL title game structure. Later, in 1949, Halas made the Bears the first team to draft an African-American player when he chose Indiana quarterback George Taliaferro in the 19th round (although Taliaferro chose to play in the All-America Football Conference instead of reporting to the Bears). When the issue arose Halas fought for equal shares of television money for all teams regardless of the size of the home city.

When someone at the Hall of Fame was cataloguing all of Halas' accomplishments, Papa Bear did sneak in a comment about how his biggest thrill in the game was that 73-0 pounding delivered to the Redskins. He kept going back to that special day.

"It has to be our 73-0 victory over the Redskins in Washington in the 1940 championship game," Halas said in rating his greatest thrill. "It centered attention on the T formation and changed the course of all pro and college football. Sid Luckman, the greatest quarterback of them all in my book, showed what could be done when all the techniques of the formation can be applied with precision." (5)

For the most part the 1940s belonged to the Chicago Bears. They won NFL titles in 1940 over the Redskins, in 1941 over the New York Giants, in 1943 over the Redskins and in 1946 over the Giants and, of course, lost that 1942 championship game to the Redskins. There was no telling just how great the Bears might have been during that decade if the team hadn't splintered because of World War II. Halas continued to believe that the great players of the first half century would still have been stars in the second half of the 20th century.

What Halas brought to the NFL with the passage of time was perspective. He was the last man standing, the last one still living that helped form the league in 1920. It seemed crazy to more recent fans that anyone might have believed that college teams had superior players than pro teams. But Halas recalled having to sell the pro game.

"What we had going for us was the great, bursting enthusiasm of the players," he said in 1972, "their genuine liking for the game and the bruising contact. That hasn't changed. The players of the present are just as intense. And that is why the game has come as far as it has. Fans in the early days responded to the all-out effort of the players. Fans now respond just the same, but in greater numbers." (6)

To this day, most Chicago Bears fans, especially those of the older variety, will say that the team's greatest quarterback of all time was Sid Luckman. He was certainly Halas' and Luckman was the signal caller for four championship teams. That's a nice cross-section of rings. During the 1920s, 1930s and 1940s, it seemed as if Halas was a personnel genius, always plucking the right players for the Bears in the draft, in trades, or as free agents.

Somehow, though, Halas appeared to lose his touch when it came to drafting, acquiring or hiring the Bears' next great quarterback. Perhaps the NFL had caught up to him. Perhaps the NFL had become too complicated for one man to wear so many hats, or rather for one man with one hat to do so many jobs. Or maybe it was as simple as Halas making the biggest blunders of his career.

Nonetheless, as Luckman's career was winding down and Halas was pursuing a replacement, the Bears' big bear got his hands on Johnny Lujack, Bobby Layne, George Blanda and either alienated (Lujack) them, misjudged their talent (Layne) or alienated and misjudged their talent (Blanda). The result was an entire decade of missteps taken at the most important position on the field. Halas even took a leave of absence from coaching occasionally, though any time a would-be successor had any difficulties he climbed down the ladder from the owner's box and reassumed control.

In the early 1960s, after a late-1950s break, Halas was back on the sidelines and he pieced together one last great club that at its best did have a shot at another crown. This was the team Halas was talking about with Marshall in the hospital – the 1963 Bears.

Many of the key players on that Bears team were aging, nearing the end of their careers, and very hungry to earn a championship to carry them into retirement. There were also some younger players mixed in, and if not a Hall of Fame quarterback on hand, then a highly competent leader with the skill to blend the components of the offense on a defensively-oriented team. That was Bill Wade, who had come to the Bears from the Los Angeles Rams in a trade.

Overall, it really was an extraordinary bunch of players. The roster included middle linebacker Bill George, who basically invented the position, Stan Jones, a lineman who was as valuable on defense as he was on offense, Doug Atkins, a defensive end who was a beast, and Mike Ditka, who was revolutionizing the tight end spot. Those four, along with Halas, became Hall of Famers. Many believe that Joe Fortunato, another linebacker, belongs in the Hall with them.

Others, from Wade to running backs Rick Casares and Ronnie Bull and center Mike Pyle to defensive end Ed O'Bradovich, linebacker Larry Morris and defensive backs Richie Pettibon and Roosevelt Taylor, all made significant contributions.

The Bears finished 11-1-2 and in that era when there were no playoffs, they had to be that good to edge out the Green Bay Packers to qualify for the championship game. The Packers, revitalized by coach Vince Lombardi, were the team of the moment, a star-studded group. Halas drummed it into his players' heads that they had to beat the Packers head-to-head in order to win the Western Division to reach the title game. He was right, the Bears did, and one of the best teams of the era did not make it into the title game. Chicago could thank the defense, which permitted just 144 points. The Bears topped the New York Giants, 14-10, for the crown.

That was a very special win, a vindication of sorts that the old man still had what it took – even though he needed very skilled assistant coaches to help out. But Halas was voted NFL coach of the year for the '63 performance. It was also his last championship.

Later in the 1960s, despite drafting superstars Dick Butkus and Gale Sayers, the Bears fell on very hard times. Their quarterback woes continued. Now into his seventies, Halas stayed on as coach through the 1967 season. When he stepped away this time at 73 after 40 seasons, he and everyone else knew it was for good. In his mind, Halas felt he was not too old to inhabit a chair in the front office. But he recognized he no longer had the stamina to nurse a sore hip up and down the sidelines between the 20-yard-lines for an entire, 60-minute game yelling at the officials.

Halas had always felt it was his God-given right to patrol the length of the field, even after rules were changed to prohibit coaches from straying too far from the coaching box. In 1958, as other teams protested, Halas still ran around at will and one day then-Commissioner Bert Bell refused to leash Halas. "My opinion is to let them go from goal line to goal line as long as they don't come on the field or interfere with the officials," Bell stated. (7)

It was one thing to get away with his old style of behavior, but when Halas couldn't will his fragile, arthritis-ridden body back and forth then it was time to quit. But quitting and quitting were two different things.

Halas turned over the coaching job to Jim Dooley, a member of the Bears' family as a former player and an assistant coach. It was a hire that was not a surprise. Dooley was a Bears No. 1 draft pick in 1952, had a productive receiving career and been a Bears assistant since 1962, most recently serving as defensive coordinator. For Dooley, it was a dream come-true to coach the Bears, but he also was aware he bore the burden of following a legend, and a legend who had an office down the hall from him since Halas, the ex-coach, was still Halas the current boss.

Dooley lasted four seasons as the coach not named Halas without putting up a winning record and suffering a record as awful as 1-13. That was enough to get that member of the family excommunicated.

Halas turned to Abe Gibron next, then Jack Pardee, who had one pretty good season, then Neill Armstrong, who was not the Neil Armstrong to walk on the moon, but did manufacture one 10-win season which to Bears fans by then seemed about as notable as the stroll far, far away.

During this time period Halas was in his full glory as an NFL elder statesman, recognized league and nationwide as a living embodiment of the fastest growing sport in America, one of those pioneers who saw the future and made it all happen. He was invited to dinners and events here and there and everywhere, but while he reveled in the role, and still participated in league meetings, Halas was distressed by the problems his team underwent on the field. This was his baby, his only family business. Halas was a winner as a player and a coach and he wanted the Bears to remain a winner.

However, he could neither hire a coach that provided sustained success, nor a quarterback that could help that coach pull it off. Until they split over money, one of Halas' favorite players during his long career was Mike Ditka. Ditka was his kind of player, hard-nosed, the kind of player who might chew nails instead of bubble-gum, who was passionate about winning and who blocked like a demon. Together, blending Ditka's skills and Halas' know-how, in the 1960s they had turned the tight end position into more of an offensive weapon.

Eventually, the two strong-willed, stubborn men had a falling out over Ditka's salary. Ditka accused Halas of being so cheap he threw nickels around like manhole covers. It was actually a brilliant insult and not far off the mark. Halas traded Ditka away and after the player retired he enjoyed a Super Bowl-winning assistant coach's job under Tom Landry with the Dallas Cowboys. Ditka was a sponge, learning all he could from the Hall of Fame mentor, but the day arrived when Ditka believed he was ready to become an NFL head coach.

Although anybody using the word "mellow" in a sentence with Mike Ditka's name or George Halas' name, never mind both, probably enjoys playing catch with hand grenades, signs of a thaw appeared. Taking note that the Bears had pretty much declined into the realm of the terrible performing teams in the NFL, Ditka wrote a rapprochement letter to Halas, saying he had always respected Papa Bear and had always considered himself a Bear. If some day Halas found himself in need of a new head coach Ditka would like to be considered.

Halas, well into his 80s, was suffering from failing health. He did not know how much time he had and he did not know if he would live long enough to see his beloved Bears rejuvenated on the field, but he wanted to play a role in reversing their fortunes. In a hire that both electrified and shocked Chicago, Halas brought Ditka back into the fold in time for the 1982 season.

It was just about the worst time for the new coach to take over because the NFL endured a messy strike that reduced the season to nine games. Nothing was proven by a 3-6 record Ditka's rookie head coaching season. But rebuilding the Bears was more than a one-season job anyway, despite this lost season.

By the fall of 1983 Ditka had started to significantly remake the roster and that season the Bears finished 8-8. It was, as he himself had suspected, too late for Halas. Halas died on October 31, in the middle of that season. But he believed he had done the right thing in anointing Ditka. That late-in-life last decision was vindicated. By 1985, the Bears were being compared to the best Halas' teams of all time and the best NFL teams of all time. They finished 15-1 in that regular season and won the Super Bowl. The Bears were the champs once more, for the first time since 1963.

Halas did not live to see one of the most glorious moments in team history come to fruition, but the man who had helped shape the foundation of a fabulously popular sport had his hand in influencing one last championship.

Papa Bear Halas was 88 when he died of heart disease and pancreatic cancer and his memorial service in its own reflective way was a major event for the league. Commissioner Pete Rozelle, team owners, and legions of players, current and former Bears, appeared to pay respects at St. Ita's Catholic Church on a windy, cool, weekday November afternoon in Chicago – it was football weather. Approximately 1,200 mourners turned out and a funeral parade followed to St. Adalbert's Cemetery in Niles.

"He touched seven decades," Rozelle said. "He was to us what Dr. James Naismith was to basketball when he put up peach baskets and invented a winter sport." (8)

The longest-running football rivalry is between the Chicago Bears and Green Bay Packers and it is amongst the most storied in American professional sport. Green Bay, Wisconsin is the smallest city to operate a pro team in any of the four American major sports and the only reason the Packers survived the financially difficult days of the league when other small towns flaked off was Halas helping fight for ways to keep the Pack going. This was particularly important when it came to revenue sharing in the way of splitting television money. It was Halas who argued loudest for equal shares, not shares divided up by the size of a team's market.

"As tough a competitor as he was, he always realized you have to help the little guys to exist, too," said Giants owner Wellington Mara. "He wouldn't give them a good player for nothing. But maybe you'd play an exhibition game for a very large contract. A couple of thousand dollars were a big thing in those days." (9)

It wasn't just the Packers, either. One had to be an insider to understand Halas' largesse because many of his loans and donations were kept secret.

"His greatest contribution was that he kept it (the NFL) going from 1920 to 1940," said Dallas Cowboys President Tex Schramm. "Nobody knows how much money he loaned people. He even kept the Chicago Cardinals going and they were in the same town." (10)

Halas touched many people in many ways. He could be gruff, but compassionate in a crisis. He could be stingy at contract time, but generous in a time of need. No one who passed through the NFL between 1920 and 1983 went home ignorant of Halas' deeds and accomplishments. He left a mark. Halas was married and had children, but joked that pro football was his mistress. Others characterized his relationship with the game as him being the father of the sport that blossomed throughout the 20th century.

One former player, a defensive tackle who was not amongst the most famous of Bears, made a long trip from Atlanta to be present at the funeral. Fred Davis, who competed for Chicago between 1946 and 1951, had tremendous admiration for the man.

"He was the father of football," Davis said. "He hated to lose, but he was a humble man, not an arrogant man." (11)

There were probably as many different opinions about George Halas the man as there were mourners in attendance, but the 1,200 of them were almost assuredly uniform in opinion that he was one of the true giants of professional football.

Chicago Bears offensive lineman **Dan Fortmann** (21) is shown, Sept. 9, 1940, in Chicago, Ill. (AP Photo/Football Hall of Fame)

BULLDOG, SAMMY, SID
AND LIFE GOES ON

Clyde "Bulldog" Turner was a rookie in 1940 and the last game of his first season was the 73-0 shellacking the Bears put on the Redskins. He had to know he wasn't going to see that every day no matter how long he played. Still, Turner won four championship rings and played for a fifth title.

He was a very good player from the start – and he got better from there. Turner was all-pro eight times and played for 13 seasons. He dominated at center and he dominated at linebacker. In 1942, he became the only linebacker to lead the NFL in pass interceptions with eight. At 6-foot-2 and 232 pounds Turner was big for the era, but what made him so devastating was that he was also as fast as a track sprinter.

If Turner had been a running back or a quarterback he would still be a household name today. But no one remembers linemen the way they remember people who handle the ball. Those who knew the game, however, recognized Turner's greatness – he was elected to the Pro Football Hall of Fame in 1966.

The running gag, only it was basically true, was that Turner was the busiest man at Chicago Bears practices because of his dual, 60-minute role on offense and defense and how once in a while coach George Halas would move him in at fullback. Turner played with such intensity and passion – and nerves – that he threw up before each game, though thankfully he didn't heave once for each position played.

"He has a keen football mind," said Bears assistant coach Carl Brumbaugh. "He's one of those rare fellows who can visualize what each player is supposed to do." (1)

Turner was feared on both sides of the ball, as a blocker and as a tackler, but he was probably at his finest as a center, a teeny bit better than he was as a linebacker. He was renowned for never making a bad snap and for opening holes large enough for the Atchison, Topeka and the Santa Fe to chug through. Turner was so good and so popular in Chicago that 25 or more years after storing his cleats he was recognized walking down the street in the Windy City.

To Chicago quarterback Sid Luckman Turner was like a big brother, a protector for him and the other guys if an opponent dared to get rough with them.

"When he walked on the field, he was all class," Luckman said. "He was motivated. He played both ways and he was a vicious football player. He looked out for all of us. If there was trouble, Bulldog was there. If we were having problems moving the ball he'd be saying, 'Just come right over me.' He always knew what he was doing." (2)

Turner was signed out of Hardin-Simmons for $2,200 and each year he engaged in such hard negotiating with Halas that he might as well have been in the trenches against a New York Giants 250-pounder. At his peak Turner earned $14,000 a year and while he thought that was fine at the time he paid for it later by not having much money for his elderly retirement.

Bulldog believed his best playing weight was 240 pounds, but Halas insisted he weigh 232 pounds and if he didn't match the coach's expectations Turner was fined. Weight was not their favorite topic for discussion since Halas charged $50 per pound over his limit. This policy was hard on a man who loved to eat and drink beer.

Only once during his Bears career did Turner fail to make All-Pro. He was in the Air Force, stationed in Colorado Springs, and played football on Saturdays for the service team, then flew out of town and rendezvoused with the Bears and played NFL games on Sundays before rushing back to the base. Turner made the All-Service team, but must have slipped a little bit because of lack of practice with the Bears.

With good reason Turner had supreme confidence and more than once announced, "I never met the man I couldn't handle on the field." The evidence of the correctness of that statement was strong. "I don't know if I could, but I did," Turner said. "A lot of 'em I wouldn't go into an alley with, but I'd meet any of 'em on the field. Some I really couldn't handle physically, but I could outsmart 'em." The Packers' Ed Neal, who weighed 303 pounds and psyched out foes across the line by breaking a beer bottle over his forearm, broke Turner's nose five times. Bulldog needed a spare helmet when he faced Neal because he was bound to have one cracked during a game. "Against me he had a habit of uppercutting with that big fist just before the play." (3)

No one said pro football in the 1940s was for the meek. Interestingly since many contemporaries would vote the honor to Turner, Bulldog said to him Bronko Nagurski was just about the toughest person in the world.

"He was 35 years old and coming out of retirement (in 1943), but I never saw anything to compare to him as far as a bruising fullback," Turner said. "If he was that tough then, he must have been a terror in his heyday." (4)

Absolutely true of Turner, as well. Turner, who said he enjoyed teaching the game, coached the American Football League's New York Titans in 1962, just for that one season, but spent most of his post-playing days in private business or farming back in the quiet of rural Texas. Late in life Turner fell on hard times. Drought wrecked his spread and he suffered financially and from ill health stemming from cancer and diabetes.

Approaching the end of his life, Turner who died at 79 in 1998, was pleased when a movement took hold to better reward pre-1959 NFL players with improved pension payments.

"That first championship game," Turner said referring to the 73-0 victory, "I got about $850. But you've got to remember I bought a new Olds 98 convertible for $700. We never really thought much about pensions. The owners didn't really have much money, either.

"Our only income was the gate receipts, but I wanted to play football. I loved football. It makes me sick I didn't get a chance to make that money (modern day salaries). It's really been a good life. We couldn't have had had more fun. I never felt anyone owed us anything." (5)

Eventually, increased payments to the old-time players were approved.

"We played because we wanted to and no one promised us anything," Turner said. "But it sure will be nice to see that first check." (6)

The 1940 Bears-Redskins championship game was remarkable in so many ways, the bloated score first and foremost, but also for the number of future Hall of Famers participating in one way or another. Besides Turner, Halas and Redskins owner George Preston Marshall, also enshrined were Sammy Baugh (1963), Wayne Millner (1968), Turk Edwards (1969), Washington coach Ray Flaherty (1976), Sid

Luckman (1965), George Musso (1982), Danny Fortmann (1965), Joe Stydahar (1967), and George McAfee (1966).

An excellent all-around team, the Bears did feature those beefy, rugged linemen that as emphatically placed a flag of ownership on the line of scrimmage as Norwegian Roald Amundsen had at the South Pole. You had Turner in the middle, but he was flanked by Fortmann, Musso and Stydahar.

Fortmann's entire NFL career spanned 1936 to 1943. It was cut short because of World War II – he was in the navy and served on a hospital ship -- but in terms of a career choice Fortmann always knew that football was a short-term venture. After graduating from the University of Chicago as a serial part-time student while being paid by the Bears, Fortmann engaged in a surgical internship in Detroit and took additional surgical training in Pittsburgh.

Fortmann entered college at Colgate when he was 16 and he was only 20 when the Bears' season began his rookie year of 1936 after being a member of the first-ever NFL draft class. He was the youngest starter in the National Football League that year and the same might very well be true every year since football players do not come straight out of high school for the pros.

"I wanted to play pro football, but I was also determined to go to med school," Fortmann said. "Without George's (Halas's) understanding and cooperation I never could have prepared for my future." (7)

As much as Halas wanted his men to focus on the task of being the best Bears they could be, he did always emphasize that they should think about and plan for the rest of their lives beyond the game. Although Fortmann was a Phi Beta Kappa scholar and had the smarts to play savvy football as well as train for another career, his biggest problem in the NFL was essentially being a shrimp.

Even by the standards of the day when linemen were much smaller than they are in the 2000s, Fortmann was too small by all measures. He was six feet tall, but when he reported to Bears training camp he weighed just 200 pounds. Although never seriously bulking up to the Turner weight class, never mind a George Musso-sized 270, Fortmann overcame his shortcoming with quick feet and superior speed. It was almost comical to suggest that Fortmann was one of "The Monsters Of The Midway." By size gauge he seemed more like an apprentice monster, an on-the-waiting-list monster once he ingested enough carbohydrates and candy bars. (He only got up to 210).

Fortmann himself was surprised to be tabbed by the Bears near the end of the '36 draft. Even then Colgate was not prominent on the radar of the college football world.

"I played at Colgate in the days when nobody from the NFL saw schools like ours," he said. "I was small and young...(but) I thought I'd give it a try. I've learned that if you try hard you'll get there." (8)

He got there, but he didn't get rich, certainly not as a rookie when the Bears paid Fortmann $1,700 for the season. His top salary was $6,000. Presumably he made considerably more as a doctor.

Once Dr. Fortmann was done with school and done with football he became a surgeon in Burbank, California. A six-time NFL All-Star guard, Fortmann must have wielded a mean scapel, as well. Besides handling his private business Fortmann was the Los Angeles Rams' team physician between 1947 and 1963. It is likely that he treated a continuous and vast number of knee injuries in that position.

Fortmann, who was elected to the Pro Football Hall of Fame in 1965, was involved in the first "play" of the 73-0 game. He was on the field for the officials' coin toss to determine who got the ball first.

"I won the toss of the coin," Fortmann said. "I was the captain and I still have the coin as a cherished souvenir. It was a silver dollar. Halas kept reminding us of that defeat (the regular-season loss to the Redskins). I played a lot of times when we were inspired, but the team that took the field that day was the highest emotionally keyed squad I ever saw." (9)

Fortmann died at age 79 in 1995.

One coincidental aspect of Fortmann's football career was how closely he was linked to Joe Stydahar. The young men did not know one another as college players, but Fortmann and Jumbo Joe got to know each other at the East-West Shrine game in San Francisco following the 1936 season and after both had been drafted by the Bears. They spent the next seven seasons playing next to each other on the Chicago line.

"It helped me tremendously to play next to Joe for so many years,"

Fortmann said. "A true partnership built up. We got to know exactly what to expect from one another." (10)

Compared to Fortmann, Stydahar, who hailed from West Virginia coal country where he was also a high school and college basketball star, was indeed jumbo-sized. He was 6-4 and weighed 235 pounds and beyond that was very large-boned so he seemed immense. Like Fortmann, Stydahar, who joined the Bears the same season, was a perennial NFL All-Star, being chosen six times between 1936 and 1946 (though he lost one year to military service). What a pair they were on the line.

Stydahar was a two-way stud, playing 60 minutes a game, though he played only one year with the Bears after World War II, retiring at 34. But Stydahar stayed in the game and in 1950 became head coach of the Los Angeles Rams.

In 1945, the Cleveland Rams met the Redskins in the NFL title game and won 15-14. The temperature at game time in Cleveland was minus-8, the coldest for an NFL title game to date, the Ice Bowl of the era. It was a bitter loss for Washington, though not in the same way the Bears' 1940 pummeling was. One reason the loss was so irritating was a first-quarter play when Washington was slapped with a safety. Sammy Baugh was throwing into the end zone, but the pass hit the goal post and instead produced two points for Cleveland.

The Rams won by a point, and then ahead of Major League Baseball by more than a decade, promptly up and moved to California. They occupied Los Angeles as a precursor of the wave of teams that would swallow up the Left Coast in pro sports in the coming decades.

Over the next few seasons the Rams slipped to pretty much a .500 team. However, in 1949, under the guidance of that old T formation whiz Clark Shaughnessy, Los Angeles finished 8-2-2. Stydahar was one of his assistants in what was seemingly a very successful season.

Owner Dan Reeves canned Shaughnessy a few months later because of his personality. Shaughnessy was feuding with some players and Stydahar. He accused Stydahar of lobbying for his job and was furious when he was ousted by Reeves and Stydahar did get the post. Coming full circle, Shaughnessy joined the Bears again as an assistant coach.

Under Stydahar the Rams had a terrific season. They finished 9-3, but that set up a post-season rich with irony. The record represented a division tie with the Bears, Stydahar's old team and current employer of Shaughnessy. LA won a playoff game 24-14 to advance to the NFL title game. But the Rams fell to the Browns, 30-28, the team that had replaced them in Cleveland.

A year later, in the 1951 season, the Rams repeated as division champs with an 8-4 mark and faced the Browns once again for the championship. This time Los Angeles and Stydahar prevailed, 24-17. It was a nice addition to Stydahar's jewelry collection since he already owned four Bears championship rings.

In the continuing Rams-Bears soap opera, however, Stydahar's charges got off to a slow start in 1952, losing exhibition games and their opener. An unhappy conversation with Reeves resulted in Stydahar being fired. His successor was former Bear Hampton Pool, who was a Stydahar teammate in that 73-0 game. With Shaughnessy, Stydahar and Pool being hired one, two, three by Reeves, he must have thought some magic was transferrable from the 73-0 smacking around the Bears gave Washington. Under Pool the Rams went 9-2.

Given that he had two division championships and one league championship on his resume, Stydahar was a proven commodity and he wasn't unemployed long. He still had a name in Chicago so that made him a natural to coach the Chicago Cardinals, which he did for two seasons that were less successful than his years in LA. In the early 1960s Stydahar returned to the Bears as an assistant coach before going into private business shortly before being inducted into the Hall of Fame.

Stydahar was only 65 when he died of a heart attack in 1977.

Although George Halas was interested in George Musso, he wasn't sure the big guy could cut it in the NFL after cutting his teeth on small-college football at Millikin University. His best offer in 1933 when Musso became available was $90 a game. Musso was a tremendous athlete in college and during those days of shorter seasons he competed on Millikin's football, basketball, baseball and track teams.

That was a hint that the young man had the versatility to make it with the Bears and he did. Musso manned the Chicago line from 1933 to 1945 and was part of four championship teams while earning All-Star recognition three times and eventually, in 1982, Hall of Fame recognition.

Musso overlapped the 1930s and 1940s Bears era and played with so many greats it could take up an entire page to list them. Besides the core of Hall of Famers around in the 1940s Musso also played with Bronko Nagurski, Red Grange and Bill Hewitt. The Bears won seven division titles with Musso in the lineup. Musso played with Nagurski at both ends of the meaty fullback's career, in his prime and when he made his comeback after a five-year layoff.

Originally, however, Grange was skeptical that Musso could make the Bears roster. A photograph of him as a basketball player sporting a mustache that some of his new teammates did not consider flattering preceded him to Chicago before Halas summoned Musso via a $3 train ride.

"This guy will never make it," Grange said. "He looks like a walrus." Later in training camp, though, Musso gained Grange's admiration and the veteran advised him that he would make the club if he merely played in a relaxed manner and utilized his potential. Musso was always thankful for the shot of confidence. (11)

Sympathetic to the older Nagurski's aches and pains, after pre-season practices in 1943 when he tried the game a second time around, Musso guided Nagurski directly to the training room. Medical attention and sports medicine as a whole were not terribly sophisticated in those days and team doctors and trainers were rare, if not non-existent. So Musso handled the chore of rubbing down Nagurski's muscles himself. It was certainly a gesture of respect for a great player who was feeling his age.

"George wants to see to it Bronko is in the best shape possible," then-Bears co-coach Luke Johnsos said. "The Moose admits the better shape Nagurski's in, the easier his job will be this season." (12) That was a combination of taking one for the team and thinking ahead.

It turned out that Musso was merely a baby at 255 pounds when he emerged from Millikin and he ate enough while with the Bears to climb up to 270 pounds. Very few NFL performers were that large at the time. In addition to his ability, the bulk gave Musso an intimidation advantage.

"George was one of the outstanding linemen of his time," Washington coach Ray Flaherty said. "His size and speed made him a difficult target, particularly on defense." (13) It went without an obvious emphasis from Flaherty that he saw plenty of Musso at the wrong time during those Bears-Redskins championship encounters.

Musso, who lived to be 90, served as a county sheriff after his playing days, and then operated a restaurant. When the telephone call came in 1982 informing Musso that he had been chosen for the Pro Football Hall of Fame, at first he didn't believe it because so much time had passed since he retired. But the call was genuine.

George McAfee was such a spectacular runner that in a future era of pro football no coach would have wasted him on defense or risked his legs in other pursuits beyond carrying the ball out of the backfield and returning punts. As a rookie in 1940 McAfee came along at the right time – and the wrong time. He was a Bears first-round draft pick and contributed to the 73-0 debacle and he was part of four title teams. But his career was also shortened by World War II.

McAfee was already a two-time champion by the time the Bears were upset by the Redskins in 1942. He was what seemed to be a million miles away in uniform in Jacksonville, Florida on the day of the contest that ended Chicago's winning streak.

"I felt bad when the Bears lost, but not because of any streak that had been broken," McAfee said. "I just wanted them to win the title." (14) They just might have if McAfee had been available.

The war service interruption cost McAfee part of his prime, but he stayed in a football uniform until 1950. Later, he did some coaching, some scouting, and even became a supervisor of officials. McAfee was spread thin on his assigned tasks as a player and did not accumulate the volume of yards and touchdowns that normally qualify a runner for the Hall of Fame. But those who saw him play knew he was one of the most electrifying players in the game and he was voted into the Hall in 1966.

While living in a nursing home, McAfee died in a terrible accident in 2009. He was 90.

Of all of the Bears Hall of Fame players who contributed to the 73-0 Redskin humiliation it is no surprise that quarterback Sid Luckman is the best-remembered and most beloved in Chicago. Part of the reason is that most of the others were linemen and Luckman more visibly led the Bears to title after title. Part of the reason is that he recorded tangible statistics for anyone to read, as opposed to measuring a player by blocks and tackles, not as readily quantified in the 1940s. And part of the reason is that despite Jim McMahon leading the 1985 Bears to a Super Bowl, the Bears have not been led by a long line of hugely achieving quarterbacks since Luckman retired in 1950.

Luckman was at the helm in the most famous game in Bears history. He was the most visible player on the club for more than a decade. He remained in Chicago and in the public eye there for the rest of his life. He worked as a Bears assistant coach for a while and went into business. But he was always around for comment and to answer questions about the old, glorious days of the Bears.

In 1948, near the end of his playing days, Luckman authored an instructional book about passing, ostensibly to provide young players and also coaches the benefit of his experience and expertise. The name of the volume was "Passing For Touchdowns." In it Luckman discussed types of passing, types of blocking, how to hold the ball, how a quarterback should move his feet and a review of the rules governing passing.

One issue that Luckman talked about was when it made the most sense to throw a pass. He noted that when passing finally became a regular part of the offense teams usually waited until they needed long yardage for a first down to give it a shot. But those days were gone by then.

"There is no set time to pass," Luckman said, speaking of the offense opening up. "Keep 'em guessing!" (15)

After retirement from the field Luckman led a long life and he watched a lot of football. The reliance on the quarterback, the long pass, frequent passing, and the skill of future generations of quarterbacks impressed him, particularly when discussing self-analysis of his own talents.

"I didn't have a quick release," Luckman said. "I wound up before I threw the ball. I didn't have what I call a great arm. If there was a reason for my success, it was the hours and hours of work I would put in after practice with my receivers. We'd go over and over their routes until we had them down perfectly." (16)

Luckman followed up his instructional book in 1949 with a more autobiographical volume, although it was highly focused on football rather than including too much about his life off the field.

By the time he retired Luckman had been a six-time NFL All-Star and the Bears family retired his No. 42 jersey. Luckman was voted into the Hall of Fame in 1965, two years after Halas and Baugh. He passed away in 1998 at 81.

Wayne Millner first appeared on the nation's football radar screen as an end for Notre Dame, where he was a two-time All-American and led a major upset of Ohio State. He began his pro career in 1936 with the Redskins, and although it was a short stay by historical standards, he was a key man on Washington's championship club of 1937. He also endured the gloom of the 73-0 beating. Millner was a Redskin from 1936 through 1941 and again in 1945, but his playing days ended there, clearly his best days interrupted by World War II.

Millner earned the praise of Ray Flaherty, his Redskins coach, soon after suiting up. He scored two touchdowns in Washington's 1937 title game.

"Talk about competitive spirit," Flaherty said of Millner. "Why, he had it by the bushel and when you put that on top of his ability and leadership you had a real football player." (17)

Millner coached the Philadelphia Eagles for most of the 1951 season, but because of an unfortunate development. Famed coach Bo McMillin had just taken the reins of the Eagles that season, but lasted just two games. He was diagnosed with the stomach cancer that led to his death in 1952 and immediately stopped coaching. Millner took over.

"It is quite a break for me being head coach, but as I said before I would give my right arm to have Bo McMillin back as the boss," Millner said. "It's something I've strived for ever since I started coaching, but I feel bad about the circumstances providing me with the opportunity." (18)

The Eagles were 2-0 when McMillin was sidelined and finished 4-8, 2-8 under Millner. That was the only season he served as a head coach in the NFL.

Millner was enshrined in the Pro Football Hall of Fame in 1968 in good company, joining old Redskins teammate Cliff Battles, Marion Motley, Art Donovan, Charley Trippi, Alex Wojciechowicz and Elroy Hirsch on the honor roll that year. He passed away at 63 in 1976.

There seemed a rush to honor the best of the Redskins players, plus Marshall, in the 1960s, after the Hall of Fame opened and Turk Edwards was one of those chosen in 1969.

Edwards was one of a small number of Redskins in the 1940 loss who had come along from Boston when the franchise shifted. He broke in with the club in 1932 and one year with Boston the two-way player spent all but 10 minutes of the regular season on the field. The 1940 campaign was the Turk's final season. He was the one who suffered the fluke knee injury during a coin toss.

Edwards, a 260-pounder whose years were typified by leather helmets and no face masks, retired after four times being chosen an NFL All-Star. He did some coaching, including running the Redskins, became an all-star automobile salesman, ran a sporting goods store and he entered county government in Washington state, not D.C. Edwards died at 65 in 1973, four years after being enshrined in the Hall of Fame.

Ray Flaherty was about as astute as they came when he was writing a playbook or walking the sidelines and the great coach was honored by being elected to the Hall of Fame in 1976, but he did make one major blunder when he was leading the Redskins. Owner George Preston Marshall more often than not had a testy relationship with his coaches and he blew through them as quickly as runway models change outfits.

But Marshall really did appreciate and believe in Flaherty once he delivered the championship goods. In quite the magnanimous gesture Marshall offered the coach 10 percent of the stock in the team. Not foreseeing that the NFL would become a billion-dollar business, Flaherty turned down the opportunity.

"They spend too much on the band," Flaherty said. (19)

Maybe he was really sick of listening to the "Hail to the Redskins" song, but it was a hasty decision, especially since Flaherty lived until 1994 and aged 90, by which time it was obvious that pro football was a going concern.

Flaherty coached the Redskins for seven seasons before joining the U.S. war effort, and oversaw four Washington division champs and two world champs. Flaherty waited a long time to accept a call from the Hall of Fame and thought he had been forgotten. He was living in Coeur d'Alene, Idaho when chosen more than three decades after leaving the Redskins.

"If I were still coaching," Flaherty said, "I'd still be stressing fundamentals. You've got to block and tackle and play defense. It's a specialist's game now, but it's still a game of fundamentals. That's how you win." (20)

Sammy Baugh kept adding to his legend following the 73-0 mistake that was the worst day of his pro football career. He spent 16 years with the Redskins, retiring after the 1952 season. By the time he quit playing ball Baugh was recognized as the greatest passer the sport had ever seen and perhaps its greatest player since he had managed to become all-league as a quarterback, defensive back and punter.

Baugh was the most popular Redskin and he was the face of the franchise. But he was a Texas guy and after each season he returned home and poured his energy into building up a ranch as a personal getaway, eventually accumulating 22,000 acres where he raised cattle. It was his private retreat, his favorite place on the planet, and whenever there was no football team demanding his allegiance Baugh spent his time in Rotan, Texas.

Between 1955 and 1959 Baugh returned to a college campus, coaching at Hardin-Simmons, the alma mater of his old neighbor Bulldog Turner. Nearly a decade into retirement Baugh was wooed to of all places New York City to coach the American Football League's New York Titans in the early 1960s. The team that was the forerunner of the New York Jets was led by Baugh during the 1960 and 1961 season, but struggled on the field and at the gate and ran into financial difficulties. Baugh was succeeded as coach in New York by Turner.

In 1963, Baugh was one of the 17 charter members selected in the first class of the Pro Football Hall of Fame. A year later he became an assistant coach for the Houston Oilers and then became head coach of that AFL original franchise. In 1966, Baugh became an assistant coach for the Detroit Lions.

Then Baugh pretty much removed himself from the football world, immersing his life in the cowboy world. The funny thing was that in 1937 when Marshall brought Baugh to Washington to show off his draft pick and asked him to dress like a cowboy, Baugh was acting a part. Later in life he really became a cowboy, working the ranch for years, raising cattle, and even becoming a rodeo competitor. He was a serious calf roper and sure enough he banged up a knee pretty badly, an injury worse than any he endured with the Redskins.

It had not been Baugh's ambition to become a pro football player when he was a youngster. When he was growing up in a single-parent home, his mother raising three children, what he most wanted was land of his own.

"From the time I was a little kid in Bell County," Baugh said, "I wanted a ranch of my own. And the best thing football did for me was to make that possible." (21)

Baugh always had that leathery, weather-beaten look about him, and as he added a few wrinkles he truly became craggy-faced. He looked as if he had been riding the range for ages in a strong wind stirring up sand. It got to the point where Baugh abandoned Washington, D.C. altogether, not because of animosity, but because of inertia and preference for Texas. He turned down the invitation to travel to Canton, Ohio for the 50th anniversary of the Hall of Fame, too. Baugh's favorite form of locomotion was horseback, his least going up in an airplane.

"I promised myself if I got to the point where I didn't have to go anywhere, I wouldn't," he said. (22)

Baugh, who lived long and stayed sharp, did welcome visitors to the homestead, though, for most of the rest of his 94 years, even after he turned over ranch operations to his sons. Many of the visitors were sportswriters and he was happy to talk about the sport that made him famous. He kept up with the game, at least on television.

"I would love to play in this day and time because of the rules," Baugh said in 1994. "When I was playing they had not one rule that would make you want to throw the ball. It was a running game and a defensive game. If you couldn't play defense, you couldn't make the team. The rules they had were terrible. You'd laugh at them. There was no protection for the passer. He could be hit until the whistle blew. You could get hurt so damned easy with a rule like that. Back when I was playing, it was easier to intercept passes because the quarterback couldn't throw the ball away." (23)

Despite all of Baugh's accomplishments and his stature in the sport, no interview was complete without touching on the depressing December day in 1940 when his team infamously lost by 73 points.

It was not his favorite topic, yet Baugh always replied to questions about the loss. Still, in one interview he lamented that sometimes the sportswriters made it sound as if that was the only game he ever played. It was a nightmare that kept on giving.

The flip side of Baugh's high-profile position with the losers was maintained by George Halas, the long-lived Bears coach-owner who was also given many opportunities to reminisce about the 73-0 result from the winner's side. He was asked many, many times about his biggest thrill or satisfaction in a lifetime in the sport and Halas never tired of answering with a grin about December 8, 1940.

"The 73 to nothing," Halas replied. (24)

The 73-0. Amen.

PART OF HISTORY

From the moment the clock ran out on the Bears' 73-0 trouncing of the Washington Redskins on that cold December afternoon in 1940 at Griffith Stadium, everyone in the football and sports world realized the game was extraordinary. It was peculiarly unique because of the point spread between two first-class teams and because it wasn't enough that the Bears had hung a crazy, crooked number on the scoreboard and shut out the foe, as well, but because a championship was at stake.

Almost immediately George Halas, Bears players, and those affiliated with the Redskins said that such a game would never come along again. And so far they are right. The decade of the 1940s passed without any result approximately 73-0, never mind in a championship game. There went the 1950s and the 1960s. It didn't happen in the 1970s or 1980s either. The 20th century came to an end with the start of a new millennium in 2000 and nothing had occurred on an NFL football field to compare to 73-0.

Fifteen seasons into a new century and the 73-0 game stands alone, a mark seemingly immune to repeat much like Joe DiMaggio's 56-game hitting streak in baseball, or Wilt Chamberlain's 100-point game in the NBA. That's 75 years and counting. The game has outlived its participants.

Eventually, football writers began taking note of each anniversary of the game that ended in a zero. They began chasing down living players and coaches who competed in the 73-0 game and relived it in print for new generations of readers.

And sometimes they didn't wait for a special anniversary. For a while Sid Luckman, who was the most gentlemanly and available elder statesman of the Bears, was routinely interviewed about the great Bears teams of the past and naturally enough the topic turned to the 73-0 game.

In Washington, it was tricky territory to remind fans of, though a history piece was always a good guise. Some sarcasm sneaked into those reviews, however. Once, a D.C. scribe wrote, "Parents found a message in the rout about which to warn prankish young sons. 'If you don't behave,' fathers of that era threatened their male offspring, 'I'll make you play for the Redskins against the Bears when you get bigger.' The result was a community of well-behaved young boys." (1)

At the time Luckman said he didn't hear too much about the game in his daily rounds, 23 years after it was played. But it never was far from the football fan's consciousness and the game kept coming back around on many of those anniversaries.

"Not too many people talk about it anymore," Luckman said, "but if you saw it you could never forget it. I guess we were the perfect football team that day. I can't imagine any club having a hotter day. But today we could never do that again. The teams are too good. The players are better, the coaching is superb and the defenses are just too smart for it to happen again." (2)

Luckman was speaking in the early days of the NFL parity theme and when he said never he meant in any game, never mind a title game. Indeed that was accurate since there has never been a regular-season game eclipsing the 73-0 spread either.

Thirty years after the game George Halas was 73 and serving as president of the National Football League, further evidence of how dug in the man was inside the sport. A Los Angeles sportswriter asked him if there was a significant meaning to the 73-0 game. Halas allowed that there was for a couple of reasons. One was that the score was so huge it got everyone's attention and another was that professional football players (still trying to escape the shadow of collegians) did something unique.

"Since then football hasn't been the same," Halas said. "That one made us major league. It showed the country the potential in professional ball. It made us accepted as professionals." Halas said he understood the game had a larger impact when it was looked at as not only a game, but the beginning of a T formation revolution. "I realized it when the requests started coming in for copies of the movies. People who had never used the T formation put it in immediately and didn't use anything else the rest of their lives." (3)

Halas learned the T formation in college playing under Bob Zuppke at Illinois and said that was all he ever used. But it had been tweaked and updated due to Clark Shaughnessy's fertile mind. Other big-name coaches employed their own offensive systems and won a lot of games, so they were not about to change. It took an avalanche of points scored by the Bears to gain nationwide attention, especially amongst open-minded coaches or those searching for something new to install.

"It stands for total offense," Halas said of the T. "You can do everything in the T formation that has to be done or that you might want to do in a football game, everything any other system can do. It's the easiest to teach in high school or college, and you can do more with it in pro ball. Clark Shaughnessy was the most helpful organizer. Clark was the first non-T formation coach to see the great possibilities in the T and nobody was more important in the organization and development of our system." (4)

Luckman, too, speaks about the 73-0 game as the coming out party for the T formation.

"That day in football was like going from the Ford Model T to the super deluxe Rolls Royce," Luckman said. (5)

Ten years after writing about the 30th anniversary of the game, the same Los Angeles sportswriter revisited it for the 40th anniversary.

"The shock was great," the history story read when the 73-0 score appeared on the national news wire, "for champions don't beat each other 73-0 – they don't, that is, unless it's 1940 and the Chicago Bears have suddenly found the key to the future of football, the T formation." (6)

The Bears piled up their 11 touchdowns that day because they cast their lot with the T formation and the rest of the league wasn't sure how to stop it, said Hall of Fame guard Danny Fortmann.

"Every 1940 pro club except the Bears used some form of the single wing," he said. "That was a slow-developing formation in which each play originated with the center throwing the ball between his legs to a running back behind him. There's a really big difference between that and the T – in which the center just hands the ball to the quarterback. Running backs hit the line much faster in the T. The defenses of the 1940s weren't ready for the T, and they weren't ready for the speed and talent Halas had. The day we played the Redskins I think we would have easily beaten any team that ever played football up to then." (7)

What is often overlooked is that the T formation wasn't new. It had been around in some form for a half century. But defenses had adapted to its old look and it fell into disuse. The Shaughnessy tweaks coupled with Halas' simple, but brilliant suggestion that the team put a man in motion gave the formation extra pop.

"Coach Halas made the big changes in my rookie year (1939)," Luckman said. Luckman said adding the man in motion and a counter play were difference makers. "When Halas put one of those three backs in motion it spread the defense, especially if the halfback was Ray Nolting, who ran the hundred in 9.8. Our fullback (Bill Osmanski), ran it in 9.9. And if he went on a counter play to the left when Nolting was in motion right, the defense was spread all over the field. That made the T formation work better than any other football system, as we proved in my second season with the Beas when we destroyed the Redskins in the 73-0 game." (8)

It was debatable whether the 73-0 win meant more to Halas or to Luckman. They both had many great triumphs in their careers and many of them together, too. They were also two prominent football figures who were frequently interviewed by sportswriters over a span of many years. That meant they did not say precisely the same thing each time they were interviewed.

Luckman offered slight variations in his commentary on the 73-0 game over the years, though they did not substantially differ. At least once he called the victory, "the greatest day I ever knew in my career." He rated it more highly than his seven-touchdown game because this was a team celebration. "After we scored our seventh or eighth touchdown," Luckman said in one telling of the goings-on on the sidelines, "one of our substitutes said, 'Gee, we've got 55 now, let's take it easy.' And just about every other guy on the bench jumped and growled at him, 'Take it easy? Heck, we want 100!'" (9)

It was more or less an anniversary of the 1940 championship game, although not a round number year, when controversy erupted over this most famous of games. Some 59 years had passed and many, though not all of the protagonists, had passed away. Sammy Baugh was the hardiest of them all, living out his days on his ranch in Texas, but always cooperative when a sportswriter called.

Of course, as it always did when talking football with Baugh about his great and memorable career, the topic eventually came to rest on the

73-0 game. It was a must. There was no way around it. For those six decades Baugh's involvement in the mess had been best recalled by his serious yet somewhat witty observation that if the Redskins had scored that touchdown when Charley Malone dropped his pass near the goal line the score would have been 73-7.

Well, this time Baugh said something else, something extra that sent the sports journalism world into a tizzy. For the first time Baugh suggested that maybe the game was not on the up-and-up. No, he did not hint or say that gamblers were involved as in the 1919 Black Sox Scandal that tarnished baseball's World Series. But he wondered aloud if all of the Redskin players had been trying their best.

Never before had been heard such discouraging words. Immediately after the game and its sad result permeated Washington owner George Preston Marshall's brain he accused his players of quitting. But he practically retracted that statement in the locker room and was never known to utter it again. Nor was anyone else at the time quoted as entertaining any such notion. To all it seemed merely a case of one team crushing the other.

In 1999, Baugh was 85 years old and he at least three times let loose with a theory that the Redskins had given up. One time he did so while talking on the radio and another time in an interview with the Associated Press. The WSCR-AM radio interview did not gain traction and may only have been heard and dismissed by a surrounding audience. Baugh said the same thing to Texas TV station WJLA. The next time around Baugh was speaking to the world through the AP, the vast news agency.

The lead on the Associated Press account of Baugh's freely offered opinion read this way: "Sammy Baugh suspects the 1940 NFL champions game – a 73-0 rout by the Chicago Bears – was not what it seemed. Fifty-nine years later, the Hall of Fame quarterback believes some of his Washington teammates tried to lose as a way to spite the Redskins' owner." (10)

After not making such a comment for about 60 years and despite having innumerable opportunities to do so, Baugh said that during the 1940 ordeal the Redskins "went through the motions" and "let the Bears do whatever they wanted to do." (11)

Yikes! The translation was straight-forward, that the Redskins had quit as Marshall suggested and had essentially thrown the NFL title game the way the Chicago White Sox threw the World Series two decades earlier, though without being tempted by gamblers. Motive is always an important element in a crime, so why would the Redskins do such a thing?

Ironically, given that the same theory was advanced for the White Sox with regard to that team's owner Charles Comiskey, Baugh said that his teammates' behavior was a backlash against Marshall, though not for being a cheapskate, but for inflaming the Bears with his newspaper rhetoric. Baugh said the Redskins were "so damn angry" at Marshall for popping off with that tirade about the Bears being crybabies that they stopped trying in the game. (12)

This reasoning did not seem terribly plausible. It was the Bears, after all, who were inspired by Marshall's statements, but now to say that the Redskins were so terribly affected by it they didn't attempt to win somehow didn't wash.

"It made us so mad," Baugh said of what Marshall did. That was believable. "Look at the game. How many times do you beat a team two weeks earlier in a real close game and two weeks later you don't do a thing? What I think doesn't matter. I don't think we even wanted to win. I never said anything. I never had anything to go on except for the way the team played. I just said I had doubts about how the game was played. They turned on Mr. Marshall. I swear they wanted to hurt Mr. Marshall more than anything. I never talked to the league because I didn't have any proof and I still don't. It doesn't keep me from thinking, though." (13)

There was that minor proof problem. A small number of players who competed in the game for each side were still alive and didn't give much credence to Baugh's all-of-a-sudden accusation. Redskin lineman Clyde Shugart did not for a moment agree with Baugh's assessment.

"Was Sammy drunk when he said that?" Shugart responded. To Shugart and anyone else questioned, Baugh's comments were fantasy. "I don't remember anything like that. I played as hard as I could, but I never saw so many holes on a line. If we were throwing the game, we wouldn't throw it 73-0." (14)

Shugart's argument was that was such a remarkable score alone would raise suspicion. In other words, 73-0 was so surreal it had to be real.

"It just looked like they didn't play," Baugh said of his mates. "I don't think we even wanted to win. If you get five guys, that's all it takes." (15)

Baugh's heretical viewpoint offended everyone, especially surviving players on both sides. To the Redskins it was an insult to their ethics. To the Bears it belittled perhaps the greatest victory in franchise history. To all it made little sense for him to issue these thoughts so many years after the fact and with no evidence.

"It took him 60 years to figure it out, huh?" derided Bears Hall of Fame tackle George Musso. "Now he says that? It doesn't make sense. We were just better that day. It's a lot of baloney." (16)

Baugh took a pounding from sports columnists around the land and fans on sports talk radio. One of the nastiest of missives appearing in the Chicago Tribune, said the AP sportswriter erred in quoting "a senile old man who was a little long on oatmeal." The same opinionated sports fellow said if Pete Rose was banned for life from baseball for betting on that sport than these Redskins "should be executed if they really dumped a championship game." Also, "Why stain Baugh's reputation at this late date just because his boat doesn't quite reach the deck?" (17)

If Baugh was revealing a long-buried, combustible secret it was not received that way. The NFL offices did not indicate there would be an investigation. No one who could be in the know stepped forward to support Baugh's position. Revisionist history was hard to come by nearly 60 years after the game. Nor was there any overt evidence to back it.

Whatever motivated Baugh – if he was confused in his old age, if he really believed he was telling the truth – nothing officially changed in the record book. The Bears won the 1940 NFL championship with the greatest blowout in pro football history and that was not going away.

Luckman, who died before Baugh dropped his bomb, was still around for the game's 50th anniversary and talked about that very thing.

"The men who played in that game, each and every one, can touch 50 years, can just touch it like it was yesterday," Luckman said, "the plays, the scoring, the touchdowns. Where have the 50 years gone?" (18)

Baugh's trip to the confessional booth, misguided or altruistic, fantasy or reality, altered nothing. No one believed him and to those who played in the most memorable football game in NFL history, the numbers 73 to nothing, as George Halas put it, were imprinted on their psyches and in the minds of all football fans.

NOTES

Introduction

1)   Smith, Red, "NFL's Greatest Content? Sacking Of Washington," New York Times, September 5, 1979.

The Setting

1)   Davis, Jeff. "Papa Bear: The Life And Legacy Of George Halas," (New York, McGraw-Hill, 2005). P. 158.

2)   Elfin, David, "The Complete Illustrated History: Washington Redskins," (Minneapolis, Minnesota, MVP Books, 2011). P. 22.

3)   Strickler, George, "Heavy Rain And The Press Upset Redskins' Drill," Chicago Tribune, December 5, 1940.

4)   Strickler, ibid.

5)   Strickler, ibid.

6)   Elfin, ibid. P. 17.

7)   Strickler, George, "Redskins Brave Frosty Day To Drill For Bear Title Game," Chicago Tribune, December 4, 1940.

Owners and Coaches

1)   Walsh, Jack, "Redskin Boss Enjoyed Being the Center of Attention," Washington Post, August 10, 1969.

2)   Addie, Bob, "Friends Gather," Washington Post, August 14, 1969.

3)   Wolff, Alexander, "Marshall Law," Sports Illustrated, October 12, 2009.

4)   Wolff, ibid.

5)   (No byline). Pro Football Hall of Fame Press Release, April 29, 1976.

6)   Elfin, David, "The Complete Illustrated History: Washington Redskins," (Minneapolis, Minnesota, MVP Books, 2011). P. 35.

7)   English, Sue, "Flaherty Joins Hall of Fame," Hall of Fame Day NFL Game Program, August 7, 1976.

8)   English, ibid.

9)   Hurley, Jim, "An Elk Gets Mad At An Irishman," Sport Magazine, December, 1947.

10)   English, ibid.

Live from Washington, D.C.

1)   Campbell, Jim, "Pro Football's First TV Game – 1939," The Coffin Corner, 1981.

2)   Campbell, ibid.

3)   Campbell, ibid.

4)   Campbell, ibid.

5)   Campbell, ibid.

6)   Barber, Red, "I Am Not A Fan," Christian Science Monitor, October 12, 1983.

Sid Luckman

1)   Winakor, Bess, "More Than 40 Years After His Brilliant Football Career Ended, Sid Luckman Is Still A Legend Around Chicago," Chicago Tribune, July 11, 1995.

2)   Winakor, ibid.

3)   Luckman, Sid, "Luckman At Quarterback: Football As A Sport And A Career," (Chicago, Ziff-Davis Publishing Company, 1949). P. VIII.

4)   Luckman, ibid. P. 55.

5)   Davis, Jeff. "Papa Bear: The Life And Legacy Of George Halas," (New York, McGraw-Hill, 2005). P. 139-140.

6)   Winakor, ibid.

7)   Winakor, ibid.

8)   Winakor, ibd.

9)   Luckman, ibid. P. 87.

10)   Luckman, ibid. P. 88.

11)   Luckman, Sid, "Passing For Touchdowns," (Chicago, Ziff-

Davis Publishing Company, 1948.) P. 117.

12) Luckman, ibid, "Passing For Touchdowns." P. 17-18.

13) Winakor, ibid.

14) Luckman, ibid. "Luckman At Quarterback." P. 87.

15) Cannon, Robert, "Sid Luckman And The Destruction Of Washington," Sports Collectors Digest, March 10, 1995.

16) Luckman, ibid. "Luckman At Quarterback." P. 88.

17) Cannon, ibid.

18) Winakor, ibid.

Slingin' Sammy Baugh

1) Elfin, David, "Washington Redskins: The Complete Illustrated History," (Minneapolis, Minnesota, MVP Books, 2011). P. 19.

2) Elfin, ibid. P. 19.

3) Holley, Joe, "Slingin' Sam," (Austin, Texas, University of Texas Press, 2012). P. 20.

4) Coffey, Jerry, "At 77, Sammy Baugh Remembers His Fancy Passing," Fort Worth Star-Telegram, October 6, 1991.

5) Elfin, ibid. P. 23.

6) Baugh, Sammy, "A Football Hero's Own Story," Part II. North American Newspaper Alliance, October 18, 1937.

7) Baugh, Sammy, "A Football Hero's Own Story," ibid. Part III, October 19, 1937.

8) Baugh, Sammy, "A Football Hero's Own Story," ibid. Part IV, October 20, 1937.

9) (No Byline), "Baugh Greatest of All – It's Unanimous," United Press International, December 13, 1937.

10) (No byline), UPI, ibid.

11) Bock, Hal, "Baugh: Redskins Lost 73-0 Game On Purpose," Associated Press, November 28, 1999.

12) Holley, ibid. P. 163.

13) Holley, ibid. 164.

14) Holley, ibid. 165.

First Quarter

1) Grosshandler, Stanley, "Do You Remember Bill Osmanski?" Sports Digest, December, 1973.

2) Grosshandler, ibid.

3) (No byline). "Bill Osmanski," Football Digest, November, 1968.

4) Povich, Shirley, "In Football History, 73-0 A Score Of Infamy," Washington Post, December 7, 1990.

5) Cannon, Robert, "Sid Luckman And The Destruction Of Washington," Sports Collectors Digest, March 10, 1995.

A Hall of Fame Line

1) (No byline), Pro Football Hall of Fame Press Release, April 1, 1982.

2) (No byline), Hall of Fame, ibid.

3) (No byline), "Dutch Vs. The Moose," Sports Illustrated, January 26, 1981.

4) Burnes, Robert L. "Now He Tackles Crime," St. Louis Globe-Democrat, (Pro Football Hall of Fame Archives, date missing).

5) (No byline) "Joe Stydahar Dies; Pro Football Star," New York Times, March 25, 1977.

6) Finch, Frank, "Jumbo Joe Stydahar Sits On Top Of World," All-Sports News, January 16, 1952.

7) Finch, ibid.

8) Smith, Don, "Dan Fortmann, Pro Football Hall Of Fame," Pro Football Hall of Fame press release, (undated), 1965.

9) (No byline), "Pro Football Hall Of Fame Admits California Surgeon," Medical Tribune, May 14, 1965.

10) Smith, ibid.

11) Smith, ibid.

12) (No byline), "Bulldog Turner," Franklin Mint press release 1942 (Pro Football Hall of Fame Archives).

13) Barr, Michael, "Remembering Bulldog Turner," (Lubbock, Texas, Texas Tech University Press, 2013). P. 35.

14) Barr, ibid. P. 48.

15) Barr, ibid. P. 49.

16) Barr, ibid. P. 58.

17) Barr, ibid. P. 69.

18) Davis, Jeff. "Papa Bear: The Life And Legacy Of George Halas," (New York, McGraw-Hill, 2005). P. 152.

19) (No byline), "Bulldog Turner," Washington Star, November 7, 1980.

20) Smith, Sam, "Ill-Fated Turner Still A Bulldog," Chicago Tribune, June 7, 1987.

Second Quarter

1) Luckman, Sid, "Luckman At Quarterback: Football As A Sport And A Career," (Chicago, Ziff-Davis Publishing Company, 1949). P. 90.

2) (No byline), "Wayne Millner," Pro Football Hall Of Fame Archives, August 1968.

3) Katzowitz, Josh, "Remember When: Dick Plasman Was Last Player To Forgo A Helmet," CBSSports.com, December 6, 2013.

4) (No byline), Pro Football Hall Of Fame Player Biography/ Archives. (No date available).

5) (No byline). "John A (Automatic Jack) Manders," The Sporting News, February 12, 1977

6) Daley, Arthur, "Among Those Honored," New York Times, December 11, 1963.

7) Daley, ibid.

8) Davis, Jeff. "Papa Bear: The Life And Legacy Of George Halas," (New York, McGraw-Hill, 2005). P. 152.

9) Davis, ibid. P. 153.

10) Luckman, ibid. P. 90

11) Davis, ibid. P. 160.

12) Artoe, Lee, "Lineman's Dream, Artoe's Big Thrill," Chicago American, February 1, 1963.

Halftime

1) (No byline), "Ray Flaherty," NFL Game Program, Broncos vs. Bears, July 31, 1976.

2) NFL program, ibid.

3) NFL program, ibid.

4) Brady, Dave, "Giant Figure Of Redskin Lore," Washington Post, September 20, 1978.

5) Brady, ibid.

6) Luckman, Sid, "Luckman At Quarterback: Football As A Sport And A Career," (Chicago, Ziff-Davis Publishing Company, 1949). P. 91.

7) Luckman, ibid. P. 91.

8) Luckman, ibid. P. 91.

Redskins Try to Dig Out

1) Atchison, Lewis F., "Turk Didn't Miss Hall Of Fame Stop," Washington Star, September 29, 1969.

2) Atchison, ibid.

3) Daley, Arthur, "Investure Of Immortality," New York Times, February 14, 1969.

4) Ragsdale, W.B. Jr., "The Redskins At 50," NFL Game Program, November 9, 1986,

5) Ragsdale, ibid.

6) Mayes, Bob, "Bears Rout 'Skins 73-0 For NFL Title: Bob Smithwick," Goldsboro (North Carolina) News-Argus, September 28, 1997.

7) Mayes, ibid.

8) Mayes, ibid.

9) Atchison, Lewis F., "Farkas Recalls Good Old Days," Washington Star (No date, Football Hall of Fame Archives).

10) Atchison, Lewis F., "Knee Well, Spirit Back, Farkas Sees Big Season With 'Skins," Washington Star, (No date, Football Hall of Fame Archives, 1942).

11) Roberts, Byron, "Wilbur Moore Played With Champions," Washington Post, August 10, 1965.

12)   Sheer, Harry, "Short Change Made Wee Willie Grid Star," Washington Star (No date, Pro Football Hall of Fame, 1943).

Third Quarter

1)   Morrison, Robert, "Profiles From The Past: NFL Aware 268-Pounder No Ghost, But Musso Later Almost Became One," (no publication identification or date, Pro Football Hall of Fame Archives.)

2)   Holley, Joe, "Slingin' Sam," (Austin, Texas, University of Texas Press, 2012). P. 168.

3)   Holley, ibid. P. 168.

4)   Holley, ibid. P. 170.

5)   Callahan, Tom, "Plenty Of McAfees," Cincinnati Enquirer, July 29, 1973.

6)   Prell, Edward, "McAfee The Magnificent," Chicago Tribune (No date, Pro Football Hall of Fame Archives, 1948).

7)   Siler, Tom, "Gorgeous George," Sport Magazine, November, 1946.

8)   Prell, ibid.

9)   (No byline), Pro Football Hall Of Fame inductee series, 1966.

10)   Pro Football Hall Of Fame, ibid.

11)   Davis, Jeff. "Papa Bear: The Life And Legacy Of George Halas," (New York, McGraw-Hill, 2005). P. 150.

12)   Siler, ibid.

13)   Luckman, Sid, "Luckman At Quarterback: Football As A Sport And A Career," (Chicago, Ziff-Davis Publishing Company, 1949). P. 91.

The Bears' Sideline

1)   Luckman, Sid, "Luckman At Quarterback: Football As A Sport And A Career," (Chicago, Ziff-Davis Publishing Company, 1949). P. 92.

2)   Luckman, ibid. P. 92.

3)   Bella, Timothy, "A Blowout Both Teams Wish To Forget," New York Times, November 25, 2012.

4)   Bella, ibid.

5)   Luckman, ibid. P. 92.

6)   Luckman, ibid. P. 92.

7)   Curran, Bob, "The Monsters Of The Midway," Sport Magazine, February, 1964.

Fourth Quarter

1)   Stellino, Vito, "Even 50 Years Later, Bears' 73-0 Rout Of Redskins Not Forgotten," Baltimore Sun, December 12, 1990.

2)   (No byline), "Fam Gets Three Pro Grid Bids," (No publication, Pro Football Hall of Fame, 1938).

3)   Pompei, Dan, "Oldest Chicago Bear Dies," Chicago Tribune, October 12, 2010.

4)   (No byline) "George Wilson: Pro Ball No Mystery To 30-Year Veteran," NFL game program, September 17, 1967.

5)   Curran, Bob, "The Monsters Of The Midway," Sport Magazine, February, 1964.

6)   Luckman, Sid, "Luckman At Quarterback: Football As A Sport And A Career," (Chicago, Ziff-Davis Publishing Company, 1949). P. 93.

7)   Luckman, ibid. P. 93.

8)   Luckman, ibid. P. 93.

9)   Luckman, ibid. P. 93.

10)   Davis, Jeff. "Papa Bear: The Life And Legacy Of George Halas," (New York, McGraw-Hill, 2005). P. 161.

11)   Curran, ibid.

Post Game

1)   Davis, Jeff. "Papa Bear: The Life And Legacy Of George Halas," (New York, McGraw-Hill, 2005). P. 161.

2)   Stellino, Vito, "Even 50 Years Later, Bears' 73-0 Rout Of Redskins Not Forgotten," Baltimore Sun, December 8, 1990.

3)   Stellino, ibid.

4)   Holley, Joe, "Slingin' Sam," (Austin, Texas, University of Texas Press, 2012). P. 172.

5)   Holley, ibid. P. 172.

6)   Holley, ibid. P. 169.

7)   Holley, ibid. P. 169.

8)   Holley, ibid. P. 169.

9)   (No byline), Pro Football Hall of Fame biography, (no date, 1982, Pro Football Hall of Fame Archives).

10)   Rennie, Rud, "Bears' 73-0 Rout Of Redskins Made History In Pro Football," New York Herald-Tribune, December 9, 1940.

11)   Strickler, George, "Bears Win World Football Title, 73-0," Chicago Tribune, December 9, 1940.

12)   Strickler, ibid.

13)   Stickler, ibid.

14)   (No byline), "Jubilant Bears Look to August – And All-Stars," Chicago Tribune Press Services, December 9, 1940.

15)   Markus, Robert, "Dec. 8, 1940 10 Different Players Score A Total Of 11 Touchdowns And The Bears Defeat The Redskins 73-0 In Washington, D.C. For The National Football League Title, Chicago Tribune, November 1, 1987.

16)   Markus, ibid.

17)   Gugger, John, "The Year, 1940: Bears Get Revenge In 73-0 Title Victory Over The Redskins, Toledo Blade, September 18, 1994.

18)   Markus, ibid.

19)   Pierson, Don, "73-0: It's Indelibly Etched In History," Chicago Tribune, December 9, 1990.

20)   Pierson, ibid.

21)   Pierson, ibid.

22)   Pierson, ibid.

23)   Pierson, ibid.

24)   Pierson, ibid.

25)   Pierson, ibid.

26)   Sherman, Ed, "Settling The Score," Chicago Tribune, October 20, 2004.

27) Hirsley, Michael, "The Monsters Of The Midway Used A T Formation To Truly Live Up To Their Nickname 60 Years Ago," Chicago Tribune, December 8, 2000.

28) Hirsley, ibid.

29) (No byline) "Jubilant Bears…" ibid.

30 (No byline), "Jubilant Bears…" ibid.

31) Whittlesey, Merrill, "Team Quit, Is Charge Of Marshall," Washington Post, December 9, 1940.

32) Whittlesey, ibid.

33) Whittlesey, ibid.

34) Whittlesey, ibid.

35) Halas, George, "A 73-0 Miracle Won't Happen Again – Halas," Chicago Tribune, July 30, 1941.

36) Halas, ibid.

1941

1) (No byline), Pro Football Hall Of Fame biography, 1965 (Pro Football Hall of Fame Archives).

2) Gugger, John, "The Year, 1940: Bears Get Revenge In 73-0 Title Victory Over The Redskins, Toledo Blade, September 18, 1994.

3) Holley, Joe, "Slingin' Sam," (Austin, Texas, University of Texas Press, 2012). P. 175.

4) Davis, Jeff. "Papa Bear: The Life And Legacy Of George Halas," (New York, McGraw-Hill, 2005). P. 169.

5) Gunn, John, "The '41 Bears The Greatest," Orange County Register/The Coffin Corner magazine, 1979.

6) Gunn, ibid.

7) Luckman, Sid, "Luckman At Quarterback: Football As A Sport And A Career," (Chicago, Ziff-Davis Publishing Company, 1949). P. 105.

8) Gugger, John, "The Year, 1940: Bears Get Revenge In 73-0 Title Victory Over The Redskins, Toledo Blade, September 18, 1994.

1942 & 1943

1) Davis, Jeff. "Papa Bear: The Life And Legacy Of George Halas," (New York, McGraw-Hill, 2005). P.173.

2) Whittlesey, Merrill, "Redskins Upset Chi-Bears, 14-6; To Capture League Championship," Washington Post, December 14, 1942.

3) Whittlesey, ibid.

4) Whittlesey, ibid.

5) Costello, Al, "New Champs 'Go Wild' After Stunning Victory," Washington Post, December 14, 1942.

6) Costello, ibid.

7) Costello, ibid.

8) Costello, ibid.

9) Costello, ibid.

10) O'Neill, Frank "Buck," "Marshall, Flaherty Sing Praises Of Valiant Redskins," Washington Times-Herald, December 14, 1942.

11) O'Neill, ibid.

12) O'Neill, ibid.

13) O'Neill, ibid.

14) O'Neill, ibid.

15) O'Neill, ibid.

16) Holley, Joe, "Slingin' Sam," (Austin, Texas, University of Texas Press, 2012). P. 198.

17) Davis, ibid. P. 174.

18) (No byline) "Profile Of A Quarterback: Sid Luckman," Oakland Tribune, October 7, 1974.

19) David, ibid. P. 187.

20) (No byline), "Marshall Escorted From Field By Police After Verbal Clash With Bear President," Washington Post, December 27, 1943.

George Preston Marshall

1) Boyle, Robert H. "All Alone By The Telephone," Sports

Illustrated, October 16, 1961.

2)   Siegel, Morris, "George Preston Marshall: Master Showman, Mastermind," NFL Game Program, October 28, 1973.

3)   Siegel, ibid.

4)   Siegel, ibid.

5)   Pollock, Ed, "Playing The Game: Redskins' Owner Helped Make Bears Football's No. 1 Team," Philadelphia Bulletin, February 5, 1963.

6)   Pollock, ibid.

7)   (No byline), "George Marshall, Charter Member Of HOF, Is Dead," Associated Press, August 10, 1969.

8)   August, Bob, "Football Loses A Stormy Giant," Cleveland Press, August 12, 1969.

9)   Durslag, Melvin, "Football's Last Rebel Is Gone," Los Angeles Herald-Examiner, August 9, 1969.

10)   Steadman, John F., "Redskin Chief Thought He'd Never Die," Baltimore News-American, August 20, 1969.

11)   Considine, Bob, "Pro Football's Two Losses," Syndicated Column, Mary 31, 1968.

12)   Kritzer, Cy, "Marshall Was A Pro Pioneer," Buffalo Evening News, August 22, 1969.

13)   Addie, Bob, "Rozelle Eulogizes Marshall As Imaginative, Dedicated," Washington Post, August 14, 1969.

14)   (No byline), "George Preston Marshall," Washington Daily News, August 14, 1969.

George Halas

1)   Smith, Red, "NFL's Greatest Contest? Sacking of Washington," New York Times, July 5, 1979.

2)   Smith, ibid.

3)   Siegel, Morris, "Old Antagonists Hold Reunion," Washington Star, August 16, 1963.

4)   Siegel, ibid.

5)   (No byline), "Grange, 73-0 Massacre Continue to Excite Halas," Associated Press, February 3, 1966.

6)   Desmond, Dan, "George S. Halas," Chicago Bears Press Release, January, 1972.

7)   Stiles, Maxwell, "OK For Halas To Roam, Says Bell," Los Angeles Mirror, October 28, 1958.

8)   Pierson, Don, "Final Farewell For A Legend," Chicago Tribune, November 4, 1983.

9)   Moran, Malcolm, "Halas Is Buried And Remembered," New York Times, November 4, 1983.

10)   (No byline), "'He Kept It Going,' Says Tex Schramm," United Press International, November 14, 1983.

11)   (No byline), "1,200 Mourners Pay Last Respects To George Halas," Associated Press, November 4, 1983.

Bulldog, Sammy, Sid and Life Goes On

1)   Prell, Edward, "Bulldog Turner Busiest Man In Bear Practices," Chicago Tribune, August 20, 1944.

2)   Weller, Steve, "Bulldog Turner: Carmel Candy On A Penny A Day," QB, (no date, Pro Football Hall of Fame Archives).

3)   (No byline), "Bulldog Turner: Never Met The Man I Couldn't Handle," American Football League press release, October 23, 1962.

4)   (No byline), "Clyde (Bulldog) Turner," NFL playoff program, December28, 1980.

5)   Smith, Sam, "Ill-Fated Turner Still A Bulldog," Chicago Tribune, June 7, 1987.

6)   Smith, ibid.

7)   Smith, Don, "Dan Fortmann," Pro Football Hall of Fame biography (no date, 1965).

8)   (No byline), "A Conversation With Dr. Dan Fortmann," NFL "Pro" game program magazine, (undated, Pro Football Hall of Fame Archives).

9)   (No byline), A Conversaton... ibid.

10)   Smith, Don, "Dan Fortmann...ibid.

11)   Smith, Don, "George Musso," Pro Football Hall of Fame biography, April 1, 1982).

12)   Prell, Edward, "Musso Becomes Dr. Lotshaw If Bronko

Needs Attention," Chicago Tribune, (no date, 1943).

13) Smith, Don, "George Musso," ibid.

14) (No byline), "The Record On Page 199," NFL game program, (undated, 1973).

15) Luckman, Sid, "Passing For Touchdowns," (Chicago, Ziff Davis Publishing Company, 1948). P. 86-87.

16) (No byline), "Profile Of A Quarterback: Sid Luckman," Oakland Tribune, October 7, 1974.

17) Powell, Charlie, "Ex-Coach Honors Millner," Canton Repository, June 18, 1968.

18) Millner, Wayne, "Coach's Corner," Eagle's Nest, November, 1951.

19) Brady, Dave, "Capitol Characters," Pro Football Weekly, February, 1976.

20) Guback, Steve, "Ray Flaherty Knows They Remember Him," Washington Star, (no date, Pro Football Hall of Fame Archives).

21) Coffey, Jerry, "At 77, Baugh Remembers His Fancy Passing," Fort Worth Star-Telegram, October 6, 1991.

22) Pierson, Don, "These Days, Baugh Enjoys The Home Field," Chicago Tribune, July 27, 2000.

23) Moore, Jonathan, "Slingin' Sammy," Associated Press, September 2, 1994.

24) Deford, Frank, "I Don't Date Any Woman Under 48," Sports Illustrated, December 5, 1977.

Part of History

1) Siegel, Morris, "Luckman Recalls 73-0 Holocaust," Washington Star, May 12, 1963.

2) Siegel, ibid.

3) Oates, Bob, "Bears' 73-0 Triumph In 1940," Los Angeles Times, May 9, 1970.

4) Oates, ibid.

5) Pierson, Don, "73-0: It's Indelibly Etched In History," Chicago Tribune, December 9, 1990.

6) Oates, Bob, "Bears' 73-0 Romp In 1940 Showed Football's Future," Los Angeles Times, December 14, 1980.

7) Oates, "Bears' 73-0 Romp," ibid.

8) Oates, "Bears' 73-0 Romp," ibid.

9) Jauss, Bill, "Bears' Luckman Dies," Chicago Tribune, July 6, 1998.

10) Bock, Hal, "Baugh Thinks Washington Tried To Lose '40 Title Game," Associated Press, November 28, 1999.

11) Verdi, Bob, "Baugh's Bitter Whine Has A Familiar Ring," Chicago Tribune, December 5, 1999.

12) Verdi, ibid.

13) Bock, ibid.

14) Bock, ibid.

15) Bock, ibid.

16) Bock, ibid.

17) Issacson, Steve, "Slammin' Sammy," Chicago Tribune, December 12, 1999.

18) Pierson, ibid.

ABOUT THE AUTHOR

Lew Freedman is a veteran sportswriter who has written numerous books about the Chicago Bears and other sports, as well as books about Alaska. He has won more than 250 journalism awards and written for the staffs of the Chicago Tribune, Philadelphia Inquirer, Anchorage Daily News and other newspapers.

Freedman and his wife Debra live in Indiana.